D1246796

DOMINION AND WEALTH

SOVIETICA

PUBLICATIONS AND MONOGRAPHS
OF THE INSTITUTE OF EAST-EUROPEAN STUDIES AT THE
UNIVERSITY OF FRIBOURG / SWITZERLAND AND
THE CENTER FOR EAST EUROPE, RUSSIA AND ASIA
AT BOSTON COLLEGE AND THE SEMINAR
FOR POLITICAL THEORY AND PHILOSOPHY
AT THE UNIVERSITY OF MUNICH

Founded by J. M. BOCHEŃSKI (Fribourg)

Edited by T. J. BLAKELEY (Boston), GUIDO KÜNG (Fribourg) *and*
NIKOLAUS LOBKOWICZ (Munich)

VOLUME 49

DONNA C. KLINE

School of Law, University of Texas at Austin, U.S.A.

DOMINION AND WEALTH

*A Critical Analysis of Karl Marx'
Theory of Commercial Law*

D. REIDEL PUBLISHING COMPANY

A MEMBER OF THE KLUWER ACADEMIC PUBLISHERS GROUP

DORDRECHT / BOSTON / LANCASTER / TOKYO

Library of Congress Cataloging in Publication Data

CIP

Kline, Donna C.
  Dominion and wealth.

  (Sovietica; v. 49)
  Bibliography: p.
  Includes index.
  1. Contracts—Great Britain—History. 2. Liberty of contract—Great Britain—
History. 3. Law and socialism—History. 4. Marx, Karl, 1818–1883. I. Title.
II. Series: Sovietica (Université de Fribourg. Ost-Europa Institut); v. 49.
KD1554.K58   1987   346.42′02′09   87–9555
ISBN 90–277–2499–7   344.206209

Published by D. Reidel Publishing Company,
P.O. Box 17, 3300 AA Dordrecht, Holland.

Sold and distributed in the U.S.A. and Canada
by Kluwer Academic Publishers,
101 Philip Drive, Assinippi Park, Norwell, MA 02061, U.S.A.

In all other countries, sold and distributed
by Kluwer Academic Publishers Group,
P.O. Box 322, 3300 AH Dordrecht, Holland.

To
Baker & Botts
which made this work both possible and necessary
and to
the Magnolia Circle
who made it worthwhile

TABLE OF CONTENTS

Preface

Donna Kline's contribution to the *Sovietica* series falls outside the strict confines of the study of Soviet Marxism-Leninism. It centers its attention on the seemingly minor question of Marx' knowledge of and attitude toward the legal theory and practice in vogue at the time he was writing studies that directly addressed issues of law and economics, and that indirectly helped to fashion the legal and economic behavior of Soviet-style regimes.

That this question is not as minor or as irrelevant to Marxism-Leninism as it might seem at first glance flows from Marx' obvious intent to do a thorough critique of all the vectors of 'bourgeois-capitalist' civilization and culture, clearly expressed in the many key texts, where 'legal relations' form at least part of the central focus. Marx' thought was forming when the 'bourgeois' law that had become self-conscious at the end of the 18th century was, following the French Revolution, trying to 'take possession' of the social-political consciousness of European-American culture, and finding itself coming up against the 'vagaries' of economic quasi-anarchy.

There is a sense in which the 'bourgeois-capitalist' efforts at developing a legal code for existing economic practice represent a sort of 'ideology in practice' to be applied to the same phenomena that Marx wanted to account for in his peculiarly Hegelian ideological critique. For, before it is a theory, economics is a practice and - in this field perhaps more than in any other - theory is constantly scrambling to keep up with or catch up with practice; and, this is what makes Donna Kline's approach instructive, fruitful and illuminating.

The author argues in this book that alienation - originally a legal term, having to do with passing ownership to another - is the point in Marx' theory, where historical materialism has to answer some hard questions about the limits between legitimate commercial transactions and economic 'oppression'. Blanket condemnations of 'capitalism' (whatever this term might mean in a given context) are easy to formulate. What is more difficult is to figure out if normal and ordinary human economic activity - and the ensuing legal entanglements - could be other than they are. For, if not, the whole Marxist enterprise is a neat little theory that can give itself any random sort of practice - which is precisely what Soviet Marxism-Leninism seems to have done.

T.J. Blakeley
Boston College

ACKNOWLEDGMENTS

This book would be incomplete without an acknowledgment of the special role of those friends whose sense of its worth and pleasure in its publication are my greatest reward in writing it: Fernando R. Casas, Leslie M. Marenchin, Bruce K. Leutwyler, and C. Glenn Cambor, M.D.

I wish to acknowledge the generous contributions of the following persons to the completion of this work: Lt. Col. and Mrs. Doil F. Kline, who tactfully inquired about its progress; Mr. Ralph B. Palmer, who endured it; Mr. James G. Ulmer, who tolerated it; Professor James P. Scanlan, who generously nutured it through long droughts of invention; Professors Bernard Rosen and Robert G. Turnbull, whose insightful criticism sharpened it; Prof. Duncan Kennedy and Prof. Roberto Mangabeira Unger whose theories on contract and society were a sufficient intellectual irritant to generate an on-going interest in that field; Prof. Harold Berman whose analysis of Soviet contract law raised the question of the necessity of contract; and Mr. Tom Thomas, whose theory of economic duress in contemporary society created the occasion to write it. My deep gratitude extends to Thomas J. Blakeley whose patience and skill transformed a manuscript into a book.

The author thanks especially those Baker & Botts word processors who worked diligently without additional salary, including in particular Ms. Sandy Robillard who saw it through to completion. A special debt is owed to Mrs. Elsbeth Baskette who made it presentable to polite society and to Mrs. Bette Hellinger who steered it safely home.

All errors and omissions are, of course, my own.

Donna C. Kline

CHAPTER ONE

An Analysis of Marx' Description of the
Will Theory of Law

I. INTRODUCTION

A. Purpose and Proposed Progress

This study consists in a critical analysis of Karl Marx' theory of
nineteenth-century commercial law in the light of the actual
nineteenth-century law of contracts. Like Marx' works, this essay
consists both in empirical study of the law and in philosophical
analysis.

It has three purposes: to place certain remarks by Marx about
philosophy of law in their historical and philosophical context,
particularly within the context of Marx' own studies of legal
philosophy; to elucidate the specific theories to which Marx was
referring by his term "juridical illusion"; and to evaluate his criticism of
those theories.

The core of this narrow endeavor is that sound criticism of Marx'
sweeping attack on capitalism should include a review of both his
empirical claims and the philosophical arguments in which they appear.
Such a review reveals that Marx' analysis is ambiguous and flawed and
that it rests upon incomplete factual premises.

The rules of contract law are the rules which govern exchange.
Freedom of contract embodies the concept of day-to-day freedom in the
exercise of economic choice. The relationship between such mundane
unfettered choice and the grander ideal of political freedom has been
much debated by such writers as Friedrich Hayek, Milton Friedman,
and Robert Nozick. Marx held that the apparent freedom of economic
action under capitalism was not freedom at all but only an illusion.
Thus, it seems worthwhile to examine Marx' critique of economic
freedom in the context of the actual rules of law which embodied that
freedom.

Marx' theory of ideology is at once a frustrating and an alluring part
of his work. Entire volumes have been expended simply in determining

1

what Marx' theory was, let alone criticizing and responding to it.[1]

Like a religious creed, the Marxist theory of ideology appears to demand allegiance, but to defy analysis. At his most opaque, Marx aspired to be both a social scientist and a rational critic of the capitalist political system. Therefore, his statements in regard to ideology, including those about the existent system of law under nineteenth-century capitalism, contain both factual and philosophical statements; capitalist ideology as a concrete social entity ambiguously fades into capitalist ideology as the immediate rival of Communism.

It is sometimes difficult to answer the most apparently simple questions about Marx' theory of ideology, as for example, the question "Did Marx believe that man in the capitalist society actually is an isolated monad?" In the essay 'On the Jewish Question', Marx said:

> None of the so-called rights of man therefore go beyond egoistic man, beyond man as a member of civil society, that is, an individual withdrawn into himself, into the confines of his private interests and private caprice, and separated from the community. In the rights of man, he is far from being conceived as a species-being, on the contrary, species-life itself, society appears as a framework external to the individuals, as a restriction of their original independence. The sole bond holding them together is natural necessity, need and private interest, the preservation of their property and their egoistic selves.[2]

Does that mean that people were *in fact* isolated, independent, and involved in a random search for self-interest, or does it mean that people, while actually united by social bonds and social institutions, subjectively *saw themselves* as isolated and independent entities, or does it mean that their contemporary social and political theory postulated that they were concerned only with private choice?

Marx tried at one and the same time to explain certain aspects of contemporary society, including the law and the marketplace; to refute other explanations of these phenomena; and to establish an alternative moral theory to that of capitalism. The fact that rival theories were themselves part of the phenomenon, as part indeed of the contemporary and alternative ideology, complicated these efforts. Marx found himself in the position of the missionary anthropologist who seeks to describe pagan religion even as he tries to destroy it.

I will not attempt to adjudicate the difficult issue of whether any ideology can contain true statements but, for purposes of discussion, assume that a statement in a case report, for example, can be true and part of the ideology of the time.

A central theme in Marx' discussion of nineteenth-century political theory is the concept of illusion. According to Marx, certain views purportedly characteristic of capitalism not only were false, but were illusions. Specifically, Marx claimed that free will as postulated by the democratic political theories was such an "illusion". That term, with its mixed connotations of objective falsity and subjective belief, has long seemed to me to be a key to comprehension and criticism of Marx' theories.

Since the issue of the nature of true freedom is a central question in evaluating the respective theories of Communism and democracy, it is necessary to examine closely Marx' claim that the capitalist democratic concept of freedom was illusory. To do so, one needs to examine Marx' description of the capitalist ideal of economic freedom and his concept of that ideology as an illusion. That examination can be carried out in a concrete examination of Marx' attempted refutation of freedom of contract, which is a narrow and relatively accessible area of study.

Marx regarded himself as a scientist, and a form of materialism, if not empiricism, formed the core of his metaphysical system. In *The German Ideology* he said that "these premises can thus be verified in a purely empirical way".[3] Two aspects of Marx' self-professed scientific viewpoint are his beliefs that moral, legal, and political systems can be studied purely as historical phenomena and that these systems are subject to the same causal laws of history which explain other social phenomena.[4]

The exact nature of the causal relationship which Marx claimed existed between the economic structure of society and the "super-structure" of society has long been a source of debate. Marx and Engels apparently disavowed a strictly materialist concept of ideology in that they apparently both did not believe that the economic structure alone shaped the ideas of a society and they attributed some causal efficacy to ideology upon the economic system while continuing to maintain that ideology was, in essence at least, causally formed by the economic system.[5]

Regardless of the precise causal structure, however, two aspects of Marx' writings on ideology are clear. First, Marx made numerous statements about the ideology of capitalism which he intended to be descriptive statements of fact; that is, Marx regarded himself as describing an existent ideology.[6] For example, in the essay 'On the Jewish Question', Marx quotes from the actual constitutions of various states to support his characterization of civil rights under capitalism.[7]

Second, Marx criticized the capitalist ideology both in theoretical terms and in terms of its factual accuracy in describing the capitalist economic and social system. His theoretical criticism of capitalist political theory can be seen in his frequent derisive rejections of social contract theories.[8]

On a factual level, while asserting that the capitalist ideology characterized political thought in the nineteenth century, he asserted that the free choice which social contract theory postulates did not exist as a matter of economic fact. In the *Grundrisse*, Marx said:

> Living labor power belongs to itself, and disposes of its own manifestation of force by means of exchange. Both sides are opposed to one another as persons. Formally, their relationship is the free and equal one of those who exchange. It appears that this is a mere semblance, and a deceptive semblance, as soon as we consider the legal relationship outside this sphere of strict economics.[9]

Consistent with his desired scientific approach to economic study, Marx himself sought empirical data for his theories.[10]

In addition to his historical reading, Marx prepared a 'Questionneur' which was published in the *Revue Socialiste*, April 20, 1880.[11] The preface appealed to the workers for responses and also to "socialists of all schools, who, desiring sound reform, must also desire *exact* and *positive* knowledge of the conditions in which the working class lives and works".[12]

Yet, Marx' own attempts at confirmation appear now somewhat sporadic and inconclusive in spite of the immense amount of factual reading that he did. For example, the extremely detailed *Eighteenth Brumaire of Louis Napoleon* cannot be easily correlated with Marx' general theories of historical change and political action.[13] As one scholar has said, that work shows "the magnificent disdain for his own theories which is characteristic of a great theorist".[14] Similarly, Marx was somewhat vague on the precise theoretical implications of the Paris commune.[15]

Marx' extensive historical and anthropological readings often appear in his own works as *ex post facto* examples illustrating his theories, rather than as an assemblage of data from which conclusions are drawn.[16] For example, his description of primitive Indian communism, which was the basis for his later general theory of the 'Asiatic' mode of production, served as an example of the allegedly communal nature of primitive property, and his history of gold was used to similar effect.[17] In all fairness, it should be noted that Ernest

Mandel has proposed a detailed analysis of the empirical bases of Marxist economics, including an extensive review of the concept of the Asiatic mode of production, which tends to contradict the above impression.[18]

Much of the subsequent factual criticism of Marx' work has been aimed at his economic claims and somewhat less at his factual description of his own time. A number of texts have been written in an attempt to explicate and analyze Marx' economics, for example, and a frequent theme in these texts is the rejection of Marx' postulated law of the increasing misery of the proletariat, which appears to have been disconfirmed by historical experience.

With respect to non-economic aspects of Marx' work, Eric Fromm, Shlomo Avineri, and Eugene Kamenka have dealt with Marx' theories of alienation and ethics. Fromm apparently accepted Marx' concept of alienation of modern man and offered little in the way of empirical support, while Avineri confidently asserted that *Capital* "shows that alienation is empirically verifiable".[19] Kamenka attempted to extricate a coherent ethical theory from Marx' remarks and did not deal extensively with the accuracy of Marx' analysis of the existent and competing ethical system, that of capitalism. Marx asserted, for example, that the ruling ideas of an age are always the ideas of the ruling class, yet he gave few specific cases to support this sweeping historical generality. Kamenka mentioned that this claim is patently false but also gave no evidence in support of his assertion.[20]

Therefore, an empirical comparison of Marx' statements about nineteenth-century ideology with the actual views held by that society can form a useful first step in a criticism of Marx' theory of ideology, and this comparison is consistent with Marx' own aims.

Having determined that an empirical examination of Marx' view of capitalist ideology is of interest, the question may be raised as to why law should be the subject of this examination, and, in particular, why the law of contract should be examined. The desirability of examining the law of Marx' time can be seen in the nature of Marx' theory of law as a part of ideology and in the nature of contract law itself.

With regard to Marx' theory of ideology, it is clear that he regarded law as part of the superstructure of society and, indeed, as playing a determining role in the relationship between the classes.[21]

In and of itself, law has certain advantages as an object of study. First, because of the nature of the case reporting system, we can examine at least part of the actual cases, including the concrete facts considered to be relevant by the courts. Such terms as "freedom", "duress", "need", etc., can and should be examined in regard to their actual extension and usage. This examination can be carried out in the study of the cases preserved by the reporters of decided cases.

Second, since Marx, in rejecting the capitalist and democratic concept of freedom, considered himself to be rejecting the existing ideology, it is necessary for us to become familiar with that ideology. Law is preserved to some extent as a datum. If one were to examine, say, the speeches in Parliament in a given year, it would be open to debate whether any particular speech represented popular or class feeling of the time. The law is by definition in Marx' theory a part of the ideological superstructure, and the law is preserved in the judges' opinions and treatises of the time. In this way, we can examine the same phenomena which perhaps were studied by Marx.

Another reason can be given for selecting law as a topic, although it will not be extensively argued here. It is popularly held among legal historians that the dominant theory of law of the nineteenth century was that the law pre-existed any given individual decision and that the judges of the nineteenth and early twentieth centuries did not regard themselves as creating new law so much as they regarded themselves as discovering already existing principles. This phenomenon itself can be argued in support of the Marxist claim that the rights of man appeared natural and pre-existent to the members of capitalist society.

The reasons for selecting the law of contract and, in particular, the law of duress lie in the inherent nature of these doctrines. First, the cases concerning these points of law represent the efforts of the courts to deal with the felt collision between economic freedom and economic need. More specifically, those cases falling within the doctrines of duress of goods or economic duress represent the courts' attempt to deal with the perception of economic need as a constraint to freedom of choice.

Second, the law of economic duress presents an interesting phenomenon in the context of Marxist thought. Even as Marx wrote, the notion of duress was beginning a course of expansion. It is commonly said by legal historians that the nineteenth century was dominated by the concept of freedom of contract, which is the concept that contracts are entered by free individuals according to their own desires and needs and that the state should not meddle with the content of those transactions. When an apparent contract was entered under duress, however, the courts refused to enforce the contract, because the coercion invalidated the requisite consent of one party. Although the view that courts should not disrupt individually chosen contracts, even where those contracts were unfair, was widely accepted during the nineteenth century, at the same time the judges increased the kinds of circumstances that were considered duress.

In the law of contracts, therefore, English and American jurists dealt with the concrete issue of freedom of economic action. As noted above, Marx repeatedly criticized the notion of economic freedom under capitalism as an illusion. For example, in the *Grundrisse* he spoke of

> the absurdity of considering free competition as being the final development of human liberty, and the negation of free competition as being the negation of human liberty and of social production founded on individual liberty. It is only free development on a limited foundation--that of the dominion of capital. This kind of individual liberty is thus at the same time the most complete suppression of all individual liberty and total subjugation of individuality to social conditions which take the form of material forces--and even of all powerful objects that are independent of the individuals relating to them.[22]

Thus, the law of duress is of great interest, because in that area of law, nineteenth-century jurists delineated the factual and legal conditions under which the will was considered to be free, and, by studying the law of duress, one can examine concrete cases of oppression and freedom as defined in the existent ideology of the time. Then, one can determine whether these actual beliefs about freedom of action were illusory.

Two objections may be raised, however, to the use of reported cases as being *eo ipso* a portion of the nineteenth-century ideology of economic freedom. First, it may be argued that reported cases do not reflect the external restraints, if any, in nineteenth-century society which may have prevented egregious cases of economic exploitation. The unknown situations where an individual complied with an extortionate contract or fled before his creditors or committed suicide or could not secure the representation of a solicitor and barrister, etc., do not appear in the case books.

Second, it may be said that we have only the expressed reasons given by the court as the basis for the decision. Class bias, general sympathies, unexpressed moral feelings, etc., do not appear upon the face of these cases.

The strongest justification for using law as a subject is that Marx himself felt that law was part of the ideological superstructure, and the common law was the law of nineteenth-century England, which was the paradigm of capitalism in Marx' writings.

With specific regard to the second objection given above, Marx

himself relied upon expressed viewpoints when he gave any evidence at
all as to the ideology of the nineteenth century. For example, he relied
upon the expressed theories of other economists, such as Ricardo,
rather than upon any analysis of their hidden motivations.

B. The Key Passage

The focal point of this study is a single passage in *The German
Ideology*, as follows:

> In civil law the existing property relations are declared to be the
> result of the general will. The *jus utendi et abutendi* itself asserts
> on the one hand the fact that private property has become entirely
> independent of the community, and on the other the illusion that
> private property itself is based solely on the private will, the
> arbitrary disposal of the thing. In practice, the *abuti* has very
> definite economic limitations for the owner of private property, if
> he does not wish to see his property and hence his *jus abutendi*
> pass into other hands, since actually the thing, considered merely
> with reference to his will, is not a thing at all, but only becomes a
> thing, true property, in intercourse, and independently of the law (*a
> relationship*, which the philosophers call an idea). This juridical
> illusion, which reduces law to the mere will, necessarily leads, in
> the further development of property relations, to the position that a
> man may have a legal title to a thing without really having the thing.
> If, for instance, the income from a piece of land disappears owing
> to competition, then the proprietor has certainly his legal title to it
> along with the *jus utendi et abutendi*. But he can do nothing with it:
> he owns nothing as a landed proprietor if he has not enough capital
> elsewhere to cultivate his land. This illusion of the jurists also
> explains the fact that for them, as for every code, it is altogether
> fortuitous that individuals enter into relations among themselves
> (e.g., contracts); it explains why they consider that these relations
> [can] be entered into or not at will, and that their content [rests]
> purely on the individual free will of the contracting parties.[23]

In the context of Marx' own study of the law, his statements about law,
including especially those in *The German Ideology*, have a certain
fascination. As discussed below, Marx (by his own account) was
relatively well-qualified to give a concrete analysis of the role of law in
the capitalist system, yet his discussion of law sometimes lacked

specificity. An exception to this lack of specificity occurred in *The German Ideology,* where he discussed particular points of contract law.

The selection of the essay *The German Ideology* and, indeed, of one key passage from that essay as the central focus of this study follows naturally from the above discussion of the reasons for undertaking an empirical comparison of existent law with Marx' analysis of law. First, Marx not only repeated in *The German Ideology* some of the themes of his earlier essays, such as 'On the Jewish Question', but here he offered specific references to certain points of contract law. Although Marx discussed Roman civil law, civil rights, and the Factory Act of 1850 in other texts, these discussions were largely historical in nature, and the examples of law were often utilized to support general historical theses. In the quoted passage from *The German Ideology,* however, Marx postulated a relationship between a theory of law and actual, particular principles of law. In that passage, Marx discussed the relationship between the theoretical emphasis upon human will and concrete rules of law. These specific points of contract law in turn reflect the general tenets of economic free-will theory which are contained in democratic political theory.

In addition, *The German Ideology* is interesting because it appears at a turning point between the early and the later Marx. It was written in collaboration between Marx and Engels, but Engels appears to have taken the subordinate role, functioning more as a secretary for Marx' ideas.

Finally, the passage in question is richly ambiguous and displays what I believe to be the range of theses that Marx loosely grouped together as his theory of ideology.

C. Ambiguities and Dilemmas

In the above-quoted passage, Marx defines the "juridical illusion" as that theory which "reduces law to the mere will".[24] It appears, therefore, that Marx is referring to the theory of jurisprudence which is generally called the "will theory of law". That theory and Marx' reactions to it are the focus of this chapter. Here, therefore, I will attempt to review briefly the role of will in theories of law and the problems Marx faced in his attempted refutation.

a. *Review of Will Theories of Law*

The idea of will occurs in philosophy of law in a number of guises, and therefore, it is difficult to speak accurately of *the* will theory of law, as if the term referred in a literal sense to some one theoretical linkage of will and law. It may be said, for example, that Austin's theory that law was the will of the sovereign is a kind of will theory of law. Rousseau held that the general will of a people determined legitimate laws. Locke apparently held that the individual consent of the governed (an act of individual will) was necessary for valid government and that society itself arose from the consent of its individual members. Savigny held that laws arose as a matter of historical fact from the common will of a people and that laws of contract and property recognized certain relationships between the individual will, other people, and the physical world. Hegel also said that contract and property law recognized the role of the individual human will in contact with others and with the physical world, although he postulated that law arose in history as a matter of the unfolding of the Idea rather than as a mere anthropological phenomenon.

The term "will theory of law", however, has a well-accepted, if not well-defined, frame of reference in jurisprudence. Specifically, it refers to the complex of theories which hold that a legal transaction consists in "a willing of some change in a person's sphere of rights to which the law, carrying out his will, gives the intended effect".[25]

These variant theories contain numerous premises both prescriptive and descriptive, and all present their own philosophical puzzles. As a general matter, Marx rejected, to some degree, all of these theories, because in both his proposed scientific theory of society and his proposed political theory, he rejected the primacy of the individual will.

Marx' analysis of the will theories of law puts him in an interesting intellectual position, because these theories are both part of the phenomenon that he is studying and rival theories. In one form or another, the will theories of law posit the efficacy of human will as a shaping force in society. That premise was denied by Marx. On the other hand, he correctly regarded various forms of that premise as key elements in nineteenth-century capitalist ideology. The will theories of law presumably, therefore, are caused by the same historical conditions that cause other elements of ideology, if Marx' theory of ideology is correct. Yet, Marx could not dismiss those theories as mere social phenomena with a particular historical origin and function; since they were the other major social theories of his time, he was concerned also to prove them wrong.[26]

Although the present work is not intended as an intellectual history of Marx' ideas, it is difficult to evaluate his discussion of the "juridical illusion" without some consideration of the philosophers to whom he attributed that illusory thesis. Moreover, as a social scientist, Marx needed to describe accurately an existent theory of law and, in his dual role as scientist and critic, Marx had to criticize real, actually held theories, not merely philosophical constructions - otherwise, he would have committed both a factual error of observation and the philosophical error of addressing his arguments to a straw man. If Marx accurately described views about will and law which were in fact part of nineteenth-century ideology of law, then those views will be found in the philosophers who subscribed to the will theory of law. In other words, the presence or absence of the ideas contained in the paragraphs above in the jurisprudence of Marx' time would show that Marx accurately described the ideas which he sought to reshape. It would *not* prove that his criticisms were in any way effective, but only that their object was not a straw man. I will argue that Marx described accurately various elements of several different will theories, but that his description was not wholly accurate as to any of them.

b. Dilemmas in Marx' Analysis

In his criticism of the will theories, Marx was faced with three conflicting positions which may be called, loosely, the dilemma of materialism and idealism, the dilemma of contract and Communism, and the dilemma of the true ideology.

First, Marx wanted to reject Hegel's idealism but to preserve the philosophical ability to criticize existing ideology. In other words, Marx rejected Hegel's idealism in favor of a materialistic stance and also rejected what he regarded as Savigny's relativism. As a materialist, Marx denied the existence of a trans-historical morality which could be used to evaluate the moral nature of any given society, but he also condemned capitalism on moral grounds as inhumane and destructive of the human spirit.

I will argue that a way out of this puzzle can be constructed from Marx' writings but that it is flawed. The proposed Marxian response is two-fold, consisting in an attempt to refute competing normative claims on factual grounds and an attempt to create a meta-ethical theory in which the true morality is that which arises from a correct perception of society and history.

The second difficulty arises from the first. Marx attempted to refute the Lockean social contract with its attendant concept of the free and autonomous individual, yet he claimed that the Communist society would be a truly free society. I will argue that Marx does not have an adequate response to this problem, although he tried to formulate an alternative concept of freedom and to make the free exchange contemplated by capitalism irrelevant.

The dilemma of the true ideology arises from the Marxist concept of false consciousness. Obviously Marx believed that the ideology of capitalism was false. Yet he must assert that some elements of that ideology (or at least some statements made in materials, such as legal writings, which are otherwise ideological texts) are correct descriptions of the existent society, or his own condemnation of that society fails. For example, in *The German Ideology* and in his notes on Mill's political economy, Marx contrasted at length the self-interested mode of exchange under capitalism with the selfless exchange that he proposed would take place under Communism.[27] According to Marx, members of a capitalist society believe that their relationships with other individuals are the result of bargaining, of mutually self-interested negotiation (in other words, of contract). Further, according to Marx, those elements characterize the alienation and exploitation of capitalist society. Thus, the alienation and exploitation of people which Marx claimed was occurring under capitalism, including during exchange relationships, occurs only if the capitalist description of the transaction is (in part, at least) true.

The notion that some aspects of capitalist ideology are correct descriptions of capitalism occurs in the passage from *The German Ideology* that is the focal point of this study. In that passage, which is quoted above, Marx says, "the *jus utendi et abutendi* [right of use and abuse] itself asserts on the one hand the fact that private property has become entirely independent of the community, and on the other the illusion that private property itself is based simply on private will".[28] The phrase "*jus utendi et abutendi*" is a Latin expression for the notion that the owner of property has the legal right to use the property in any way which he sees fit, literally "to use and abuse". That notion correctly expresses the legal concept of private property, and it is, therefore, part of the capitalist ideology. With regard to that phrase, Marx said that it expressed both a true proposition (that property was "independent of community"; i.e., that it was not subject to being used for the benefit of or according to the decision of all members of society) and a false proposition (that the use of property depended on the arbitrary will of the owner). Thus, Marx' condemnation of capitalist ideology must permit him to retain those elements which he believed to be true and to reject those which he believed to be false.

II. MARX' UNIVERSITY STUDY

An examination of Marx' study of law and philosophy reveals the influence of Hegel and Savigny.

During the period when Marx was a student, two great rival theories struggled for dominance in the byzantine world of German academia: the historical realism of Savigny and the idealism of Hegel. To some extent, the followers of Hegel predominated for a time in Germany, although Savigny had enormous intellectual influence in England and the United States. Many influential scholars and judges, including Oliver Wendell Holmes, adopted wholesale his analysis of contract law. The historical record of Marx' studies tends to show that he was much influenced by Hegelian law professors, although he also developed an acquaintance with Savigny's work. It also shows that he acquired a substantial grasp of actual rules of law, as well as the theoretical analyses of these rules.

Relatively little is known of Marx' specific studies at the universities of Bonn and Berlin, which he attended from October 1835 to March 30, 1841. We do know that his father intended that he become an attorney and that, at least while he was at the University of Bonn, he seemed "to be reconciled to becoming a lawyer".[29]

The available records, both of his course work and of his reading, show that Marx was studying both law and legal philosophy at the University of Bonn, where he attended six courses in the Winter and four in the Summer of 1835-1836, some of which were courses in law. Robert Payne suggests that Marx was "developing a considerable knowledge of its finer points".[30]

In October 1836, Marx moved to the University of Berlin. Franz Mehring notes that Marx put his name down for only twelve lectures during his years at the University of Berlin, "including for the most part the obligatory lectures on jurisprudence, and even of these twelve he probably heard very few".[31]

Both Payne and Mehring refer to the letter which Marx wrote to his father in 1837, which describes in some detail Marx' first year at the University of Berlin.[32] The letter describes Marx' course of study during that year and reveals the extent of his reading on law, as well as his philosophical inclination. Marx noted that he had read some works by Thibault, who was the proponent of a German civil code after the model of the Napoleonic code. Marx had also translated the *Pandex*, which are works on Roman law, into German. In the letter, Marx noted that he had read Savigny's "scholarly work on possession" and lists other works that he had read, as follows: Klein's book on criminal law, Feuerbach's and Grollmann's works on criminal law, Kraemer's *De Verborum Significatione*, Wenning-Ingehein's *Pandect System*, Muhlenbruch's *Doctrina Pandectarum*, and some of Lauterbach's works on civil and ecclesiastical law, as well as various works on the history of Roman and German law.[33]

Although the emphasis on treatises on law, rather than upon collections of cases, differs from the present-day method of American legal education, the subjects (property, criminal law, and contracts) remain the staples of formal legal studies. Marx included a two-page outline of a proposed essay on law, which demonstrates his study of the actual law by its references to many technical legal terms such as "*donatio*" (gift).

Marx diligently attended the lectures of Eduard Gans in the Summer of 1838. Gans lectured both on criminal law and on the then-new Prussian civil code, and he reported the "excellent diligence" which Marx displayed at both these courses.[34] Interestingly, Marx also attended Savigny's course on Roman law, and Savigny indicated that Marx was "outstandingly assiduous" in his attendance. In *Karl Marx: An Intimate Biography,* Padover notes that Savigny and Gans had both been students of Hegel. Payne notes that Marx also attended a course that Winter on the laws of inheritance, rather cynically adding, "perhaps because he was beginning to be anxious about his own inheritance".[35]

Although no independent source, such as letters, reveals in such detail what Marx read in the years at the University of Berlin subsequent to the 1837 letter, it appears that he must have continued to read in the works of the historical school represented by Savigny, because only five years later, in 1842, he wrote 'The Philosophical Manifesto of the Historical School of Law'.[36]

In the 1837 letter, Marx indicated expressly to his father that the philosophy of law was ever more interesting to him than his concrete legal studies. In the proposed essay which he mentioned in the 1837 letter, he intended to construct a coherent philosophy of law and compared his embryonic theory with that of Savigny.[37] This early interest is evidenced in his later work, where Marx relatively seldom referred specifically to concrete examples of existent law, emphasizing instead various philosophies of law, including those of Hegel, Savigny, and Rousseau.[38] His later work, however, is not without specific references to existent laws and legal systems. Marx discussed Roman civil law, for example, at some length in *The German Ideology*, and his knowledge may plausibly be attributed to the extensive readings on Roman law documented in the 1837 letter.[39]   Significantly, one of Savigny's most famous works was his *Treatise on Roman Law*. Marx also later wrote about civil rights, including specific examples from the constitutions of various states, as in the essay 'On the Jewish Question'.[40] In *Capital*, he referred ex- pressly to English regulatory laws, such as the Factory Act of 1850, which controlled the permitted hours of work for factory workers.[41]   Also, of course, in the key passage quoted earlier, Marx referred to specific points of property and contract.

Marx' early allegiance to the young Hegelian movement while he was at the University of Berlin led naturally to his opposition to Savigny and his followers. Eduard Gans, whose courses Marx attended, was a Hegelian philosopher of law, and according to Mehring, Gans' influence can be seen in the polemical 'On the Historical School of Law', which Marx wrote against Savigny's and Hugo's theories.[42]

III. TEXTUAL INDICATIONS OF ATTRIBUTION

The textual evidence as to precisely which theory (or theories) Marx intended to discuss is sometimes scant.

In the course of his voracious reading and production of essays, Marx read and referred to many legal philosophers, social commentators, and economists.   For example, Macchiavelli, Campanella, Hobbes, Spinoza, Hugo, Grotius, Rousseau, Fichte, Hegel, and Montesquieu were all mentioned in the space of a brief page from the leading article in No. 179 of the *Kölnische Zeitung*.[43]

Marx, however, varied in the degree of care with which he identified the subject of his criticism. For example, Easton and Guddat note that Marx' criticism of Gustav Hugo in his article 'The Philosophical Manifesto of the Historical School of Law', written for the *Rheinische Zeitung* in early 1842, could have been directed at Savigny.[44] The only specific reference to Savigny in the essay, how- ever, is the indirect reference contained in the following sentence: "In designating Herr Hugo as the ancestor and creator of the historical school, we act in the very spirit of that school as proved by the most famous historical juris program for Hugo's doctoral anniversary."[45] Easton and Guddat, in editing this passage, note that Marx was referring then to Savigny's *The Tenth of May, 1788: A Contribution to the History of Jurisprudence, Berlin, 1838.*[46]

In his writings, Marx mingled together his rejections of Hegel and Savigny. In his 'Contribution to the Critique of Hegel's Philosophy of Law. Introduction', written in Paris in 1843, Marx referred generally to the historical school of law, in which Savigny was a prominent figure, in the following sentence: "German philosophy of law and state is the only German history which is *al pari* with the official modern reality."[47] The reference to the "official modern reality" may refer to Savigny's office as Minister of Justice, in that according to Marx, Savigny's historical theory of law both legitimated the existing government and directly influenced government policy. A more specific reference was contained in that same essay: "A school of thought that legitimizes today's infamy by yesterday's, a school to which history shows only its *a posteriori*--the Historical School of Law--might have invented German history if it were not an invention of German history."[48]

In addition to Gustav Hugo, Bruno Bauer, Feuerbach, and Max Stirner were frequent targets of specific attack by Marx. In his book *From Hegel to Marx: Studies in the Intellectual Development of Karl Marx,* Sidney Hook devotes a chapter to the analysis of the relationship between Max Stirner and Karl Marx and notes that Marx wrote an entire book on Stirner.[49] Marx devoted an essay ('On the Jewish Question') to the views of Bruno Bauer and referred at various times in that essay to Rousseau, Voltaire, Saint-Simon, Adam Smith, Sismondi and Cherbuliez, Ricardo, and Proudhon. The full title of *The German Ideology* is translated in the *Collected Works* as *The German Ideology: Critique of Modern German Philosophy According to its Representatives Feuerbach, B. Bauer, and Stirner, and of German Socialism According to its Various Prophets.*

Marx' attention in his early works to his rejection of Hegelian philosophy does not need extensive discussion here. His essays 'Toward the Critique of Hegel's Philosophy of Law' and 'Critique of Hegel's Philosophy of the State' are perhaps the most detailed of any of Marx' works in their attention to a particular theory. Yet, in the essay 'Toward the Critique of Hegel's Philosophy of Law; Introduction', Marx did not deal extensively with Hegel's theories of particular aspects of the positive law of property and contracts, nor did he do so in the 'Critique of Hegel's Philosophy of the State'. Except as contained in *The German Ideology*, which was written between November 1845 and October 1846, Marx does not appear to have expressly written about Hegel's treatment of positive law in his own early works, but by Volume III of the *Grundrisse*, written between 1852 and 1858, he felt sufficiently confident to say: "Nothing could be more comical than Hegel's analysis of private property in land. Free private property in land, a very recent product, is not, according to Hegel, a definite social relation, but a relation of man as an individual to Nature ..."[50]

The text of the key passage under consideration here does not give the name of the philosopher or philosophers to whom Marx was addressing his criticism. Easton and Guddat note that according to its title, *The German Ideology* dealt with the work of Feuerbach, but they also assert that it "analyzes the 'illusions' of the Hegelian speculation and asserts the empirical premises of historical explanation".[51] Certainly in his early writings Marx was much occupied with his proposed refutation of Feuerbach's work, which was in turn closely related to his rejection of Hegelian idealism. However, to limit analysis of the quoted passage to merely another essay on Feuerbach would be to narrow unduly the range of Marx' criticism of contemporary legal theory.

It is important not to be too hasty in progressing from the reference to a theory which "reduces law to mere will" to a specific form of the will theory of law. As noted above, the concept of will plays the dominant role in most, if not all, common theories of law in the nineteenth century. In the *Grundrisse*, Marx criticized the same theory of law, which he identified in these terms: "In historical fact, the theorists who considered force as the basis of law were directly opposed to those who saw will as the basis of law."[52] The distinction which Marx made in the *Grundrisse* between theories based on will and those based on the idea of force might possibly rule out Hobbes as the target for Marx' criticism, but it and the above definition together still encompass a large number of theories of law; on its face, the "juridical illusion" could characterize a number of philosophers.

It seems likely that Marx was referring to a group of otherwise disparate philosophers or, more accurately, to a complex of ideas common to some degree to a disparate group of philosophers, including Hegel, Savigny, Rousseau, Locke, and even, to an extent, Austin. That complex of ideas centers on the basic concept that the essence of law is human will. It may include such ideas as that individual or general will brings law into being and that particular rules of law represent and regulate relations of separate human wills.[53]

There is some evidence in *The German Ideology* itself that Marx intended to sweep the bulk of eighteenth- and nineteenth-century legal theory within the reach of his criticism: "The modern French, English and American writers all express the opinion that the state exists only for the sake of private property so that this view has also been generally accepted by the average man." Easton and Guddat translate the latter phrase more metaphysically as "this fact has entered into the consciousness of the ordinary man."[54]

In the next section, I suggest that the complex of ideas about will and law actually contains two distinct will theories of law, one about the basis of law and one about the nature of legally significant facts. After that, I argue that the ideas which Marx called the "juridical illusion" are found principally in three philosophers: Hegel, Savigny, and to a lesser degree, Locke. Throughout these sections, I will develop the idea that Marx shifted from one kind of will theory to another and that his criticisms, therefore, vary in efficacy and direction.

I believe that the theories of Savigny and Hegel represented two magnetic poles to which Marx was drawn in turn; alternatively attracted by Savigny's concrete historical studies and Hegel's powerful dialectic, Marx wanted simultaneously to reject Hegelian idealism and to avoid Savigny's historicism, at least insofar as the latter appeared to legitimize *all* existing institutions.

IV. ANALYSIS OF THE WILL THEORY OF LAW

Assuming that Marx' "juridical illusion" refers to a will theory of law, this section provides an analysis of the kind of theories Marx was discussing. As noted above, however, Marx' reference to the theory "which reduces law to mere will" does not unambiguously pick out one variant of the theories of law which include the idea of will. Specifically, Marx' reference may include, but is not necessarily limited to, the will theory of law in the narrow sense of the view that legal relationships are determined by acts of will.

In this first section I will endeavor to show that the general idea of a will theory of law actually contains two related positions, which are that law as a social institution is based on human will and that the law recognizes relationships which arise out of the will of the parties. I call these two positions, respectively, the basis will theory of law and the recognition will theory of law. Both of these will theories of law are theories about the nature of law.

Further, both of these theories can have normative, as well as descriptive, content; i.e., both theories can contain premises about the way laws ought to be as well as about the factual or descriptive nature of those laws as social institutions. Finally, these theories can occur in reported cases as well as in philosophical writings.

When a court states a proposition about will and law, however, that statement may be a theoretical statement about the nature of law, including a factual claim; or a normative claim; or, finally, a rule of law, e.g. a statement of the legal effect of an act of will. Succeeding sections will examine these variants.

A. The Will Theory as Meta-Legal Principle

This section analyzes the will theory of law as a theory about the nature of law, which is descriptive or factual in the sense that any theory about the nature of society is intended to describe and explain a particular phenomenon.

a. The Nature of Meta-Legal Statements

In ethics, statements about the nature of ethical discourse, such as statements about the nature of the good or about the nature of rights, are termed "meta-ethical", meaning that these statements are not themselves statements with an imperative or normative content, but are rather descriptive sentences about the nature of normative statements. For example, the statement "The term 'good' does not refer to a quality" is a meta-ethical statement, while the statement "Pleasure is good" is an ethical or value statement.[55]

The will theories of law are about the phenomenon of law itself and are not statements of rules of law. They are, therefore, meta-legal statements. The prefix "meta" is used loosely here, rather than in the technical sense of a meta-language.

b. The Truth Conditions of Meta-Legal Statements

The distinction between meta-legal statements and rules of law affects the truth conditions of the will theories. A meta-legal statement may be one concerned with the nature of the law or one which expresses a normative statement about laws, such as "All laws ought to be in conformity with the general will." It does not express, however, a rule of law, such as "All valid contracts require a meeting of the minds." To avoid confusion, the term "meta-legal" is here used to refer to those theories which are not normative theories; the latter will be referred to as "normative will theories". A meta-legal statement is one concerned with the nature of law, not one which expresses either a normative statement, such as "All laws ought to be in conformity with the general will", or a rule of law, such as "All valid contracts require a meeting of the minds." Thus, the meta-legal statements are neither statements of rules of law nor prescriptive statements, and therefore, they suffer none of the problems associated with determining the truth of those statements.

As meta-legal statements, both the basis will theory and the recognition will theory are statements of purported fact, not statements of rules. As such, they are susceptible to being refuted on the grounds that they are simply false or that some of the terms are non-referring. Thus, to the extent their theories contain such statements of purported fact, Savigny, Hegel, and the social contract theorists may be refuted on either or both of these grounds.

As can be seen by the discussion of Hegel's and Savigny's philosophy of property law and contract below, the nature of law is considered a factual matter in the sense of being a statement about the world; Hegel and Savigny treated their description of property and contract (including the free will aspects) as factual descriptions. Indeed, this is one reason for loosely characterizing these statements as meta-legal statements.

c. Two Forms of Will Theories

There are, however, two forms of this meta-legal will theory of law, two will theories, so to speak. One is the theory that the phenomenon of law, of rule-governed social order or dispute resolution, is based on human will; that theory is called here, reasonably, the "basis will theory". The other, which is called the "recognition will theory", is the theory that the law recognizes or governs the relationship between individual wills or between the individual will and physical objects.

1. The Basis Will Theory

The basis will theory is basically a historical theory about the nature or origin of law as a social phenomenon, that is, about the origin of rule-governed order as a social relationship. The basis will theory itself can have two narrower forms: as an attempted historical account either of the general phenomenon of law in the broad sense of rule-governed social order or of the specific, positive rules of law by which a given society is ordered.

A hypothetical example of the will theory of law as a general historical thesis would be the following proposition:

Law (rule-governed social order) arose in the course of history because, at some determinate point, individuals decided that theirs would be a rule-governed relationship.

In a parallel manner, the basis will theory of law may be offered as a factual explanation of what causes laws in a present-day society. One may say that "laws are created by the will of those governed by them" or "the people choose their representatives, and these representatives decide upon the rules which will govern the people" or "the will of the sovereign is the law". All are examples of a basis will theory of the origin of existent laws.

2. The Recognition Will Theory

The recognition will theory is not concerned with the causes of law as a social phenomenon, but with the nature of that phenomenon. Under a recognition will theory, it could be a matter of indifference what caused the rules in society to exist, and it would be consistent with a recognition will theory to postulate, for example, that law exists because the species with the most harmonious and regulated social order has the best chance of survival.

The recognition will theory in the context of contracts and property postulates that the laws of property and contract recognize, enforce, or govern expressions of the individual will; to put it another way, that acts of will create legal relationships. On this theory, property law expresses the rules governing the exercise of human will over an external object, and contract law reflects the meeting of two wills, to paraphrase the legal maxim.

A less metaphysical (but still meta-legal) version is to read the recognition will theory as containing simple statements of facts about a specific society, rather than as general statements about the nature of law and human will. Specifically, a cultural interpretation of a recognition will theory of nineteenth-century law is that the existent (nineteenth-century) laws of contract and property provide for the free expression of human will. Although Savigny and Hegel agreed with that proposition, it differs somewhat from Hegel's theories at least in that it expresses only a contingent proposition about a given set of laws and does not purport to express a universal truth about human will.

The above cultural interpretation is included in this catalogue of possible interpretations of the phrase "juridical illusion" for two reasons. First, nineteenth-century legal treatise writers and judges apparently believed that as a matter of fact various legal propositions accurately described their society, as will be discussed below. Second, the cultural interpretation fits in the context of the passage under consideration and with certain other criticisms by Marx of freedom of contract. Specifically in the passage from *The German Ideology*, the conclusions which Marx discussed as following from the juridical illusion are all concerned with actual freedom of action in nineteenth-century capitalist society, e.g., the actual ability to use property, as opposed to the abstract legal right to use it.

An interesting aspect of both the recognition and basis theories is that both are susceptible of relativistic versions. In other words, one may hold that members of a society would always choose certain principles if each had his or her free way or that the laws chosen will vary depending on the social circumstances. That is, one may hold with Savigny that laws properly vary, depending on the historical conditions of the people, or with Locke that the people ought to choose laws which reflect the one true and underlying relationship between an individual and his labor. The question of whether and to what extent laws vary depends in part on whether one holds that the relationships between individuals and between individuals and things vary. Hegel, Savigny, and Locke all held that there were certain fundamental aspects to the relationships between individuals and each other and the world, which were that the individual related to others and objects on terms of dominance in an individual way: e.g., "This object is mine if I have created it by my own labor and its 'mineness' consists in my possessing it and excluding you from having it." Savigny believed that the proper expression of that relationship could and would vary from communal to private property depending on economic and historical conditions. Marx' great rejection of the will theory was to argue that the relationship itself was malleable, so that a fundamentally different non-contractual non-dominance relationship could obtain in the ideal society.

3. Logical Relationship of the Basis and Recognition Will Theories

It is possible to hold one of these theories without subscribing to the other. It would be logically possible, for example, to hold that a rule-governed society was inevitably caused by historical forces (and not by human will), but that the characteristic element of these rules is the action of the human will. The three theories of interest here

(Savigny, Hegel, and the social contract theories) varied in their combination of the two theories.

Certain aspects of each of the three philosophers considered as candidates for holders of the "will theory of law" would lead to their being considered to have held both a recognition and a basis will theory. To some degree, Hegel, Savigny, and Locke all felt that the rules of law which governed such matters as contract and property were concerned with the human will. Not only did Savigny and Hegel treat the essential nature of law as will, but both of them held that specific rules of law follow from this nature.

As can be seen in the following discussion of Hegel's and Savigny's philosophy of property law and contract, the nature of law was considered by them as a factual matter in the sense of being a statement about the world. Hegel and Savigny treated their description of property and contract (including the free will aspects) as factual descriptions. Locke did so also, as can be seen in his description of the state of nature. Indeed, this is one reason for loosely characterizing these statements as meta-legal statements.

Since Hegel believed that property was a matter of the relationship of the human will to the objective world and that it required the recognition of other individuals for its validity, it is plausible to say that Hegel would not adhere to any view which postulated the existence of law itself as a matter for human decision. For Hegel, laws, such as the law of contract, expressed the true nature of the relationship between people and the world; these laws exist not as a matter of decision, but as a matter of necessary fact.

Hegel similarly held that contracts of exchange consist of the mutual willing of the exchange of mutually recognized items of property. Not only did Savigny and Hegel treat the essential nature of law as will, but both of them held that specific rules of law follow from this nature. Hegel, for example, argued that the rule that invalidates a contract where the consideration on one side is inadequate *(laesio enormis)* expressed a necessary element of contracts, which is the exchange of property recognized by both sides (as a matter of the meeting of their common will) as equivalent in value. Thus, Hegel could be said to hold a recognition will theory but not a basis will theory.

Savigny appears to hold a theory which would contain at least some variant of both the basis and recognition will theories. He believed that law originates in the common will of a nation and that the nature of contract and property law consists in the recognition of the relationships of the human will to others and to the physical world. The will of a people creates the law, and especially, of course, the common law. Yet, at the same time, Savigny held that the essence of contract and property law is human will, the relationship of the individual will to things and to other people. For example, Savigny treated contracts as the domination of one will over another in a limited sphere of action.

Similarly, at least some versions of social contract theory would hold both a recognition and a basis will theory. It appears that Locke and Rousseau can be plausibly interpreted as believing in some form of historical social contract, while believing that social relationships were essentially a matter of the will of the parties. According to classic will theory, society is as it is because people have come together and agreed to live under certain rules.

B. The Will Theory as Moral Principle

A will theory of law can take the form of a normative principle of political philosophy, one having to do with the question of which laws are valid or which laws are morally correct.

One form of this normative theory is that those laws are just (or obligatory) which are derived from the will of the governed; this is the view that a law is valid if, and only if, the persons governed by that law have agreed so to be governed. In other words, this is the normative form of the social contract theory. Naturally, this version of the social contract is capable of a large number of permutations.[56] Some remarks which Marx made in describing the will theory of law suggest that he had a normative theory in mind, and he was concerned to reject social contract theory.

Clearly, the above normative interpretation is consistent with the basis will theory. That is, the premise that laws are created by a communal act of will is consistent with the premise that a law is valid only if the persons governed have consented to it.

It is not at all clear that the social contract interpretation is necessarily consistent with the view that, as a matter of fact, law is the expression of human will, i.e., with the recognition will theory. The reason for this possible inconsistency is that the recognition will theory, as stated by Hegel and Savigny, treated law as expressing the true relationships of one will to another or of one will to an object, not as expressing a decision about the desired form of those relationships. The law of adverse possession, for example, on Hegel's view, is the law not because it was agreed to in an effort to resolve old title disputes but because it expressed the true relationship between usage, will, and the ownership of physical objects.

The normative theory does not entail the basis will theory; i.e., the "ought" statement does not follow from the "is" statement and vice versa. Under the basis will theory, the society or law created by the will is not necessarily valid or just; as a factual theory, it contains no expression on this matter. Under the normative theory, however, an ordered society may or may not be *created* by the will of the people, but laws are *valid* only if all persons (or a specified portion of them) will themselves to be bound by those laws. (The term "valid" is used in this discussion as a shorthand term for "legitimate", "morally binding", or one of the variety of other terms which have been used to refer to the obligation of a member of a society to obey the law.)[57]

A normative theory about will and law need not consist in the social contract theory of legitimate societies. Rather, it may consist in the principle that the law ought to recognize relationships willed by individuals, that acts of will ought morally to create legal relationships. Such a view would be, for example, that the laws of contract and property ought to further the free exercise of the human will.

The question arises of the consistency of this normative version of the recognition theory with other facets of the will theories. Here it is not clear that every normative recognition theory will be consistent with a normative version of social contract theory. The principle that "the law ought to recognize as legally binding such acts of will as promises" might conflict with the premise that "those laws are valid to which people consent" if the people should consent to a non-contractual system of exchange. Thus, a normative recognition theory may conflict with a normative basis theory.

Once again, the reason for including this particular normative version of the recognition theory here is its presence in judicial thinking of the time. In both the law of contracts and of property, restrictions on the free exercise of property rights were frowned on. For example, restrictions on the alienation of property were generally prohibited, with certain technical exceptions. Similarly, restrictions on the right to enter contracts were discouraged. An example of this is that labor cases prior to the enactment of the National Labor Relations Act often protected both the worker's right to strike and the factory owner's right to blacklist union workers, since both these actions fell within the individual's right to determine with whom he would contract and upon what terms.

If the "juridical illusion" refers to a normative theory, however, then certain problems are raised for Marx. As noted above, Marx regarded himself as a social scientist, not as a mere utopian reformer arguing that his version of society was more fair or more just. He is in danger of being just such a reformer, however, if he is attempting to refute a normative theory on purely normative grounds. It is argued later that although Marx may well have used the term "juridical illusion" to refer ambiguously to a complex of beliefs which include the normative propositions discussed above, he should, if he is consistent in his role as social scientist, be pointing out factual, not moral, flaws in the opposing theories. Additionally, it will be argued that Marx was unsuccessful in this venture.

C. The Will Theory as an Axiom of Law

The phrase "juridical illusion" may also refer simply to a law. The term "juridical illusion" itself connotes a relationship with courts, and the phrase is used by Marx synonymously with the "illusion of lawyers".

General statements about the relationship of will and law appear in nineteenth-century cases as part of the courts' reasoning and are therefore to be considered either as rules of law or as factual or theoretical views of the judges. In any event, such statements form part of the current ideology.

One court's views on freedom of contract and property were clearly expressed in 1905 in the case of *Berry v. Donovan*, as follows:

The right to dispose of one's labor as he wills is incident to the freedom of the individual, which lies at the foundation of the government in all countries that maintain principles of civil liberty.[58]

In that context, the principle that the law is (rightfully) intended to promote free exercise of will over oneself and one's relationships appears as one of the premises upon which the court bases its decision. It may be considered to be an axiom of law because it appears in the printed records of the decision in the same fashion as the other rules of the decision, because it is a premise in the court's argument, and because it concerns legal rights.

At this point, I wish to digress long enough to discuss the nature of the statements contained in reported cases. Lawyers and scholars often speak as if not every statement in a judicial opinion (nor every premise in a legal argument) is a rule of law. First, of course some of the statements in an opinion are factual remarks about the particular situation, since the usual model for legal reasoning is that general rules of law are applied to specific facts. Second, a judge may mix statements of social policy or sociological theory in with his premises of law. So, for example, the Supreme Court in the leading desegregation case, *Brown v. Board of Education,* apparently based its holding in part on sociological data concerning the deleterious effects of school segregation on black youngsters. Moreover, a court might also, and on similar terms, include any of the will theories of law. Theoretical statements like "The law of contract ought to (or does) further certainty in business dealings" can be found in cases along with specific rules, such as "Acceptances are effective upon being sent but revocations only upon receipt."

One of the difficulties of an analysis of judicial thought is that the nature of the premises of the court's reasoning is not differentiated. That is, similar but not identical sentences may express different kinds of statements, which in turn are subject to different kinds of proof. Thus, a given sentence may express a descriptive statement, which may be more or less theoretical or observational, a meta-legal statement, and a rule of law. The following sentence from *Dunn v. Chambers* will serve as an example:

> Every man is presumed to be capable of managing his own affairs; and whether his bargains are wise or unwise is not, ordinarily, a legitimate subject of inquiry, in a court either of legal or equitable jurisdiction.[59]

That sentence arguably comprises four distinct kinds of proposition.

First, the sentence states two rules of law. One is the presumption in the law that a party to a contract was competent to make the contract. That assumption is expressed by the rule that one seeking to repudiate a contract on the ground that one party to it was not capable of giving a valid consent - as where the person was under age - carries a heavy burden of proof. Further, it is also a rule that the unfairness or imprudence of the bargain is not usually a legal ground to unwind the contract. Thus, the court in *Dunn v. Chambers* accurately stated the law.

Second, however, the idea that each individual is the best judge of his own affairs is a descriptive premise about the role of each individual as an autonomous member of society, capable of appointing his own needs.

Third, the concept of the legitimacy of a court's evaluating contracts for fairness or prudence is a moral concept; that is, the thought expressed is that it would be wrong for a court to have such power.

Finally, the phrase concerning the legitimacy of a court's reviewing contracts for fairness also can express a recognition theory of law, whether normative or not. The sentence can be taken as expressing the proposition that a court cannot properly undo a transaction entered into by a competent individual because correct decisions reflect the recognition of the individual's willed acts.

The nature of rules is itself subject to some philosophical subtlety. It was noted earlier that if the "juridical illusion" refers to a will theory of law and if that theory is a descriptive theory, then the theory may be refuted on factual grounds; the truth conditions for the theory are, relatively speaking, simple. To the extent that the "juridical illusion" refers to rules of law, some complexity is created by virtue of their ambiguous nature.

The statement "Each player shall be given three chances to hit the ball" is a constitutive rule of the game of baseball; it is part of the network of rules which effectively define that game and distinguish it from other games, such as basketball. Similarly, the rule that "Three of a kind beat two pair" is a rule of the card game of poker.

The sense in which these rules can be true or false is difficult to understand. If these odd statements are true at all, they are true only in the limited context of the game being played. If spoken at the Astrodome in the Summer when the Astros are playing, the proposition that each player (although not each person attending) will be given three chances to hit the ball may well be true. The statement may well be false if spoken at the Astrodome in the winter when the Oilers are playing football.

In certain limited contexts, then, four things may be said about the truth or falsity of rule statements such as the proposition P, where P is a statement of the kind "Three of a kind beat two pair": (1) the truth of the statement that "P is a rule of the game of poker" is evaluated by certain criteria which may differ from those used to determine the truth of P itself; (2) the proposition P may be true or false as an objective description of events; (3) the proposition P may be meaningless if the game of which it is a rule does not exist; and (4) when the proposition P is used to express a rule, it is not susceptible to being true or false, although the statement "P is a rule of the game of poker" may be true or false.

The question, then, is: what is the status of the will theories of law when incorporated in a judicial opinion? Indeed, what is the metaphysical status of the statements of rules? Is the statement "Each person has the right to enter such contracts as he chooses" a mere statement of one of the lesser rules of the game of capitalism with no more objective truth value than the statement "Do not pass Go; do not collect two hundred dollars"?

Law is part of capitalist ideology, and Marx attempted to refute the economic and sociological model portrayed by the will theory of law, as well as to impeach the political model of social contract. How can such a refutation be made as to the factual truth of these statements if they are rules? It would be possible for Marx to try to criticize the rules on the grounds that they were unjust, but then Marx would be dealing with normative, rather than ordinary, objective, statements of fact.

The question of whether Marx' remarks accurately describe remarks by judges and courts will be discussed later. Since the purpose of our study is not to evaluate the linguistic nature of rules, I will assume that, to the extent the "juridical illusion" refers to some form of the will theories as expressed by judges, those statements may be taken as descriptive statements about society, as well as rules. The answer, then, is to embrace the ambiguous nature of these statements - to permit them, so to speak, to function both as rules and as ordinary objective statements, whether descriptive or theoretical.

V. ANALYSIS OF THE KEY PASSAGE

For purposes of discussion, the key passage quoted above can be separated into seven different theses, as follows:

Thesis I: This juridical illusion, which reduces law to mere will, in further development of property relationships necessarily leads to one's having legal title to a thing without actually having it.

Thesis II: If, for example, the income from a piece of land is lost due to competition, the owner, to be sure, has his legal title to it along with the *jus utendi and abutendi.*

Thesis III: But he cannot do anything with it.

Thesis IV: If he does not have enough capital to cultivate his land, he owns nothing as a landed proprietor.

Thesis V: The illusion of lawyers also explains why for them, as

for every code, it is altogether accidental that individuals enter into relationships with one another, for
example, make contractual agreements.

Thesis VI: The illusion of lawyers also explains the view that
these relationships can be entered into or not at will.

Thesis VII: The illusion of lawyers also explains why they hold
the view that the content of these relationships rests
entirely on the individual free will of the contracting
parties.

Upon analysis, it can be seen that these apparently simple sentences are
rich with theoretical implications but are lamentably ambiguous. This
section is devoted to analyzing these theses, including particularly the
role of the "juridical illusion".[60]

It can be seen that the above theses fall into two groups. Theses I
and V through VII postulate relationships between the "juridical
illusion" and other aspects of legal theory, while Theses II through IV
comment specifically on the relationship between financial conditions
and title to real property. The statements about the "juridical illusion"
are the most interesting and will be analyzed the most closely.

At this point, it may be useful to put the present discussion in
perspective. This section of our account is not concerned with the accuracy of Marx' characterization of will theory as an illusion; rather, it is
concerned only with the content of that claimed illusion - with the
belief, not with its alleged falsity. The illusory nature of this belief, in
Marx' view, will be analyzed in the section of this paper which deals
with Marx' criticism of the will theory of law and its implications.

Basically, Theses I, V, VI, and VII are four statements about the
consequences of the "juridical illusion". As will be discussed further
below, it is not clear whether these statements are claims about the
psychology of capitalist lawyers, about the historical development of
ideology, or about the alleged logical consequences of the will theory of
law. For the purposes of this discussion, however, the four theses will
be analyzed by breaking them into their component parts and then by
examining the proper linkage between these parts.

A. The "Juridical Illusion" as Will Theory of Law

Assuming that Marx' supposed "juridical illusion" is identical with a will theory of law, the discussion in this section concerns the nature of that theory. For present simplicity's sake, the will theory of law may be assumed to consist of one sentence, as follows: "Will is the foundation of law". The question becomes, then, what sort of statement is that? As noted above, it may be a meta-legal statement, a moral principle, or an axiom of law.

The earlier analysis of will theories of law provides a useful framework for analysis of the juridical illusion. That framework consisted in two versions of a will theory (the basis and recognition theories). Although there are numerous variants on these theories, the following two premises express the general principle of each alternative:

1.   The laws of property and contract are created by the will of the people in the society where that law is in force. (Basis will theory)

2.   The laws of property and contract recognize or express the relationship between one individual's will and an object or another's will. (Recognition will theory)[61]

In addition to the textual support for the assertion that Marx was discussing, in some form, Savigny or Hegel or the social contract theorists, there is some textual support for the proposition that Marx was concerned with a meta-legal version of the will theory of law.

The general basis will theory interpretation of the "juridical illusion" is supported by various passages in the *Grundrisse*.[62] Marx there referred to the will theory of law as being a theory which ascribed both the origin of the law and the creation of particular laws to acts of will or decisions.

The narrower basis will theory as to the origin of specific laws was also mentioned by Marx in the *Grundrisse*, where he said: "[T]he individuals who rule under these conditions, quite apart from the fact that their power has to constitute itself as a State, must give their will, as it is determined by these definite circumstances, a general expression as the rule of the State, as law." Marx, of course quickly rejects that thesis, saying, "Just as the bodily weight of individuals does not depend upon their ideal will or caprice, so it does not depend on them whether they embody their will in law... ."[63]

Indeed, the basis will theory and the recognition will theory are intertwined in the key passage from *The German Ideology*. Marx first said there: "In civil law the existing property relationships are declared to be the result of the general will." He followed that remark with the statement that "[t]he *jus utendi and abutendi* itself asserts…the illusion that private property itself is based solely on the private will… ."[64] The former statement reflects the basis will theory, while the latter reflects a recognition will theory.

As will be discussed further below, the basis and recognition theories embody various views about the formation of society and human nature, which views Marx rejected. The basis theory holds that humans' will creates society; Marx held that economic forces shaped society. The recognition theory holds that law (or correct law) reflects the existing (or true) relationships among individuals; Marx held that society's rules *sometimes* recognized existing social relationships but that when those social relationships reached a certain point, legal rules did not reflect society accurately and that at some time in the future law would not exist at all. More specifically, Marx rejected the idea that there were universal, true, or natural relationships of domination and exclusion between people. He also rejected, at least in part, the premise that exchange relationships were freely chosen.

Although the descriptive meta-legal readings of the will theory referred to by Marx as the "juridical illusion" are consistent with the Marxist texts and with at least some of the views expressed by the philosophers here considered, two other interpretations are possible: to interpret the "juridical illusion" as a normative principle or as an axiom of law. These interpretations will be discussed in passing only, since the meta-legal reading is more plausible in the context.

B.   Analysis of the Result Propositions

The propositions which, according to Marx, follow from the will theory of law (called here the "result propositions") are characterized by being more specific and concrete than the "juridical illusion". Theses I and V through VII deal with specific aspects of property and contract, containing relatively concrete statements about these phenomena:

1.   Legal title is separable from economic usage.

2.   It is altogether accidental that individuals enter contracts.

3.   Contracts can be entered into or not at will.

4.   The content (substantive terms) of contracts rests entirely on the individual free will of the contracting parties.

These four statements are themselves susceptible to three different kinds of interpretations: as meta-legal (or non-legal) statements of fact, as rules of law, and as normative claims. Although again these interpretations are not mutually exclusive, it will be seen that not all of the four statements lend themselves equally to each of the possible readings.

One may assume that Marx considered these four claims as part of the then existing ideology, specifically capitalistic legal theory. Yet, the kind of criticism of that ideology that can be made varies with the sort of statement under consideration. For example, if the "juridical illusion" refers to the basis will theory, then Marx could be claiming, alternately, that that will theory is flawed because it leads to allegedly false factual claims or to false rules of law or to false normative claims. In his quest for the moral neutralism of the scientist, however, Marx wanted to avoid basing his criticism of the factual premises of capitalistic economics upon a moral assault - he wanted to demonstrate that that economics was false, not merely that he offered a more desirable Utopia.

a. As Meta-Legal Statements

As descriptive meta-legal statements, the result propositions can be plausibly cast as follows:

1a. Ownership of physical objects is separate and distinct from the economic ability to make use of the object.

2a. It is not necessary that individuals enter into relationships with each other; people do not *ab initio* stand in relationships of obligation to each other.

3a. Contractual obligations arise solely because the parties freely decide to enter into agreements; no external constraint forces people to do so.

4a. The terms of these contracts (the obligation which is undertaken) are likewise freely decided by the parties.

The first and most obvious aspect of these statements is that they are statements of fact; while these statements are not unambiguous, their

truth conditions lack the complexity and controversy of rule and normative statements. Specifically, in the context of the nineteenth-century
worship of science and of Marx' own commitment to empiricism, these
appear to be statements which are susceptible to demonstration or
refutation by the scientific formulation of a social theory or by simple
scientific observation.

If, as Marx claimed, these factual views were held by the ideologists of the nineteenth century and *if* these factual claims could be
proven false, then Marx could claim to have refuted certain tenets of
capitalist political philosophy on a purely scientific ground. Further, he
would have shown that the capitalist view that will creates law led to a
false conclusion.

Implicit in the above remarks is the fact that Marx, in order to score
a telling point against capitalist ideology, must actually prove two
premises: first, that these factual perceptions were actually held by
members of capitalist society and, second, that, as a matter of fact, they
are false. Here, then, the concept of illusion surfaces in this discussion;
if Marx is to show, as he boasted, that these ideas are the illusions of
capitalism, he must show that these were false ideas held by capitalists. In a later section, I will consider whether Marx succeeded in either
of these aims.

The second point about the above factual claims is that their scope
remains unclear. That is, are these statements which refer to a certain
society, probably to nineteenth-century English and American society,
or are they intended as universal descriptions of the human condition?
If meant as universal, then to be true they must hold throughout the
historical permutations of societal conditions (unless the theory allows
for historical distortions of these facts about human nature), but if they
are intended *only* as referring to one particular culture, then they cannot
be impeached by a mere showing of historical cultural variance, i.e., by
simply showing that not all cultures conform to those premises.[65]

The dichotomy can best be seen with regard to result proposition
2a, above. As a universal premise, it might be implied in many social
contract theories, since those theories tend to postulate that man is by
nature isolated and alone and that societal relationships are secondary
features adopted as a matter of choice. On the other hand, as a premise
specifically referring to nineteenth-century society, the thesis
corresponds to the popular view that the nineteenth century was a time
of unbridled liberty of individual choice, i.e., one in which individuals
were essentially unrelated to one another, in contrast to the Middle
Ages, where status, rather than choice, determined the bulk of the
individual's social alliances. Both Marx and Sir Henry Maine adopted

some form of that historical comparison. A related point, with regard to statement 2a again, turns on the meaning of "accidental". As discussed below, the term may refer to characteristics which are not essential elements of human nature, or it may refer to an absence of some sort of historical necessity, or it may refer to the relationships of individuals in an actual society. In the last sense, of course, the concept is congruent with Marx' and Maine's views which contrasted capitalism with feudalism along the lines of the contract/status distinction. Under that contrast, an individual's personal identity under capitalism is complete and fully formed without the addition of his societal relationships; he is, to use Marx' idea, a "monad". Thus, his societal relationships are accidental to his identity because they are not necessary to it; that is, the identity is complete in all essential aspects without those relationships. Under feudalism, according to Marx and Maine, one's relationships determined one's identity so that a person simply was a peasant or a lord or a burgher, and such relationships were necessary components of one's identity.

The third point with regard to the above four factual premises concerns statement 3a, which seems to be a tautological definition of the term "contract". A contract consists in a meeting of the minds, and if both wills were not free, no binding actual agreement was entered.[66]

Finally, the four factual assertions contain a crucial unclarity: what are they about? Are these statements about things (or at least relationships) which can be said to exist independently of any particular society? Do the terms in these statements indelibly refer to a given society? Are there societies in which such terms as "contract" would be non-referring and where, therefore, the statements containing these sentences would be meaningless or false? As will be argued further below, for Marx these statements are all to a degree societally dependent.[67]

b. As Rules of Law

These four result propositions may also be interpreted as stating rules of law, as follows:

1b.   The economic use made of property is not one of the criteria for title to it.

2b.   Each person is legally unrelated to another prior to entering contracts.

3b. Contractual obligations arise solely because the parties freely decide to enter into agreements; no external constraint forces persons to do so.

4b. Each person has the legal right to decide upon what terms, if any, he or she will enter any given contract; the terms of contractual obligations are set by consent.

First, the legal interpretation of Premise 2 is somewhat strained because the term "accidental" is a rather metaphysical term.[68] The concept of something being accidental does not fit handily into the framework of a legal rule, although it may well be contained in the framework of legal thought.

The legal interpretation of result propositions 3b and 4b renders 2b somewhat superfluous. The reason for this is that 3b and 4b express the lack of a prior legal obligation which characterized at least exchange relationships in nineteenth-century law. The concept that consensual (as opposed to societally imposed) obligations characterize a given society (which may be the nub of the accidental concept in the legal context) is better and more naturally expressed by the two later premises. In fact, of course, statements 2b through 4b summarize the classical principles of freedom of contract which dominated nineteenth-century contract law.

As with the descriptive claims described in the previous section, Marx needed first to establish that the legal interpretations were in fact the law. If they are in fact rules of law, he could have ventured upon three different routes of criticism. He could have argued that these laws were not just or fair *or* that the relationship of the will to the world is not as described *or* that the factual or societal presupposition for the rights does not exist. In other words, Marx might have argued that the rule in statement 3b above is not a just law and, therefore, that it either is not or should not be the law. Marx might, on the other hand, have attempted to show that although a given rule was an element in the positive law of a particular society, it was not expressive of a truth about man and nature; in other words, he would have attempted to show that the factual statement was false. Finally, Marx might have argued that statement 3b presupposes statement 3a and then attempted to show that 3a was factually false, thus showing that even if society ostensibly afforded the legal rights described in 3b, their exercise was impossible.

c. As Normative Principles

The result propositions can also be interpreted as normative statements, as follows:

1c.   One's right to property vis-à-vis the other members of society ought not to be affected by the use which one is economically able to make of the property.

2c.   It is not morally necessary that individuals enter into relationships with each other; persons do not ab initio stand in relationships of obligation to each other.

3c.   Valid or binding contractual obligations arise solely because the parties freely decide to enter into agreements; no external constraint forces persons to do so.

4c.   The terms of morally binding agreements are likewise free-decided by the parties.

Once again, in order for Marx' criticisms, if any, of these normative principles to be telling as a criticism of capitalism, he must show first that these principles were in fact held by capitalists and then that they were false. Like the legal interpretations, these readings can be considered as purely descriptive statements concerning a particular society, so that the amplified proposition, "In 1850 in Britain and the United States, there was no moral obligation to enter any particular contract" would be true or false depending on the actual social mores of that period. On a relativistic theory of ethics, of course, that is the only sense in which the statement can be meaningfully said to be true or false. On any objective theory of ethics, on the other hand, the statement could be true or false as a matter of fact. The question for Marx is a delicate one; if the will theory led to morally unacceptable claims, then it is flawed, but Marx cannot rely on a universal theory of ethics to refute these normative claims as false.

C. Analysis of the Connection Between the Juridical
    Illusion and the Result Propositions

The next step in this step-by-step analysis is to consider what these
theses are about, that is, what sort of claims are these? The key theses
may be read as expressing three separate sorts of claims: claims about
psychology, being the relationships between certain subjective beliefs;
claims about the relationship between certain components of ideology as
a matter of historical causation; and claims about logical entailments.

This section of our account is devoted only to brief descriptions of
the three kinds of connections which Marx may have been postulating
between a will theory of law and various more concrete statements
about law and society. The question of whether either the actual legal
system or the various theorists actually held any of these views is post-
poned until later.

The point of elucidating these various connections is to expand
further our concept of what Marx must show about the various aspects
of capitalist ideology which he is attempting to describe and criticize.
If, pursuant to the historical or psychological viewpoints, he argued that
having a certain idea causes one to hold also to another idea, then he
must show that either the jurisprudence or the actual law of the day
contained both these ideas. Specifically, if those who held the will
theory of law in some form did not also believe in freedom of contract, then Marx will be confronted with a counter-example to this
proposed causal theory. On the other hand, Marx could have offered a
proposed logical argument that the juridical illusion entailed certain
consequences, whether or not these consequences were actually
believed by those who held a will theory, and that those consequences
are false.

Further, a historical or psychological interpretation raises the
question of the genetic fallacy; what does it matter that ideas are
historically formed together?

a. *Subjective Interpretation of Theses I, V, VI, and VII*

The first possible interpretation of Theses I, V, VI, and VII is that they
are statements about the psychology of actual lawyers in the nineteenth
century. In this sense, ideology is treated as being a subjective
phenomenon, perhaps a set of beliefs or concepts, and the "juridical
illusion" would then be seen as an element of that ideology which is a
unique subjective phenomenon, viz., a psychological phenomenon

occurring in lawyers and consisting in a persistent false belief about the relationship of will and law. For example, on this interpretation, Marx would say that a lawyer subscribing to the capitalist ideology would believe that, as a matter of fact, contracts are entered because people decide to enter them, that each person had a legal right to make those decisions, and that such a state of affairs was morally desirable.[69]

The subjective interpretation is supported to some degree by the language used by Marx, since it is consistent with the terms "illusion" and "explains for them" which occur in the text. The specific reference to lawyers and the notion of explaining why someone holds a particular belief suggest psychological claims about certain people's subjective beliefs, rather than matters of social theory. The term *gerechtlich*, which Easton and Guddat have translated as "juridical" is used to signify matters having to do with lawyers and courts. While too much stress should not be placed on the point, *gerechtlich* may be contrasted with *rechtswissenschaftlich*, which refers to matters of jurisprudence or legal philosophy.

This subjective reading is further supported by references to subjective perception and "consciousness" in the following passage, where shortly after the above-quoted key paragraph, Marx cryptically noted:

> Why ideologists turn everything upside down. Clerics, jurists, politicians. Jurists, politicians (statesmen in general), moralists, clerics.
>
> For this ideological subdivision within a class:
>
> 1. *The occupation assumes an independent existence owing to division of labor:* everyone thinks of his craft as the true one. The judge, for example, applies the code, he therefore regards legislation as the real active driving force.
>
> Respect for their goods because their occupation involves the universal. Idea of law, Idea of state. The matter is turned upside down in ordinary consciousness.[70]

The subjective interpretation has two aspects. First, it treats the component elements of an ideology as being subjective beliefs. Second, it postulates that the connection between two ideological beliefs is causal. It does not necessarily follow from the fact that the elements of ideology are subjective beliefs or perceptions that the relationship between them is a causal one, but terms like "necessarily leads to" and "explain", in the context of Marx' avowed devotion to science, suggest a causal link.[71]

Further, earlier in *The German Ideology*, Marx proposed his theory
of consciousness, which included the forms of consciousness corresponding to various forms of ideology, such as religion. Marx'
theory of consciousness was, of course, that ideas about the world
reflected the material conditions of production. He said: "The phantoms
formed in the brains of men are also, necessarily, sublimates of their
material life-process, which is empirically verifiable and bound to material premises."[72] This discussion of the natural history of ideas,
suggests that Marx might have postulated in the key passage a link
between two subjective ideas.

Marx' claim of a causal relationship between historical conditions
and mental processes blurs the distinction, however, between a
historical account and a psychological account. The difference intended
here is that between ideology considered as an existent thing (perhaps a
theoretical entity in social science) and the subjective ideas which
individuals have which correspond to elements of that proposed entity;
a claim about the former would be a historical thesis, about the latter a
psychological one.

The difference between the historical and psychological readings is
that the former postulates a connection between elements of the social
superstructure while the latter looks primarily to elements of the
individual's mental processes.

b. Historical Interpretation

Another interpretation of Theses I, V, VI, and VII is as premises about
the course of history. On this interpretation, the juridical illusion causes
certain other developments in the superstructure of the society. Thus,
Marx might have said:

> Where the dominant legal theory includes the principle that societal
> rules are properly concerned only with individual decision making,
> then those societal rules will regulate the ownership of property in a
> manner which separates societal recognition of property ownership
> from the economic reality of being able to deal with the property.

Such phrases as "leads to the development" suggest a historical
sequence: that is, for example, that the concept of law as will precedes
historically (or causes) the separation of title from economic usage.

Moreover, Marx suggested that this development was inevitable or, at least, that the elements were causally connected.[73]

c. The Logical Interpretation

The term "necessarily" in Thesis I inevitably suggests to the twentieth-century American philosopher a statement about a logical truth.

An example of this hypothetical "logical" interpretation would be stated as follows:

> The statement "Rules of law concern only the exercise of will" logically entails the statement "Legal title, which consists in the rules of law governing ownership, is entirely separate from the economic realities of possession."

Marx apparently meant something stronger than an assertion of mere consistency or an interesting observation that these concepts generally go together; words such as "explains" and "necessarily" rule out such a loose interpretation and suggest the relationship of logical necessity.

VI. HEGEL, SAVIGNY, AND LOCKE AS WILL THEORISTS

One step in understanding Marx' view of the will theory and evaluating his proposed criticism of it is to examine the theories of Hegel, Savigny, and more briefly, Locke, to see the degree to which they can be considered "will" theorists in any relevant sense. The second step will be to see whether Marx' description of the will theories accurately describes any of these three philosophers, and the third is to see whether his criticisms are telling.

A. General Principles of Hegel's and Savigny's Legal Philosophy

Savigny and Hegel influenced Marx' philosophy of law; Marx studied and wrote about both philosophers, although his greatest interest was in Hegel. Both earlier writers expressed strong convictions concerning the role of the human will in law. Hegel said, for example: "The basis of right is, in general, mind; its precise place and point of origin is the will."[74] Savigny's works on Roman law and contract law are almost entirely devoted to explanations of the role of the will in legal relations.

The two schools of thought were opposed, however, on both theo-retical and political matters. Although their analyses of property and contract law agreed remarkably, particularly on the role of the will, Hegel and Savigny differed as to the nature of law in general. Morever, the followers of the two schools differed on matters of German politics.

On a theoretical level, Hegel distinguished law from a philosophical point of view from actual laws: the law, considered philosophically, consisted of general principles and universal definitions, while positive law consisted in the individual cases in which abstract principles are worked out. Like Montesquieu, he held that the positive law should not be regarded abstractly but rather should be studied as one element in the totality which made up the character of a nation. Hegel concluded that Savigny's historicism was useful but that it "did not fall within the province of a philosophy of law, because a particular existent law might be grounded in the historical circumstances and yet be 'wrong and irrational in its essential character'".[75]

Savigny held that the true principles of law for a given society were revealed by the actual material course of history and said in contrast to Hegel's grand, abstract enterprise:

> In the earliest times to which authentic history extends, the law will be found to have already attained a fixed character, peculiar to the people, like their language, manners and constitution. Nay, these phenomena have no separate existence, they are but the particular facilities and tendencies of an individual people, inseparably united in nature, and only wearing the semblance of distinct attributes to one view. That which binds them into one whole is the common conviction of the people, the kindred consciousness of an inward necessity, excluding all notion of an accidental and arbitrary origin.[76]

Savigny rejected the concept of a universal natural law as expounded by Hegel and developed an explicitly relativistic theory, arguing:

> As a People changes throughout its whole sphere of life in the course of time, the same holds true of its system of Right as a branch of that life. Right is not fixed or stable at any particular time. It develops with the People. It attaches itself to the national character at its different stages of culture, and it adapts itself to the changing wants and requirements of the People.[77]

These two theories, however, did have certain general elements in common, particularly in considering actual historical and social conditions as at least part of the nature of law.

On a political level in the early nineteenth century, it was proposed that Germany adopt a code of civil law to replace the common law and also to replace the hated *Code Napoléon*. Many jurists of a more Hegelian persuasion supported the adoption of a rational, logical code in place of the supposedly anarchic common law comprised of individual case decisions. Savigny, however, served as Minister of Justice and therefore had a practical, as well as a theoretical, influence on German law. He opposed the civil code, preferring the historical process of the common law, by which law arose from the unconstrained will of the people. Savigny was successful in his own time, and a German civil code was not adopted until the end of the nineteenth century.[78]

B. Hegel on Property and Contract

This section consists of a consideration of Hegel's remarks on contract and property law with brief comparisons to those made by Marx in the *Grundrisse* passage.

In his *Philosophy of Right*, Hegel clearly developed a recognition will theory of property in which the relationship of individual will to property is the essential element of ownership. Moreover, Hegel distinguished the universal nature of dominion from the varying individual facts of possession and desire. Among the relevant passages are the following:

> 45.   To have power over a thing *ab extra* constitutes possession. The particular aspect of the matter, the fact that I make something my own as a result of my natural need, impulse, and caprice is the particular interest satisfied by possession. But I as free will am an object to myself in what I possess and thereby also for the first time am an actual will, and this is the aspect which constitutes the category of *property*, the true and right factor in possession.

> 49.   In relation to external things, the rational aspect is that I possess property, but the particular aspect comprises subjective aims, needs, arbitrariness, abilities, external circumstances and so forth (See Paragraph 45). On these, mere possession as such

depends, but this particular aspect has in this sphere of abstract
personality not yet been established as identical with freedom.
What and how much I possess, therefore, is a matter of indifference so far as rights are concerned.

62.   My merely partial or temporary use of a thing, like my
partial or temporary possession of it (a possession which itself is
simply the partial or temporary possibility of using it) is therefore to
be distinguished from ownership of the thing itself. If the whole
and entire use of a thing were mine, while the abstract ownership
was supposed to be someone else's, then the thing as mine would
be penetrated through and through by my will (See Paragraphs 52
and 61) and at the same time there would remain in the thing
something impenetrable by me, namely the will, the empty will, of
another... Ownership therefore is in essence free and complete.[79]

Hegel then quoted from Paragraph II.4 of the *Institutes of
Justinian*:

*usufructus est jus alienis rebus utendifruendi salva rerum
substantia... Ne tamen in universum inutiles essent proprietates,
semper abscendente usufructu, placuit certis modis extingui
usufructum et ad proprietatem reverti.*

and noted "Placuit! A *'proprietas SEMPER abscendente usufructu'*
would not [be] mere *inutilis*, it would be no *proprietas* at all"; that is,
"Property forever lacking the right to the fruits of the property would
not be merely useless, it would not be property at all."[80]
Two additional Hegelian paragraphs on property are the following:

64.   The form given to a possession and its mark are
themselves externalities but for the subjective presence of the will
which alone constitutes the meaning and value of externalities. This
presence, however, which is use, employment or some other mode
in which the will expresses itself, is an event in time, and what is
objective in time is the continuance of this expression of the will.
Without this the thing becomes a *res nullius,* because it has been
deprived of the actuality of the will and possession. Therefore I
gain or lose possession of property through prescription.

Prescription, therefore, has not been introduced into law solely from an external consideration running counter to right in the strict sense, i.e. with a view to truncating the disputes and confusions which old claims would introduce into the security of property. On the contrary, prescription rests at bottom on the specific character of property as "real", on the fact that the will to possess something must express itself.[81]

Thus, Hegel clearly adhered to a recognition will theory of private property; that is, he held that private property was constituted by the relationship of the individual human will to a physical object. The laws of property recognized or expressed these relationships. When an individual has the power to exercise his will over an object, to do with it as he pleases, then, according to Hegel, he possesses it. That exercise of will over the physical world is for Hegel the essence of property.

The individual's motive in obtaining possession, e.g., to satisfy his hunger or his curiosity, is not the essential element of property; rather, that essential element consists of the act of exercising will over the object, in obtaining possession, which act remains the same in many objects. Moreover, that power over an object properly excludes the exercise of any other individual's will in connection with the object. The concrete circumstances of the possession are merely the visible reflection of the subjective exercise of the will.

On Hegel's theory, therefore, private property is not merely a transitory phenomenon of a given economic period; rather, as Marx accurately noted, Hegel believed that property was the fundamental relationship between the individual will and nature, the physical world.

The fact of possession, however, is determined for Hegel by just such "particular aspects" as "subjective aims, needs, arbitrariness, abilities, external circumstances and so forth". Possession, therefore, is for Hegel a matter of particular fact, but property is not identical with mere possession; rather, physical possession of an object simply signifies the existence of the will's unfettered dominion over the object.

In contrast, Marx stressed the social nature of property, arguing that property was part of the relationship of persons in a society. For Marx, the need and want which impelled individuals to enter into contracts for the exchange of property were not "matters of indifference so far as rights are concerned".[82]

Second, Hegel emphasized the universal nature of the will/object relationship which constituted possession. The "natural need, impulse, and caprice" which motivated the individual to acquire possessions were to Hegel simply "the particular interest satisfied by possession". The relationship between individual will and object which was necessary in order to satisfy those particular desires remained constant, even as the desires varied.

Marx, of course, denied the universal nature of private property and denied that the one true relationship of the individual to nature was represented in private property.[83]

As to contracts, Hegel said:

> 71.   One aspect of property is that it is existent as an external thing, and in this respect property exists for other external things and is connected with their necessity and contingency. But it is also existent as an embodiment of the will, and from this point of view the "other" for which it exists can only be the will of another person. This relation of will to will is the true and proper ground in which freedom is existent... The sphere of contract is made up of this mediation whereby I hold property not merely by means of a thing and my subjective will, but by means of another person's will as well and so hold it in virtue of my participation in a common will.

> Reason makes it just as necessary for men to enter into contractual relationships - gift, exchange, trade, etc. - as to possess property (see Remark to Paragraph 45). While all they are conscious of is that they are led to make contracts by need in general, by benevolence, advantage, etc., the fact remains that they are led to do this by reason of the real existence of free personality, "real" here meaning "present in the will alone".

> 77.   Since in real contract each party retains the same property with which he enters the contract and which at the same time he surrenders, what thus remains identical throughout as the property implicit in the contract is distinct from the external things whose owners alter when the exchange is made. What remains identical is the value, in respect of which the subjects of the contract are equal to one another whatever the qualitative external differences of the things exchanged.

> The legal provision that *laesio enormis* annuls the obligation arising out of the making of a contract has its source, therefore, in the concept of contract, particularly in this moment of it, that the contracting party by alienating his property still remains a property owner and, more precisely, an owner of the quantitative equivalent of what he alienates.

78.   The distinction between property and possession, the substantive and external aspects of ownership (See Paragraph 45) appears in the sphere of contract as the distinction between a common will and its actualization or between a covenant and its performance.[84]

With regard to contracts as with property, Hegel distinguished the particular conditions of any given contract from what he considered to be the underlying realities, which was the relation of one individual will to other individuals' wills. Needs, desires, benevolence, etc., are accidental, in the sense that these qualities did not on Hegel's view affect the nature of the contract; both contract and property are constituted by the exercise of will, irrespective of the motive, such as need, for that exercise.   Indeed, need or mere preference is not, according to Hegel, even the cause of people entering into contracts nor of their acquiring possession of things, as indicated by the remark to Paragraph 71, where he said: "The fact remains that they [individuals] are led to do this [enter contracts] by reason implicit within them."

From the face of the paragraphs quoted above, it appears that Hegel held a recognition will theory of contracts, that is, a theory which postulated that will was the essence of contractual relations, which relations were expressed in the law. Hegel may also be said to have held a metaphysical and abstract form of the basis will theory, since he held that the state and other political entities were the emanation or manifestation of pure Spirit.

C. Savigny on Property and Contract

Marx, as has been discussed above, frequently criticized the historical school of law, the leader of which was Friedrich Karl von Savigny. Yet, on the surface it would appear that Marx had much in common with Savigny, since both wished to ground the study of law in general upon the study of positive law as an actual historical phenomenon. This section consists of a consideration of Savigny's theories of contract and property in the context of his general theory of law as compared briefly to Marx' statements on these issues.

a. Relationship of Marx' Theories to Savigny's

Whether or not Marx consciously adopted Savigny's historical and anti-idealist viewpoint, we can find in Savigny's work traces of the theories of property and contract which Marx rejected in *The German Ideology*. Before beginning our examination of Savigny's remarks on contracts and property, it may be worthwhile to examine some of Savigny's general principles, including examples of all of those rejected by Marx and those which appear to be parallel to Marx' views, since although Marx' analysis of Hegel is well known, his analysis of Savigny is not.

1. Themes Common to Marx and Savigny

Marx' rejection of law as a phenomenon independent of history seems to be echoed in Savigny's statement in 'Of the Vocation of Our Age for Legislation and Jurisprudence', where he said that law, like language, was simply the historical expression of the "kindred consciousness" of a particular people.[85]

The idea that law is a historical phenomenon, a product of the historical condition of a given people, also occurs in Marx' work. For example, in *The German Ideology*, Marx said: "It must not be forgotten that law has just as little an independent history as religion."[86] Similarly, earlier in the same essay, Marx argued that when an ideology is scientifically examined, it will be seen to be the product of actual people's "material life-process". "Morality, religion, metaphysics, and all the rest of ideology as well as the forms of consciousness corresponding to these, thus no longer retain the semblance of independence."[87] Law and language as the products of history, thus, were linked by Marx as they were by Savigny. Both Savigny and Marx rejected the premise that the laws of a given society reflected universal normative truths, and both held that a society's laws reflected its particular historical situation. In addition to the material quoted above, Savigny argued as follows:

> The historical spirit, too, is the only protection against a species of self-delusion, which is ever and anon reviving in particular men, as well as in whole nations and ages: namely, the holding that what is peculiar to ourselves is common to human nature in general. Thus, in times past, by the omission of certain prominent peculiarities, a natural law was formed out of the *Institutes of Justinian*, which

was looked upon as the immediate emanation of reason. There is no one now who would not regard this proceeding with pity; and yet we meet with people daily who hold their juridical notions and opinions to be the offspring of pure reason, for no earthly reason but that they are ignorant of their origin. When we lose sight of our individual connection with the great entirety of the world and its history, we necessarily see our thoughts in a false light of universality and originality.[88]

Marx offered an explanation of the apparent universality of the contemporary society's rules in 'On the Jewish Question', arguing that "the *droits de l'homme* appear as *droits naturels* because conscious activity is concentrated on the political act".[89] That is, the rights of man (as given by the French and American revolutions) appear to be the "natural" rights of man, according to Marx, because of the psychological effects of the particular society upon the perceptions of the members of the society. Similarly, in *The German Ideology*, Marx said:

This conception of history, which is common to all historians particularly since the eighteenth century, will necessarily come up against the phenomenon that ever more abstract ideas hold sway, i.e., ideas which increasingly take on the form of universality... [each new dominant class] has to give its ideas the form of universality and present them as the only rational, universally valid ones.[90]

It is implied in Marx' work and expressly stated by Savigny that people who were aware of law's historical nature would not be deluded into believing that those laws are the universal products of reason.

2. *Theses of Savigny which Marx Rejected*

Yet, despite their similarities, Savigny expressed several theses which Marx rejected. The concept of free will, as espoused by Savigny and rejected by Marx, appears both in the general concept of freedom in society and in the specific concept of will as the basis of property and contract.

In Chapter I of his *Treatise on Roman Law*, Savigny said:

In order that free creatures thus put in each other's presence are able to mutually aid each other and not harm each other in the deployment of their activity, it is necessary that an invisible line of demarcation circumscribe the limits within which the parallel development of these individuals finds independence and security. The rule which fixes these limits and guarantees this liberty is called law.[91]

This may be compared with the view criticized by Marx in the essay 'On the Jewish Question', which is:

Liberty is thus the right to do and perform anything that does not harm others. The limits within which each can act *without harming* others is determined by law just as the boundary between two fields is marked by a stake. This is the liberty of man viewed as an isolated monad, withdrawn into himself.[92]

On the relationship of man to man under law, Savigny also said:

Within the point of view where we are placed, each legal relationship appears to us as a relationship of person to person, determined by a rule of law, and this determining rule of law assigns to each individual a domain where his will reigns independent of any other will.

But in the outside world, one first encounters nature, which is not free, then other free wills like one's own, that is to say, persons foreign to our own personality.[93]

This view of civil society as composed of men "strangers to ourselves" can be seen in Marx' notes from his studies in the Summer of 1844, where he says: "Each of us sees in his product only the objectification of his own selfish need, and therefore in the product of the other, the objectification of a different selfish need, independent of him and alien to him."[94]

Marx rejected the particulars of Savigny's theory of history. Savigny held that the history of a social phenomenon such as the law flowed from the history of a people and their general will, while Marx thought that law, language, and religion were the reflection in consciousness of the material conditions of production.

Marx also rejected the normative consequences which Savigny and his followers drew from their historical studies, which was that the correct law of a given period could be deduced from the history of the positive law of that period. Savigny said: "That, consequently, by which according to this theory, the common law and the provincial laws are to become truly useful and unobjectionable as authorities, is the strict historical method of jurisprudence... Its object is to trace every established system to its root, and thereby to discover an organic principle... ."[95]

Marx vehemently criticized that position in his article 'The Philosophical Manifesto of the Historical School of Law' for failing to take into account whether the positive law was rational, that is, for failing to allow for criticism of existing institutions. Marx characterized this theory as holding that "the pimple is as positive as the skin", and argued that "But only very little criticism is needed to recognize sordid old ideas behind all the fragrant modern phrases... ."[96]

Although Marx fervently rejected the concept in the 'Philosophical Manifesto' essay that whatever is, is good, his own position on this issue remains unclear. In his criticism of Hegel, Marx turned to a materialist concept of history, and he also rejected the concept of a universal good or ideal, as can be seen in the above-quoted statements from *The German Ideology*. Moreover, even though Savigny's theory may form part of the actual German ideology of the nineteenth century, Marx wished to deny that it represented accurately the actual conditions in society.

b. Savigny's Theories of Property and Contract

In his *Treatise on Roman Law*, Savigny said of property:

> We cannot dominate unfree nature in its totality, but in a determinate portion detached from the whole. The portion thus detached is called "thing", and thus begins the first possible species of rights, the right to a thing which, in its most pure and complete form, is called "property".[97]

Similarly, in his *Treatise on the Law of Obligation*, he said:

> To the contrary, it is necessary to note an essential analogy between obligations and relationships of the law of things of which property forms the base. It is true that in property we do not find the isolated persons who are the essence of obligation. But in the end these two institutions have a common character in that obligation, like property, consists in the domination of one person over a fraction of the exterior world. Also, they [property and contract]

constitute together the law of goods, of which they are the two
correlative parts; in effect, the law of things comprehends the
principles of the law of goods, an abstraction taken from the entire
relationship of man to man, inasmuch as that relation is precisely
the object of obligations... .[98]

Thus, Savigny expressed a recognition will theory of contract and
property, similar in appearance to that of Hegel, in which property
consists in the exercise of human will over physical objects, just as
contract consists in the domination voluntarily accepted of one person's
will over another's.
Savigny based his theory of jurisprudence upon extensive historical
study, and he thought that the institution of property was, as a matter of
historical fact, the relationship between human will and the objective,
physical world. To that extent, at least, Savigny slipped into a
universal mode, and therefore, some of his remarks upon property and
contract appear indistinguishable from those of Hegel.[99]
Savigny also held a will theory of contract, saying:

But if we wish to resume a legal relationship which establishes our
domination over another person without destroying his liberty, a
right which resembles property and yet is distinguished from it, it is
necessary that our domination not dominate the entire other person,
but only one of his acts, and then that act restrained from the
arbitrary liberty of the other person passes under the rule of our
will. The legal relationships by virtue of which we rule over a
specific act of another person are called "obligation".

One calls declarations of will that species of juridical fact which
not only are free acts but, according to the will of the agent, have
for their immediate end to engender or destroy a legal relationship.[100]

Thus, for Savigny as for Hegel, contracts represented the relationship of one will to another. Savigny believed that a contract consisted in one free will's acquiring the right to direct an action of another
free will, which nonetheless remained free.
For Savigny, therefore, statements relating to the exercise of will,
such as "I promise to do X", were "juridical facts", facts that
determined the existence of a particular legal relation. In the passage
from which the second quotation was taken, Savigny argued that only
two factual conditions, violence and error, could cast any doubt upon

the validity of an apparent free commitment of the will and discussed the notion of free will as affected by the threats of violence. These issues will be considered later in the context of nineteenth-century law.

D. Locke on the Will Theory

Elements of what may be called a will theory of law may be seen in the writings of John Locke. As the social contract theory is well known, only a brief mention will be made of these elements.

To begin, Locke characterized the hypothetical state of nature as "a state of perfect freedom to order their actions and dispose of their possessions and persons as they think fit, within the bounds of the law of nature, without asking leave, or depending on the will of any other man".[101]

Property in land is acquired, according to Locke, by the labor of cultivation, and property in any physical thing by the labor of gathering or producing it, since "[w]hatsoever, then, he removes out of the state that nature hath provided and left it at, he hath mixed his labour with, and joined to it something that is his own, and thereby makes it his property."[102]

Locke further believed that the state was caused or created by the will of the persons governed by it. "The beginning of politic society depends upon the consent of the individuals to join into, and make one society; who when they are thus incorporated, might set up what form of government they thought fit."[103]

Although Locke did not speak specifically of the role of the will in law, several elements of a will theory of law may be discerned in the above remarks.

First, Locke did not assert, in so many words, that title to property arose from the exercise of the will over a physical object; rather, he asserted that title was established by the expenditure of labor on the object. Yet, such labor may be said to be the result of an exercise of will by the laborer, and it indisputably entailed, in Locke's view, the right to dispose of the result as one chose. Indeed, Locke's position may be compared with Hegel's remarks on the necessity of actual use of the property to establish the presence of the will over the property. In this sense, then, Locke may be held to have asserted that property was the result of the exercise of will, through labor, over a physical object, and hence, it is fair to say that Locke held a recognition theory of property.

Second, Locke may be described as having a basis will theory of the origin of law. The state and the laws composing it are both brought into being by and made valid by the consent of the governed. As he said: "That which begins and actually constitutes any political society is nothing but the consent of any number of freemen capable of a majority to unite and incorporate into such a society. And this is that, and that only, which did or could give beginning to any lawful government in the world."[104] The concept of consent necessarily includes the concept of will, and therefore, in Locke's view, the will of the individual creates and legitimates the law.

It is perhaps obvious that a strong normative element is incorporated in the above analysis. Locke clearly held normative versions of the basis and recognition will theories; indeed, depending on the extent to which he regarded the state of nature as historical fact, he may not have held to a strong form of non-normative basis will theory, at least to the original constitution of society.

In Locke's view, the relationships between individuals are established by consent, with the possible exception of the relationships of children to their parents. In this sense, the notions that contracts are entered arbitrarily by individuals and that their content is a matter of the free will of the parties may be easily seen in Locke's work. Locke also regarded individuals in the state of nature as essentially unrelated, and to this extent, it may be argued that he would consider the relationships among people as "accidental", that is, as not derived from the nature of human beings, but from their free decisions.

In light of the comments by Hegel and by Marx on the subject of title and use, certain remarks by Rousseau may also bear examination. Rousseau said that one of the criteria of the right of the first occupant of real estate was "that one takes possession not by a vain ceremony, but by labor and cultivation, the only sign of property that others ought to respect in the absence of legal titles".[105] This is interesting, since it seems to commit Rousseau to precisely the position described by Marx, viz., that legal title may be had in the absence of use of the property. Yet, at the same time, like Hegel, Rousseau emphasized the importance of actual use of the property as the essential element of ownership.

Although the attribution of the specific premises of *The German Ideology* cannot be made, perhaps, as clearly with regard to Locke as with regard to Hegel and Savigny, it seems reasonable to include Locke within that category of philosophers to whom Marx may have been directing his remarks. There is no particular reason to exclude other social contract theorists, such as Rousseau, from this category, and indeed, given Marx' remark about all contemporary thinkers' belief that the state was established for the protection of property, it would be plausible to conclude that Marx directed his remarks at the entire class of social contract theorists within the category of theories which he rejected. Locke has been chosen for convenience and not with any idea of excluding the others from consideration.

E. Conclusion and Summary of These Will Theories

In the above material, it can be seen that the term "will theory of law" describes some aspects of the legal philosophy developed by Hegel, Savigny, and Locke.

First, it may be said that all three philosophers espoused some form of a basis will theory. Savigny held that the law at a given historical moment was the expression of the common consciousness of the people of that society. Hegel held that abstract right consisted in the acts of the free will. The precise causation of that relationship is more unclear in Hegel than in Savigny, particularly as positive law is only the application of the universal concept of right to particular conditions. Locke held that the state arose by the consent of free individuals. Here again, the causation is left unclear since it is open to question whether Locke regarded the state of nature, out of which civil society arose, to have been an actual historical state (in which case the necessary consent would have caused the state to exist) or as an illustrative device or method of argument (in which case the issue of causation in the historical sense is left open).

Second, it may be said that all three philosophers held a form of recognition will theory in that all felt that the laws of contract and property were fundamentally a matter of the relations of the individual will to the world of physical objects and to other persons. All three asserted that the law simply recognized and regulated relationships which existed prior to the adoption or application of the law. Hegel and Savigny, one working from the concept of pure right and the other from historical example and both drawing heavily on the *Institutes of Justinian*, for example, clearly believed that the will of the individual simply stood in certain relationships with nature and with other wills and that the law simply reflected those relationships. It is not clear how Savigny stood on the apparently universal nature of his claims in this regard; it would appear that he could hold that, in some form, the basic relationships (will/nature and will/will) were universal parts of the human condition but that the precise form of those relationships could vary from society to society. For example, Savigny noted that in a society where slavery exists, there is a group of people who cannot stand in a contractual relation with another (the master totally dominates the will of the slave), whereas in contracts, only a small number of acts are brought within the compass of another's will.

Finally, it is noticeable that all three philosophers used the term "will" in the context of property and contract law to refer to a free and individual will. Savigny held that law originated from the will of the people, from a *Volksgeist* which was not unlike Rousseau's general will; Locke, on the other hand, held that society, including its laws, arose (or was made legitimate) by the consent of its individuals but still related the state to will and right in some abstract way. All discussed the *individual* will, however, when they discussed the specifics of contract and property.

Moreover, the individual will which they considered was in differing senses a free will. For Locke, the will was free in that it was free from the imposition of other individuals. For Savigny, it was necessary for the will to be free in order that its actions should be juridical acts, i.e., acts with a legal significance, and such freedom existed only if the will of another had not physically replaced the individual's own will.

CHAPTER TWO

An Examination of the Accuracy
of Marx' Description of the Will Theory

It is time at last to turn to an evaluation of Marx' criticism of the will theory of law as exemplified by Savigny, Hegel, and Locke. Given Marx' extensive criticism of Hegel and of social contract theory, it is, of course, impossible to address every argument which Marx raised. Therefore, as a foundation, this chapter will consider the accuracy of Marx' descriptions of the will theories, including the accuracy of his attribution of certain consequences to these theories. In later sections, Marx' attempt to develop a third alternative to Savigny and Hegel and the apparent genetic fallacy in Marx' rejection of these philosophers will be discussed.

Again, since Marx cast his remarks as criticisms of an existent ideology, the first question is whether the actual ideology did in fact hold the complex of positions which Marx ascribed to it; that is, did Hegel, for example, hold a will theory of law which not only contained the premises ascribed to it by Marx but also lacked consideration of the practical consequences raised by Marx. As a philosopher, Marx would be guilty of having created a straw man opponent if the will theory of law was not as he had described it, and as an empirical social scientist, he would be guilty of a factual error.

In Chapter One, the comparisons between Marx' comments on the will theories and the works of Hegel, Savigny, and Locke show that Marx has succeeded in describing part of the ideology of the nineteenth century, and his criticisms, therefore, are not directed entirely at straw men. In particular, to the extent that Hegel, Savigny, and Locke formed a part of the ideology of nineteenth-century capitalism, which seems indisputable, Marx almost paraphrased parts of their works, particularly those of Hegel, as his statement of existent German ideology. For example, Marx' description of capitalistic exchange in his notes on Mill, which will be discussed further herein, almost echoes Savigny and Locke in some respects.

Upon detailed examination of the theses from *The German Ideology* in the context of these philosophers, however, it becomes apparent that Marx' description is not wholly accurate. In this more complex comparison, the relation of the will theory to the result propositions is of primary importance. Each thesis proposed by Marx in the key passage will be examined in turn.

I. THESIS I (LEGAL TITLE AND ECONOMIC REALITY)

Marx made two statements concerning the separation of legal title (and
its associated rights) from economic reality. Basically, Marx
characterized the will theory as holding that the law, including property
rights, rested entirely on the individual will, irrespective of any
consideration of practical ability to exercise the will. Thus, he said that
the will theory held that "private property is based simply on private
will", and to that supposed theory he contrasted two alleged instances
of practical reality, as follows:

1.   The right to consume (*jus abutendi*) the property is limited by
     the practical consequence that exercise of this right may lead to
     loss of the property; and

2.   The legal owner of property may be unable to use the property
     if he lacks the funds necessary to make use of the property.

The first task is to return to the description of Locke, Savigny, and
Hegel given above and to see whether they held the specific views
attributed by Marx to those holding the "juridical illusion". Then the
question can be raised as to whether the will theory committed them in
some way to those views.

A. Descriptive Accuracy

Since we already know that these philosophers were will theorists, the
portion of Thesis I in which we are here interested is the possibility of
"having legal title to a thing without actually having it". It has been
noted that there are three possible interpretations of Marx' remark about
title and economic reality: a meta-legal, a legal, and a normative interpretation. It remains to be seen whether any of the three philosophers
held the view that legal title was separable from economic usage in any
of these forms.

a. Locke - Accuracy

It is unclear whether Locke can accurately be described as holding any
of these views. As noted, Locke in *Two Treatises of Civil Government*
did not extensively discuss the existent rules of law and, therefore, it is

difficult to say whether he was aware of the extent to which, in law, title to property is separable from economic usage of it. With regard to a meta-legal interpretation or a normative interpretation, there is some evidence that Locke did not hold the view that title was separable from use.

Here, one must separate the meta-legal statement into its two forms: a description of the contemporary actual society and a general description of the social entity called "property". With regard to the former, I have not found any discussion in the *Two Treatises*. With regard to the latter, however, Locke said that property was constituted by the admixture of labor with an object, as by the cultivation of land. Therefore, Locke would not agree that property in general was separable from at least some form of economic usage of the land; it is not known whether he would have felt that the concept of property included the idea of having sufficient capital to be a landed proprietor.

As to the normative interpretation, there is perhaps somewhat more evidence that Locke did not hold the view that title was rightly separable from use, since he believed that in the state of nature one should not possess more than one could profitably use.

b. Hegel - Accuracy

As with Locke, it is difficult to determine whether Hegel held the view discussed above if it relates to actual nineteenth-century laws. Hegel did not extensively discuss the German society in which he lived, but rather he explored the nature of the universal concept of property. Similarly, Hegel did not dwell on specific legal rules of contemporary society as a topic for his discussion, although he did analyze, for example, certain instances of Roman law as examples of the general concept of property. In that regard, therefore, he could criticize the careless Roman jurist who wrongly, in Hegel's opinion, analyzed the separation of the *usufruct* from the title.

Further, it is difficult in Hegel's *Philosophy of Right* to draw a bright dividing line between normative and other statements. His statements about property are about property rights, i.e., about what entitles one to claim ownership of an object, and therefore, they are to that extent normative, as being about rights. On the other hand, Hegel regarded property as being a relationship between the individual and things, and that relationship was essentially an objective fact about the exercise of the subjective will over the physical world. Thus, the clearest and most central question is whether Hegel held the general meta-legal view about the relationship of ownership and utilization.

Substantial evidence suggests that Hegel did not hold the view that

title could or should be separable from usage. There are three indications of this in the texts discussed above. These indications consist in
Hegel's use of the word "power" in defining possession, in his statement that use cannot wholly be separated from ownership and, finally,
in his observation that without active use of the property, possession is
simply an empty form.

The first of these is Hegel's description of the separation of *usufructus* (use) from *proprietas* (title). The passage which Hegel quoted
from the *Institutes of Justinian* can be loosely translated as follows:

> The *usufruct* is the right of alienation of the fruits of a thing, apart
> from the substance of the thing... . However, property, always
> lacking the *usufruct*, would be generally useless [and] it is pleasing
> to extinguish the *usufruct* by certain methods and return [this right]
> to the property.[1]

The rule refers to the situation in which one person has the right to
use the property while another has legal title. Hegel scornfully asserted
that so-called "property" permanently lacking the right of use is not
property at all ("a 'proprietas SEMPER abscedente usufructu' would
not be mere *inutilis*, it would be no *proprietas* at all").

The term "*usufructu*", however, means the "right to the use of the
property". Therefore, perhaps Hegel spoke of the owner's having the
right to the use of the property, not of the economic utilization of that
right. He may have been saying that the *right* to use and consume property as one wills is true ownership and that, therefore, a title theoretically separate from that right would be a nullity. To the extent that
Hegel is understood as talking about rights alone, then perhaps, assuming that the right may be totally separate from actual power to use,
Marx' practical characterization of Hegel's version of the will theory
may apply. This limiting but consistent interpretation of Hegel's remarks, however, is not reinforced by an examination of his comments
on property in general and adverse possession in particular.

Second, in the above-quoted passages, Hegel closely connected the
concepts of use and title. Hegel said: "The form given to a possession
and its mark are themselves externalities", which may be read as
encompassing both the particular form of physical possession and title
("its mark").

Hegel also said: "In relation to external things, the rational aspect is
that I possess property, but the particular aspect comprises subjective
aims, needs, arbitrariness, abilities, external circumstances and so
forth... . On these, mere possession as such depends...." and prior to
that he said: "To have power over a thing *ab extra* constitutes
possession." It is noteworthy that Hegel tied the concept of property

first to power over an object, which connotes an actual ability to act upon the object and, second, linked the concept of possession to such practical matters as abilities and external circumstances. Although Hegel said in Paragraph 64 that the subjective presence of the will alone gives meaning to the externalities of the possession, he also noted that

> This presence, however, which is use, employment or some other mode in which the will expresses itself, is an event in time, and what is objective in time is the continuance of this expression of the will. Without this the thing becomes a *res nullius*, because it has been deprived of the actuality of the will and possession.[1]

In other words, actual physical use of the property represents the exercise of the will's dominion over the physical object and is therefore essential to the concept of property. This is consistent with Hegel's earlier remarks concerning the separation of the right to use the property from title. Just as *proprietas* (ownership) cannot be separated from the *right* to use the property, so it cannot be separated from the *actual use* of the property.

The third point of interest is that Marx' description of the will theory's separation of title from economic use did not encompass the doctrine of adverse possession, which indeed would seem to contradict the Marxist claims about capitalist ideology, since adverse possession by its nature consists in the acquisition of title by actual use. In general, the doctrine of adverse possession concerns the means by which title to property may be acquired by one who uses the property for a set period of years, where the user does not have title when the use began. The rationale which is often given for that doctrine is that it helps to clear up uncertainty of title and that the open and notorious use of the property by a stranger is plain notice to its owner that his ownership interest is challenged.

In contrast to that pragmatic justification, Hegel said that the adverse possession rules in fact embodied a will criterion for true ownership, and he tied his conceptual point about physical possession and title to the actual point of property law - adverse possession. According to Hegel, the doctrine of adverse possession was not simply a way of clearing up old title disputes but expressed the nature of property law. In the adverse possession situation, title (which should represent the right of the owner to exercise his will over the property) is apparently in one person while another person manifests his will in the property by using it. If the situation could continue, according to Hegel, then the will of the person using the property would encounter at every turn the will of the alleged owner, which would be an impossibility. Hegel asserted therefore that title passes to the actual user, just as the right to use the property (*usufruct*) was not permitted to remain separate from the *proprietas*.

Hegel's theory as a whole seems inconsistent with the position attributed by Marx to the will theory of law, although there may not be a direct contradiction. Hegel held that the will's dominion over an object was the essence of property, and to that extent, he would seem to hold that private property was based on private will. On the other hand, Hegel clearly rejected any theory of property which would separate the title to property from the actual use of the property. Hegel did not expressly say that an owner who can no longer use the property because of economic conditions should be deprived of title, and he did say that "What and how much I possess, therefore, is a matter of indifference so far as rights are concerned" which would seem to be the metaphysical position to which Marx contrasts the pragmatic economic fact that without capital, title to property may not convey the power to use it. Since Hegel claimed that property without use was not even property, then it appears that he accepted one view characterized by Marx as a necessary consequence of the will theory of law, i.e., that "the thing considered only with reference to his will, is not anything at all but only becomes actual property through interaction". Hegel, however, rejected the idea that legal title is properly separable from usage. That is, Hegel said that the use of the property is essential to the concept of ownership and that ownership cannot exist in the absence of the use of the property. It seems, therefore, that Marx has not accurately described the content of Hegel's theory of property.

The relationship between Marx and Hegel, however, is complex, and on this point of law it is difficult to disentangle the two theories. Indeed, it seems that Marx takes Hegel's view of the impossibility of separating use from title and attempts to turn it against the will theory.

c. Savigny - Accuracy

Although rather less space has been given herein to Savigny's theory of property than his theory of contracts, the Marxian version of the separation of title and use cannot be squarely attributed to Savigny any more than to Hegel. Where Hegel used the word "power", Savigny used the term "domination", which can also refer both to a right (which might be separate from the economic ability to utilize the property) and to the actual ability to use the property.

B. Entailment: Psychological, Historical, and Logical Necessity

At this point, then, given that it is unclear from the texts quoted whether any of these three philosophers can be said to have adopted whole-heartedly the concept that the title to property could (or should) be separated from the power to use the property, it seems appropriate to turn to the issue of whether these philosophers were necessarily committed to that position by virtue of their adherence to the will theory. As explained above, the statement that "[t]his juridical illusion which reduces law to mere will ... necessarily leads to one's having legal title to a thing without actually having it" (Thesis I) is susceptible to three interpretations. It can be read as a statement about the connections between certain subjective beliefs, as a premise about history, and as a statement of entailment.

a. Psychological Necessity

This short section addresses the question of whether a person psychologically must believe that title can be separated from use if he or she believes in the will theory of law.

As discussed above, the use of the word "explains" in the last of the seven theses suggests that these statements are intended as descriptions of psychological causation, rather than as logical arguments. That analysis in turn suggests that Marx held that these beliefs were actually found in the beliefs held by philosophers of his time, at least those who adhered to some form of the will theory of law. Therefore, it would seem that some inkling of the belief in the accidental nature of contracts should be found in the philosophers herein discussed as holding varieties of a will theory of law.

The fact that the three philosophers arguably did not accept the separation of title from use casts considerable doubt upon the psychological claim that the subjective belief that property is a matter of will leads directly to the belief that title to property exists independently of the utilization of the property.

b. Historical Necessity

Even if it is not true (as discussed above) that one is psychologically compelled to hold certain views, it could be that in the course of history, the separation of title from usage always appeared when the will theory of law was the dominant ideology.

With regard to the historical interpretation, Hegel himself pointed to the two rules of law which cast doubt upon that interpretation, the prohibited separation of use and title in Roman law and the doctrine of adverse possession. The fact that the *usufruct* could not be permanently severed from the title suggests strongly that in the actual (Roman) law the utilization of the property was not entirely irrelevant to the question of title. The *usufruct*, however, as noted above, was the *right* to the uses and fruits of the property, not perhaps the fact of the employment of the property. The doctrine of adverse possession, however, squarely linked the actual use of the property, as by cultivation, with the title, and Hegel believed that that fact reflected the law's recognition of the true state of the will's relationship to the property. That is, the thing belonged to the person whose will dominated it, and in the case of adverse possession, that person is the user of the property, not the person who ostensibly holds the title. Thus, Hegel's recognition of historical instances of actual laws where use and title were linked (together with Locke's belief that they ought to be linked) casts doubt on the proposition that the will theory is historically linked to that view.[2]

c. Logical Necessity

With the historical issue in at least some doubt, it remains to be seen whether the will theory of law in some form entails the title/use separation. Given the two forms of the will theory, the relevant questions are as follows: "Does the premise that law is *caused* by acts of will entail the statement that the title to property is entirely separable from the utilization of the property?" and "Does the premise that law *recognizes* relations of the will entail the statement that title to property is entirely separable from the utilization of the property?"

With regard to the basis will theory, it is immediately apparent that the will theory does not, without more, entail the separation premise. There is simply no connection between the two statements.

That conclusion is supported by the fact that those philosophers who held some form of a basis will theory, such as Locke, Rousseau, and Savigny, generally also held that the general will had a range of possible alternative systems of law. In the social contract theory, presumably the contracting individuals could elect among various governmental forms. Locke and Rousseau said that the will is constrained to an extent by natural law, so that matters of property are not entirely variable by legislation. Savigny spoke of the "inward necessity" of law but also recognized the cultural (and therefore legal) variations among peoples in different historical circumstances. It would surely seem that on those theories the specific legal relationship between the empty *indicia* of ownership, such as title, and the actual cultivation of the property would be subject to some variability at the will of the law-creating individuals.

With regard to the recognition will theory, it may at first seem more plausible that the will theory itself contains the premise of separability. In fact, however, the premise that law reflects will does not entail that title must be separate from use, unless the concept of title is contained within the concept of the will's domination over things.

Presumably an expanded version of Marx' argument as to a recognition will theory version of Thesis I would proceed something like this:

1. The law of property reflects the domination of an individual will over an object, such as land, and the law is concerned with nothing else.

2. Legal title is the law's recognition of the dominant will's relationship to the object.

3. Since the law is concerned only with the relationship of the will to the object, title rests only on that relationship and on nothing else.

4. Since title cannot be affected by or involve anything other than the will/object relationship, it cannot be affected by or involve the particular economic factors which may affect the individual's concrete ability to exercise his will in a particular manner with the property.

5. Therefore, title must be separate from the economics of the situation.

The Marxian argument is, however, fallacious, since it presupposes that the will's relationship to the object does not include the will's actual exercise of its power over the object. To put it another way, the argument begs the question by assuming that the will/object relationship is concerned only with right and not with power and, therefore, that title, which is a matter of the right to the property, is necessarily utterly independent of the ability to exercise the rights conferred.

Thus, Marx' remark concerning the necessary consequence of the will theory of law is not true of the will theories which we have examined, which include the major theories of the period. To that extent, at least, Marx has failed to describe an existent theory; the conclusion which he proposes neither follows from the theory nor is expressly included in it.

II. THESIS V (CONTRACT AS ACCIDENT)

Since Theses II, III, and IV are primarily conclusions about Thesis I, it is appropriate to turn directly to Thesis V.

That thesis deals with the "accidental" nature of contracts, and like most of the sentences with which we are dealing, it is highly ambiguous. In light of both its philosophical freight and Marx' discussion of the practical overtones of property ownership earlier in the paragraph, the term "accidental" can refer either to a concept of necessity based on the nature of individuals as, for example, concerning the characteristics which comprise individual identity, or to a concept of practical necessity as, for example, including economic pressures which narrow one's choices. That term could also include actions based on whimsy or personal caprice, meaning therefore "arbitrary".[3]

A. Contract and Human Nature

If "accidental" is interpreted as referring to a concept of necessity based on the nature of individuals, then Thesis V attributes to lawyers under the spell of the will theory of law the belief that it is not inherent in the nature of human beings to enter into contracts (or other relationships) with each other. That alleged belief would stand in contrast to Marx' belief that man is inherently social.[4]

a. Locke - Contract and Human Nature

Locke's social contract theory is based upon the image or metaphor of man in the state of nature in which each individual lives a fundamentally isolated existence. Production, labor, and property exist prior to the time that the individual enters into any relationship with another noble savage; even the plunder of one by another presupposes that the spoils belonged to the victim. For Locke, the individual's identity is theoretically assured in advance of his membership in society, and in this sense, Locke believed that social relationships, including contracts, are accidental to the individual. Locke's postulation of the state of nature suggests, however, that the underlying relations of domination, such as the dominion rightfully acquired by labor, are part of human nature and, therefore, that such relationships are not accidental in the sense that people could theoretically structure their relationship with each other and with objects differently.

b. Hegel - Contract and Human Nature

Attribution to Hegel of the belief in the accidental nature of contracts presents much greater difficulty, if only because those passages where Hegel spoke jointly of the state, necessity, and individuality are among the most opaque of his usually obscure works. On the one hand, Hegel rejected the individualism of Kant and glorified the supposedly universal qualities of the state. On the other hand, Hegel, as Marx noted, contrasted civil society and the family, "the spheres of private rights and private welfare", with the universal ends of the state.

Marx' specific comments on the relevant passages of Hegel deserve examination in this regard. In his manuscript on Hegel's political philosophy, Marx analyzed several of Hegel's passages as dealing with the separation of modern society into two conceptual spheres: civil society, which was described as the realm of private and individual desires, and the state. Marx quoted several passages from Hegel in the course of his analysis in the manuscript 'Contribution to the Critique of Hegel's Philosophy of Law', of which the following are the relevant portions:

§261. Over against the spheres of civil law and personal welfare, the family and civil society, the state is on the one hand an external necessity.... On the other hand, however, the state is their immanent end, and its strength lies in the unity of its ultimate general purpose with the particular interest of individuals....[5]

§264. Since they themselves possess spiritual natures and therefore unite in themselves the two poles, namely, explicitly knowing and willing individuality and the generality which knows and wills what is substantial, the individuals who make up the multitude acquire their rights on these two counts only insofar as they are actual both as private and as substantial persons.... In these spheres [the family and civil] society they attain partly the first of these rights directly and partly the second in that they have their essential self-consciousness in the institutions as the inherently general aspect of their particular interest, and partly in that these institutions furnish them in the corporation with an occupation and an activity directed to a general purpose....[6]

Just as civil society is the battlefield of the individual private interests of all against all, so here the struggle of private interests against particular common concerns.... It is the secret of the patriotism of the citizens in this respect, that they know the state to be their substance because it is the state which backs their particular spheres... .[7]

Marx argued that Hegel's concept of the state presupposed the existence of civil society - in other words, of society as a motley collection of isolated individuals with private interests.[8] It is apparent that Marx linked that presupposition with the claim that contracts were believed to be accidental.

Marx' claim about the will theory, then, would be as follows: If the complete individual, conceptually or in historical fact, predates the relationship, then the relationship is accidental to that individual.

The question is, of course, whether that linkage is correct, and it seems to me that it is not, at least not to the degree that both concepts can be found in Hegel. It would seem that, even if the concept or historical fact of a state presupposed the concept of isolated individuals, that presupposition would not be inconsistent with the premise that individual persons necessarily united into societies. Indeed, Hegel said, as quoted by Marx in the Easton and Guddat translation: "[T]hey find their essential self-consciousness in social institutions", and the term "essential" implies that such social self-consciousness is an inherent element of the individual's composition, in contrast to the concept of accidental. In Locke's description of the state of nature, the choice of a stateless existence seems to be a distinct possibility; Hegel's unclear language of "necessity" and "immanent aim" does not give rise to the same clear possibility.

Indeed, there is considerable textual support for the position that Hegel held quite the opposite view. In Paragraph 71, which is quoted in Chapter One, Hegel said: "Reason makes it just as necessary for men to enter into contractual relationships... . While all they are conscious of is that they are led to make contracts by need in general...the fact remains that they are led to do this by reason of the real existence of free personality... ." The existence of the will, according to Hegel, renders necessary its entry into certain relations with others, viz. the relations of contract.

For Hegel, the needs which impelled people to enter into contracts are indeed accidental, in the sense that these needs are not the necessary element of the contract. On the other hand, Hegel did not believe that it is "accidental" in the sense of non-necessary that people enter into contracts. Rather, people enter contracts because free will exists and acts in the exchange relationship of contract. The relation which connects parties to a contract, on Hegel's view, is not a relation such as worker/capitalist but a relation of wills vis-à-vis a particular piece of property, where one possesses and the other recognizes the possession.

c. Savigny - Contract and Human Nature

Since I have not found in Savigny the same self-conscious discussion of necessity which lurks in Hegel, it is necessary to resort to inference to determine whether Savigny would have said that contracts and other social relationships were accidental in the context of the concept of the individual. Here, one is tempted by Marx' reasoning: since Savigny theorized that contracts were the exercise of one individual will over another separate will, surely he must have thought that such contractual relations were accidental to a whole and entire concept of the individual. As in Marx' analysis of Hegel, however, this analysis fails.

It is true that in Savigny's analysis of historical instances of contract law he treated the individual as pre-existing, at least conceptually, the contractual relationship. That fragment of analysis, however, does not rule out a variety of statements about the necessity of social or contractual relationships to individual human beings. One might consistently say, on Savigny's theories, for example, that individuals lacked a complete identity until they had exercised their wills in the peculiar fashion described as contractual; or one might say that individuals sought social relationships with others and that such seeking was a necessary part of their character.

In summary, then, the relevant texts are inconclusive or lacking, and the argument that Savigny or Hegel must have believed that contracts were accidental vis-à-vis individuals, because they completely separated conceptually the individual from his social relationships must be rejected. Thus, while Marx has apparently described a characteristic of the social contract theory as expounded by Locke, it would appear that he has not described a clear or salient characteristic of the works of Savigny or Hegel.

B. Contract and Practical Necessity

As noted earlier, the term "accidental" may also refer to a concept of practical necessity, i.e., to the economic and physical constraints - such as the necessity of obtaining food in order to survive - which influence actions. In this sense, the relevant concept is that of arbitrary choice, of an unfettered election among alternatives. That interpretation is textually supported by Marx' equation of private property and the "arbitrary disposal of the thing".[9] On this reading, Marx would be attributing to the will theorist the view that individuals did not enter contracts because of various concrete pressures, but rather that they entered contracts solely as a matter of arbitrary choice.

There is little or no textual support for that position. Locke spoke expressly of the pressures which induced individuals to join together for protection. Hegel referred to the fact that individuals "are led to make contracts by need". Savigny discussed extensively the relationship between physical force, violence, etc., and contracts.

C. Alternative Social Relationships

There are two additional views to which Marx might have been referring and which remain to be discussed. These are the view that the real world of individuals is distinct from the theoretical idea of contracts and the view that there are alternate forms of social relationships.

With regard to the former, the passage under consideration might be considered an oblique reference to Marx' frequent criticism of philosophers that their works were concerned with abstract entities rather than with concrete individuals. As discussed above, although that criticism may be justly leveled at Hegel, Savigny is to a degree exempt from it; although Savigny dealt in what he believed to be the universal concepts underlying a given legal system, he nonetheless based his theories upon concrete historical research.

The latter point is more interesting. The question is whether individuals could arrange their social relationships other than by contract. In this sense, then, the term "accidental" would refer both to a lack of conceptual necessity and to a lack of historical necessity.

It has been noted that there is a suggestion in Hegel that the contractual relationship is the necessary form of free relationships among individual wills. Savigny apparently believed that contract simply was the only relationship of mutual domination between two free wills. Locke certainly recognized that other relationships, such as domination by force, were possible but held that at least the only binding societal relationship was by contract, other than that between parent and child. A key concept here is that of *freely* entered relationships; as to those relationships, all three philosophers probably held that free agreement was a necessary element of a binding relationship, although entry into that or any particular compact was not, perhaps, conceptually necessary in order for individuals to exist.

It should be noted that, to some extent, Locke, Hegel, and Savigny were talking about relationships which were binding or which gave rise to obligation. There is no reason to suppose that any of them was unaware that people sometimes acted out of charity or love, but these motives did not constitute a relationship of obligation between one individual and another. All three philosophers probably held that people were not by nature obligated or willing to exchange goods on the basis of need rather than agreement.

Marx, however, must tread a fine line here, for he must on the one hand deny that contract, as it dominated legal thinking in the nineteenth century, was simply a historical accident (because he believed to some degree in the concept of a causal, necessary development of history), and yet at the same time he must hold that it is not the necessary or natural relationship between individuals (except, perhaps, under capitalism) because he proposed an entirely different structure of societal relationship. In particular, Marx wished to restructure the producer/-consumer relationship from self-interested exchange or bargaining to some other form of relationship, where allegedly the relationship would be one of mutual recognition of need.[10] Contractually based exchange is characterized by Marx as follows:

> Political economy - like the real process - starts out from the relation of man to man as that of property owner to property owner. If man is presupposed as property owner, i.e., therefore as an exclusive owner, who proves his personality and both distinguishes himself from, and enters into relations with, other men through this exclusive ownership...then the loss or surrender of private property is an alienation of man, as it is of private property itself... . The case of violence excepted - what causes me to alienate my private property to another man? Political economy replies correctly: necessity, need. The other man is also a property owner, but he is the owner of another thing, which I lack and cannot and will not do without, which seems to me a necessity for the completion of my existence and the realisation of my nature... . The social connection or social relationship between the two property owners is therefore that of reciprocity in alienation... . Exchange or barter is therefore the social act, the species-act, the community, the social intercourse and integration of men within private ownership and therefore the external, alienated species-act.[11]

The Communist producer and consumer in Marx' theory are related as follows:

> In my production I would have objectified my individuality, its specific character, and therefore enjoyed not only an individual manifestation of my life during the activity, but also when looking at the object I would have the individual pleasure of knowing my personality to be objective.... In your enjoyment or use of my product I would have the direct enjoyment both of being conscious

of having satisfied a human need by my work... and of having thus created an object corresponding to the need... .[12]

Marx goes on to argue that exchange under Communism would result in each party being the mediator between the other and the species and receiving the other's love. Further, according to Marx, each party's activity would confirm his individual nature.

Therefore, whether or not the will theory included the premises that contracts are accidental in a historical or conceptual sense, Marx clearly held that contract law was not a historical accident but that it did not express the necessary or natural relationship of individuals.

III. THESES VI AND VII (CONTRACT AND FREE WILL)

The result propositions of Theses VI and VII refer respectively to the premises that entry into a contract and the terms of that contract are the result of decisions made by two free wills. It is immediately apparent that all three philosophers rested their concept of contract upon some concept of a free will. Several questions remain in this area, however. Basically, these fall into two areas; first, even allowing for the fact that Savigny, Hegel, and Locke held some form of free will theory, what meaning does the term "explains" have, and second, what exactly did these various philosophers mean by their concept of free will? The former idea is important in an analysis of Marx' work because it helps to delineate the internal relationships, as Marx saw them, of ideology, and the latter issue is important because it bears on the Marxist concept of necessity. These questions will be dealt with in the following material more by indirection than by direct confrontation.

Since all three philosophers clearly held some form of these theses (subject to the reservations discussed above with regard to "accidental"), this section will discuss first, whether these philosophers believed that as a matter of fact contracts were entered into freely and, second, whether the will theory entails the premise that contracts arise from acts of free will.

Whatever exactly the word "explains" expresses, the question would seem to be whether the will theory of contracts leads in some way to the premise that the existence and terms of contracts rest entirely on the decisions of the parties concerned. As noted above, the latter part of each thesis ("these relationships can be entered into or not at will", etc.) is itself susceptible to three possible interpretations: a descriptive meta-legal interpretation, a normative interpretation, and a legal interpretation. The descriptive interpretation and the normative are the most interesting here, and it is not necessary to distinguish the general version of the meta-legal thesis from that referring specifically to the positive law of England and America.[13]

A. Description of the Philosophers' Views

Under the descriptive interpretation, these sentences describe purported states of affairs in which the free will of individuals in a society is unconstrained when it comes to entering contracts, so that both the terms and the very fact of the agreement rest entirely upon the will of the parties.

A normative interpretation of the same premises would be that the individual ought to be unconstrained in contractual decisions.

An exhaustive or even extensive analysis of the concept of free will cannot be attempted here, and the version of the free will controversy which will be considered here is the issue of the necessity of a range of choices for the "true" exercise of free will.[14] This appears to be the version to which Marx directed his attention.

Earlier in the section of *The German Ideology* under discussion, Marx contrasts the possession of title with the actual economic ability to do anything with the property. More clearly, in the same paragraph, Marx said:

> The *jus utendi et abutendi*...itself asserts...the illusion that private property itself is based solely on the private will, the arbitrary disposal of the thing. In practice, the *abuti* has very definite economic limitations for the owner of private property if he does not wish to see his property and hence his *jus abutendi* pass into other hands, since the thing, considered merely with reference to his will, is not a thing at all but only becomes a thing, true property in intercourse and independently of the law.[15]

Thus, Marx contrasted the theoretical right of property ownership to dispose of the object solely as one wills, free of any external constraint, with the fact that certain actions with regard to the property will result in the loss of ownership. It seems, therefore, that Marx concerned himself here more with the issue of constraint as a barrier to the exercise of the free will than with causation as the negation of free will.

a. Free Choice as Fact

It would appear, then, that Marx intended to attribute to the will theorists a view that the act of will involved in entering contracts was an arbitrary one free of any external constraint, such as economic considerations. It remains to be seen whether any of the three theorists held such a view of the free will involved in their concept of contracts.

1. Locke - Free Choice

Locke suggested that men entered into the social contract freely but with the desire to unite for their mutual protection and benefit; the choice to remain outside the social contract, even in Locke's imagined state of nature, was not unattended by adverse consequences. Those adverse consequences constrain the exercise of the will in the sphere of contractual decisions just as the possible loss of the property constrains the improvident property owner.

Locke said, for example:

> Though in the state of nature he hath such a right, yet the enjoyment of it is very uncertain and constantly exposed to the invasion of others... This makes him willing to quit this condition which, however free, is full of fears and continual dangers.[16]

In that paragraph, then, Locke proposed a pre-social state both free and full of dangers; the existence of fear rendered the state of nature undesirable but nonetheless free.

Thus, it cannot be said that Locke held the views that contracts "can be entered into or not at will" or that "the content of these relationships rests *purely* on the individual free will of the contracting parties" if those attributed views are taken to mean that the practical consequences do not affect the exercise of the will.

2. Savigny - Free Choice

The philosophy of Savigny on this point can best be seen in his analysis of duress and contract law, which is also of interest in that it is parallel to the analysis of that problem by some modern jurists. Savigny linked the concepts of fraud, physical violence, and mistake in his analysis of those conditions which invalidate contracts.[17]

According to Savigny, neither mistake (such as a mistake as to the quality of goods) nor fear (such as fear of adverse consequences if the contract were not signed) would invalidate a contract unless they were produced by the act of one of the parties to the contract. Savigny put it thus:

In both cases, it is necessary to carefully distinguish the internal state of the agent and the immoral influence of another man. In the spirit of the agent we find, on the one side, fear; on the other, error: both are equally indifferent with regard to the existence of a true declaration of will and are without influence on its efficacy. But both acquire a particular character when they are the result of an immoral action from without. Fear then appears as violence, and error as fraud; and there is between those two terms a complete parallelism.[18]

The complete parallelism in the law to which Savigny referred is that both fraud and violence invalidate a contract, i.e., that an apparent contract entered into under those circumstances is not enforceable in court and is not a true or valid contract - literally, there is no contract because there is no actual assent. Savigny, however, rejected the common explanation that such influences negate the existence of a real consent which is required for a valid contract; rather, he maintained that the will remains free under such influences, but the immorality of the persons inflicting them entitles the state to refuse to enforce the contract.[19] That is the reason, according to Savigny, that it is generally held that mere error does not invalidate a contract; if the error is not caused by the other party to the contract (i.e., if it is not fraud), then there is no reason not to enforce the contract, because the requisites for a valid contract (mutual free agreement) are present.

Savigny, however, held that sometimes violence could negate the existence of the free will. He distinguished two kinds of violent action which one individual could take toward another. One sort of violence was physical restraint, "which reduces each who is the object of it to a purely passive state. A signature obtained by physically guiding the hand of another is no more his signature than is a counterfeit, although both have the outward appearance of being so."[20] To such violence, Savigny contrasted the exercise of influence over the will of another by fear. The law, both of modern Europe and of ancient Rome, provided that contracts obtained by fear could be repudiated by the person coerced. Savigny said, however:

Nothing is more natural, at first glance, than to consider liberty and violence as incompatible things and to conclude that where there is violence there cannot be liberty. However, a more attentive examination must cause one to abandon this doctrine. We need not occupy ourselves in the speculative difficulties that the philosophical definition of liberty presents. In the domain of law, we consider liberty in its visible appearance, that is to say, as the faculty of choosing among several alternatives. *Thus, there is no doubt that one who is constrained or rather threatened retains that faculty. In effect, he can choose between three alternatives; to perform the act which is dictated to him, to repulse (the domination) by his resistance, or finally to accept the evil with which he is threatened.* [21]

Thus, Savigny did not believe that contracts could be "entered into or not at will" if that is taken to mean that valid contracts require the unfettered will of the parties. So long as the constraint is not wrong-fully being employed by the other party to the contract, the existence of fear, etc., does not invalidate the contract. On Savigny's view, fear may influence one's choice, but the fact of choice remains. It cannot plausibly be said, then, that Savigny felt that contracts were entered into with an absence of external pressure and constraint.

3. Hegel - Free Choice

The complexity of his concepts of free will and individual liberty render it very difficult to analyze Hegel's position in this regard. In the context both of property and contract, however, Hegel referred to the concept of need. That fact is of interest because need would seem to bear the same relationship to contract as economic constraint of other kinds bears to property, according to Marx. That is, it would seem that need and deprivation could constrain the postulated free will in regard to entering contracts just as the lack of capital could constrain the ability to use property.

Hegel said that although both property and contract appear to exist for the satisfaction of the needs of the individual, actually both property and contract are themselves the substantive end of the exercise of the free personality.[22] Apparently Hegel believed that people perceived themselves as entering into contracts and possessing objects in order to satisfy their needs, but that in fact they entered into those relationships in order to exercise their will over the external world of physical objects and in association with other individuals. Thus, in the specific context of contracts and property, Hegel's concept of the free will remains obscure; need, etc., are not irrelevant to the actual contracts entered, but yet the essence of those activities is the exercise of the free personality.

It appears that Hegel would agree in some form with the premise of the theory described by Marx which holds that "these relationships can be entered into or not at will", since Hegel asserted that persons are led to enter contracts by "the idea of the real existence of the free personality". Moreover, Hegel held that such motives as need and subjective desire are extraneous to the true nature of contracts. Hegel, however, did not deny the existence of need as the motive on the individual's part for entering into a particular contract and indeed said that property was connected to "their necessity and contingency". It is true that Hegel believed that "the essence of a contract was the will alone", but this does not entail that he was unaware of the extraneous pressures upon persons.

The above remarks apply also to an attempt to evaluate Hegel's statement in light of the claim by Marx that the terms of the contract depend on free will. To this topic is added, however, Hegel's discussion of *laesio enormis*.

That rule of law held that a contract was invalid if one party received a grossly inadequate compensation. It was the law on the continent, but it was not adopted in England.

According to Hegel, the rule of *laesio enormis,* like adverse possession in property law, expressed the inner conceptual workings of contract - the two individuals meeting and exchanging property for *property*. One form of property is exchanged for another, but the core of property, as a mutual recognition of the expression of will over external objects, remains the same for each party. To this extent, then, it would seem that for Hegel, the terms of a valid contract are not completely and arbitrarily set because the *values* of the items exchanged must be in some way equal. One may compare this view of the exchange relationship with that set out by Marx and quoted above; on the one hand, the notion of reciprocity of exchange appears in both, as does the emphasis on the relational and exclusionary nature of private property but, on the other hand, Marx seems to contemplate a relation of mutual exploitation and perhaps a kind of inherent unfairness, whereas Hegel required a kind of equality. That equality could pre-sumably be, however, an equality of desperation.

First, it may be confidently said that all three philosophers believed that the concept of a valid contract required a free will on the part of both parties. Second, it may also be said that none of the three equated that free will with a will totally unconstrained by external factors and acting altogether arbitrarily, that is, in complete disregard of the consequences of the action. To the contrary, it is clear that Locke and Savigny recognized the influence of external considerations upon the will but denied that such considerations, however powerful, negated the free will which was a prerequisite to a valid contract. Given his reference to needs as a motive for entering contracts, it is unlikely that even Hegel believed that as a matter of fact individuals entered into contracts purely in order to satisfy an unfettered whim.

While these three philosophers may not have been committed to the view that the will had unconstrained free choice, however, they were committed to the view that the contractual relation, both as to its existence and its terms, consisted in the results of certain acts of will.

b. Free Choice as Good

Given those conclusions, it is time to turn to the question of whether these three philosophers held a normative version of Theses VI and VII. Such a normative version of these statements would be, for example, that "it is morally correct that a contract be entered into or not depending on the will of the parties" or "persons ought to be allowed to determine the terms of their own agreements".

All three philosophers held some form of those views, varying in part upon their concept of free will. That is, all thought that contracts were entered into by an act of will, that that state of affairs was morally desirable, and that consent was a proper ground for moral obligation. It should be noted, however, that given their varying concepts of free will, the moral view did not include a belief that the exercise of free will ought properly be completely unfettered or that all pressures which might bear upon one's decision must morally be removed.

B. Entailment

The remaining question in this section of the conclusion is whether the result propositions of Theses VI and VII follow from the will theory of law. These logical arguments can take a multitude of forms, given the number of permutations of the possible premises that have been discussed. There are four basic possible questions, as follows:

(1)   Does the basis will theory entail the proposition that people in fact have an unfettered choice as to their contracts and the content of those contracts?

(2)   Does the recognition will theory entail the proposition that in fact people have an unfettered choice, etc.?

(3)   Does the basis will theory entail the proposition that in fact contracts arise from the acts of free will of the parties?

(4)   Does the recognition will theory entail the proposition that in fact contracts arise from the acts of free will of the parties?

Clearly, if (1) or (2) above is answered affirmatively, then the philosophy of Hegel, Savigny, and Locke will contain an inconsistency.

The answers to (1) and (2), however, are negative. Both theories require only that there exist certain relationships between the will and other wills, which is the relationship of mutual agreement or dominion. It is not necessary to either theory that these relationships be entered into under any particular set of economic circumstances.

As to argument (3) above, the basis will theory does not entail that all contracts arise from the acts of free will of the parties; it would be possible to hold that, for example, the social contract was based on free consent without requiring that all social relationships thereafter arise likewise. The two views are, however, consistent and compatible, particularly if one holds, as Locke did, that contract is the basic fabric of society.

The status of (4) above is more complicated, because the two premises are closely related. If it is held that the law recognizes relationships entered into as a matter of will and if people enter an exchange relationship by mutual consent, which is an example of contract, then it follows that the law will recognize and enforce such contracts. In that argument, however, the existence of the contractual relationship is built in. There are other relationships based on will which the law could recognize. For example, slavery is the complete domination (albeit usually without consent) of one will over the other.

The last but very complex question which remains is whether the normative versions of the predicate premises follow from the various will theories discussed. The immediate problem is that of the transition from "is" to "ought", if one attempts to construct an argument from the descriptive meta-legal versions of the basis or recognition theories to the normative version of the predicates. Thus, there are difficulties with arguing that if the law is as a matter of fact based on will, it ought to enforce agreements entered as an act of will. The normative to normative arguments, however, do not present that particular problem.

It is not altogether clear, however, that the normative contractual premises follow from the normative version of the basis will theory. There is a strong tendency to feel that the enforcement of contracts does follow from the basis theory, on the ground that if the only valid laws are those consented to by the governed, what other basis can there be for the origin of a legal relationship from man to man? That is the context in which the private lawmaking aspect of contracts has so much appeal; if the moral basis for social organization is consent, should not the law enforce, then, consensual relations (and no others) among the individual members of society?

The recognition theory sequence is clearer and more simple: if the law properly recognizes only relationships of will, then it ought properly to recognize and thus enforce those agreements entered into as an act of will and no others.

IV. CONCLUSION

Thus, although Marx' description of the will theory of law accurately reflects various facets of that theory, it distorts others and, like a twisted mirror, reflects them only incompletely.

CHAPTER THREE

Duress and Free Will in Nineteenth-Century
Contract Law

I. INTRODUCTION

A. Purpose and Summary

This chapter presents an analysis of certain features of contract law in the mid-nineteenth century. That analysis provides a ground for the evaluation of Marx' statements about law as purported empirical descriptions of the ideology of the time.

As discussed above, according to Marx the will theory of law resulted in the adoption by lawyers and jurists of a will theory of contracts. The specific legal doctrines which allegedly followed from the will theory of law are specified by Marx in the result propositions of Theses I, V, VI, and VII: that is, the four result propositions are (1) that use can be separated from title; (2) that contracts are "accidental;" (3) that they can be entered into or not at will; and (4) that their terms can be varied at will. It also has been noted that Marx' statements contain substantial ambiguity.

The question, therefore, is whether some form of those result propositions is found in the actual case law of the period. This chapter describes the law, and Chapter Four contains a more detailed analysis of the accuracy of Marx' description. Three conclusions will become clear. First, it will become apparent that the result propositions express accurately a central doctrine of nineteenth-century Anglo-American law - freedom of contract. Marx' description of that doctrine, however, contains a crucial unclarity, which arises from the fact that the result propositions can be taken either as statements of rules of law or as factual claims. The truth conditions of these kinds of statements differ, and hence, the role that these statements can play in any criticism of capitalist ideology differs. Second, as a matter of fact, the extent to which these result propositions accurately describe nineteenth-century ideology varies substantially, depending on whether they purport to be statements of the law or statements of fact; as will be seen, the cases clearly reveal that these premises were part of contract law but that their factual content was not unequivocally accepted. Third, the relationship of the judges' beliefs about the world to the legal rules indicates that the true concept of freedom of contract was essentially freedom from oppression by another individual and not unfettered freedom of choice.

The premises in *The German Ideology*, however, are not merely a random set of premises about contract law; rather, they deal with the role of will in contracts and, more specifically, with the concept of contracts as consensual relationships. Therefore, this chapter deals not only with the general doctrine of freedom of contract, but with the doctrines of duress and undue influence.

The doctrines of duress and undue influence delineated the circumstances under which the law considered that an apparent contract was not in fact an actual contract because it did not in fact result from an act of free will. It is in these doctrines, therefore, that one finds the most detailed and concrete development of the concept of will which the nineteenth-century judge actually believed was requisite to a valid contract. It is here that we will find the precise nature of the views which Marx called illusory.

Some comment is appropriate concerning this long and perhaps somewhat dull chapter. The chapter contains a considerable amount of information about the general law of contracts and certain widely-held theories about such matters as the relationship of these laws to the industrialization of England. This material is included to provide a framework of information for those whose main study is not the law, and also, it is hoped, to point out indirectly the large number of interesting questions which this area of law presents in the context of the Marxist analysis. Those who find this uninteresting or repetitive may wish to concentrate on Section V which describes the law of economic duress and undue influence and upon Section VI which summarizes the role of will theory in contract law - which provide together a groundwork for the critical analysis to follow in Chapters Four and Five.

B. Method and Progress

The general structure of this discussion is from the general to the specific. It proceeds from an analysis of the broad doctrine of freedom of contract to the specific doctrine of duress, ending with consideration of the evidentiary support for the presence or absence of free will as recorded by the courts. In view of the breadth of the subject matter, the doctrine of freedom of contract is first discussed in general terms, and some historical background is provided. Second, the law of duress is discussed in greater detail and with reference to several specific cases. Finally, I have gathered some cases which deal with the issue of undue influence, since these cases also concern the conditions under which a party to a contract may be said to have gone through the motions of entering a contract without in fact assenting to its terms.

In preparing this chapter, I have followed the same procedures for legal research which I would use if I were to research the law today. In order of preference, I have looked for controlling cases, which are cases themselves referred to as authoritative in subsequent decisions, often-cited encyclopedias of law or treatises on the law, and historical sources.

In this research, therefore, I have followed those canons of authority, both express and unspoken, which are relied on by lawyers today. That is, for example, an attorney looks first for a case which has been relied upon by subsequent courts, since such reliance establishes that the earlier decision was not regarded as an aberration.

In the context of the legal research for this chapter, I have, of course, not been concerned with whether these cases were repudiated in a later period as the doctrine of duress developed; I have rejected only those cases which were criticized or repudiated as being incorrect at the approximate time of Marx' analysis and commentary.

During the nineteenth century, as today, there were texts and encyclopedias of law, such as *Parsons on Contracts*[1] which, although not the product of a state decision-making body, were nonetheless regarded as accurate and authoritative statements of law. I have regarded these as less authoritative than the case law but as still useful sources. Among other sources, I have used *The American and English Encyclopedia of Law*[2] and *A New Abridgment of the Law ("Bacon's Abridgment")*.[3]

With the exception of those works which were partly historical and in popular use during the period in question and which, therefore, form a part of the data, I have not relied extensively on works of legal history or theory. The reason for this is that the topic of freedom of contract is heavily laden with ideological freight. For example, it has been tied both to the idea of political liberty, as in the works of Friedrich A. Hayek[4] and Robert Nozick[5], to the normative concept of a promise in the illuminating *Contract as Promise* by Charles Fried[6], and to the rise of industrial capitalism and other social factors in nineteenth-century Britain as in the book, *The Transformation of American Law*, by Morton Horowitz[7], and the excellent study, *The Rise and FAll of Freedom of Contract*, by P.S. Atiyah.[8]

C. Selected Areas of Law - Limitations on the Subject

There are two issues which arise in the area of contracts and which are of great interest but which, for reasons of length, cannot be dealt with in this study.

The first of these issues is whether reported decisions actually represent the reasoning of the court in any real psychological or historical sense. Are these decisions mere rationalistic façades for the judge's subjective intuition of how the case ought in some sense to come out? Did judges really decide in accordance with their class or economic biases? Was the law formulated to favor the development of capital, and did judges really decide in accordance with what they thought was socially desirable or useful for the expansion of the English or American economy? Although fascinating, these analyses of the "real" bases of legal decisions or the "real" motives of judges are beyond the scope of this paper.

Another fascinating issue in this area is whether contracts in some sense exist; i.e., should the term "contract" be quantified over. In law a contract clearly can exist independently of any physical manifestations, such as a writing, and to the extent that it is considered to do so by the courts, the contract becomes an elusive entity, fully as elusive as propositions, sentences, ideas, and beliefs. The courts in the mid-nineteenth century were fond of saying that a contract did not *exist* where there was no meeting of the minds, and it may well be that they thought of the contract as fully as existent as the will, which is itself metaphysically elusive. While it is necessary to discuss here the conditions under which a given act of will, free or not, may be said to exist, the merits of this position as a matter of ontology (and the merits of the proposition that contracts exist) are beyond the scope of this work.

Also, for similar reasons, I have deliberately avoided certain areas of law. First, I have avoided cases dealing expressly with the transfer of property, since this area is diffuse and since the disposition was usually in a contractual form which would therefore appear in the duress/undue influence cases if relevant. Further, Marx' claim that the economic use of property is irrelevant to title is difficult to prove or disprove, since the claim is essentially a negative one, viz., that the courts did not consider economic usage in determining title. Although this may be true, the doctrine of adverse possession, as discussed above in the context of Savigny's and Hegel's works, seems to refute that very broad claim which, in any event, is not related to the central theme of this account. On the other hand, of course, the law recognized such economic relationships as leases, in which the use of the property might be separated from title (although leases of course conveyed a right to possession). More clearly, the law recognized indirectly, and society clearly countenanced, such social and economic relationships as hiring workers (who had no title to the land) to use it. Thus, the separation of title from use is not developed further herein.

Freedom of contract is closely related to the general freedom to use one's property as one wishes. One can dispose of property in other ways than by its sale, of course. For example, one can consume it, destroy it, give it away, or devise it by will. The right to determine the terms upon which one would sell it, however, was generally considered in the nineteenth century to be a corollary of the right to do with it as one pleased, which is, of course, the right which Marx referred to as the *jus utendi* and *abutendi*, the right to use and to abuse. For this reason, the discussion applicable to contracts is also generally applicable to Marx' remarks on the freedom of an individual to use his property as he chose.

Labor was considered a form of property, and the same freedom to contract was granted with regard to employment contracts as with regard to other forms of contracts, such as contracts of sale. Indeed, Locke, for example, referred to labor as a kind of property and, in general, the courts made no distinction between transfers of property and employment contracts, with regard to the legal grounds for the validity of the contract. Courts expressly considered that the right to determine the terms upon which one worked was a vital aspect of the general freedom of contract.[9]

I have, however, avoided cases concerning labor law because that area of law was complicated by the statutes governing union activity in the mid-nineteenth century. It should be noted, however, that these cases reveal very interesting features of the mid-century conceptions of freedom of contract, duress, and economic pressure. Naturally, by virtue of its very subject matter, the common law of labor organization would be of interest in a Marxist context, both in terms of a historical survey of the legal framework with which Marx may have been familiar and as an examination of the historical response to Marxism. It is interesting to note, for example, that Mr. Justice Holmes specifically mentioned the "socialist threat" in at least one opinion on labor issues. Atiyah even-handedly describes the court's concern with possible coercion of individual workmen by unions, and with the paradoxical question of whether workers or businessmen could lawfully agree among themselves not to work or to trade except upon certain terms.[10]

The issue of coercion frequently arose in labor cases. It has been argued that modern labor law consists in equalizing the employer's supposed economic power so as to prevent the employer from inflicting duress on the workers. Dickinson suggests in 'New Conceptions of Contract in Labor Relations' that "the theory underlying the whole mass of labor law is that it is a way of countervailing and overcoming the employer's supposed superiority of position - a way of preventing economic duress by the employer".[11]

The issue of economic power as coercion was also raised by

employers who sought to invalidate contracts entered under the pressure of a strike upon the grounds that these contracts were the product of coercion. In 1917, Justice Brandeis wrote:

> But coercion, in a legal sense, is not exerted when a union merely endeavors to induce employees to join a union with the intention thereafter to order a strike unless the employer consents to unionize his shop. Such pressure is not coercion in a legal sense. The employer is free either to accept the agreement or the disadvantage.[12]

Dickinson has observed that this doctrine expressly rejects the thesis that "no basic difference exists between economic duress and physical duress".[13]

Similar cases were decided on the technical ground that the worker has the right to labor upon such terms as he sees fit and, therefore, a threat to refuse to labor, i.e., to strike, is a threat to do what one has a right to do, and therefore not a wrongful threat, and therefore not duress.[14]

D.   Selected Areas of Law - Time Span

A word is appropriate about the time span within which the cases considered herein fall. As a general rule, I have limited my selection of cases to be discussed extensively to those dated within twenty years of the publication of *The German Ideology* in 1845, although I have been more lenient in the selection of authorities for basic principles of law. I have not been overly strict in the selection of cases, but I feel that a case's relevance to this analysis decreases as its distance from the mid-1840s increases.

A mixture of practical and theoretical considerations have influenced my selection of this time period.

Among the theoretical considerations is the fact that the law, particularly that of duress, was in a period of change at that time. The doctrine of freedom of contract is traditionally considered to have been expanding then at a rapid rate to keep pace with the requirements of an industrialized society.[15] Paradoxically, however, the law of duress was becoming in some ways more lenient. Even as the courts rejected a role as the supervisors of the fairness of contracts, they expanded the grounds upon which a contract could be invalidated for duress practiced on one of the parties. For example, as will be discussed below, the law progressed from a strictly objective standard to a subjective standard in the evaluation of the effect of threats upon the individual. That involved a rejection of the original rule that a threat would invalidate a contract only if it was sufficient to induce fear in a man of reasonable courage in favor of the present rule that a threat would invalidate a contract if it in fact terrified the particular person in question. Moreover, the concept of economic duress, as opposed to other sorts of coercion, was developing during this period.

It is worth noting that that apparent paradox may be dissolved by observing that increased deference to individual decision and increased protection of the will from coercion are consistent with a legal theory grounded on the primacy of the subjective wishes of the individual. On a more practical level, it would be desirable to ascertain the state of the law at exactly the time Marx was writing. But, on the one hand, if one restricted oneself only to cases prior to Marx' actual date of publication (which would at least ensure that they were cases of which Marx in some sense should have been aware), one might be forced to reject clear cases and important statements of the law somewhat after Marx' date of publication, even though those cases were entirely consonant with the law existing at the time of publication. Further, Marx regarded himself as writing about capitalism as an existent social phenomenon and, as is well known, Marx considered that the para- digms of capitalism were England and the United States.[16] Therefore, to limit oneself to cases decided prior to the date of Marx' publication would be to risk distorting the subject of study by ignoring the forward- looking aspects of Marx' writings; if Marx is accurate, the tendencies which he describes should increase as capitalism develops. On the other hand, if one did not limit the time period at all, one would risk distorting the sample and, indeed, obtaining a confused picture of law by virtue of the changes which were then in process.

II. A GENERAL REVIEW OF THE DOCTRINE OF FREEDOM OF CONTRACT

Freedom of contract formed an essential element in the commercial law of the nineteenth century, and because of the role of consent in contract law, the doctrine had to be harmonized with the tenets of the will theory of law. Further, as we will see in the duress cases, it had to be reconciled with perceived social and economic reality.

A. Basic Elements of the Law of Contract

The law of contract required only two things for a valid contract:

1. that there be a meeting of the minds of the parties and

2.   that there be a mutual exchange of consideration.

Holdsworth says in *A History of English Law*:

> That the essence of contract is agreement, and the essence of
> agreement is a union of wills, was as clearly recognized by the
> lawyers of the sixteenth century as it is recognized by us. "The
> agreement of the minds of the parties", it was said in 1553, "is the
> only thing the law respects in contracts"; and in 1551 agreement
> had been defined as the "union, collection, copulation, and con-
> junction of two or more minds in anything done or to be done".[17]

The concept of the meeting of the minds is the notion that a contract
consists in both parties' mutually agreeing on the terms of the
obligation.[18] It followed from this concept, for example, that mutual
mistake or fraud would invalidate a contract because, although each
party thought that he understood the terms of the contract, neither of the
parties understood the terms in the same manner as the other. There
was literally no meeting of the minds on mutually agreeable terms.
     The second basic element of a valid contract is consideration, which
is in essence an exchange of values. Consideration is now defined as a
benefit to one party or a detriment to the other. This means that one can
be obligated where one receives no benefit from the transaction except
the satisfaction of knowing that the other person has done something.
For example, one can offer a reward for the capture of a dangerous
criminal. The capture of the criminal does not confer any benefit on the
person offering the reward but, nonetheless, that person is bound to
pay the reward because the person claiming it has gone to the trouble of
capturing the criminal.
     The effect of this rule is that courts would not (and will not today,
as a general matter) enforce a contract where no value had been
exchanged. Thus, a court would not compel a person to make a
promised gift because the person receiving the gift has not given
anything in exchange. Any value would suffice, however; no parity
was required. This rule of law was referred to as "the peppercorn
theory" of consideration, because even the giving of a peppercorn
would be sufficient to make the contract enforceable.
     The effect of a contract's being invalid at law may be worth
discussing here. On the one hand, a court would not force the other
party to perform if the contract were not valid. Similarly, a court would
not award damages for the breach of an invalid contract.

B. Statement and Restatement of the Doctrine

The doctrine of freedom of contract, loosely stated, consists in the concept that each person is free to obligate himself legally to perform any action on such terms as he or she decides. In the case of *Printing and Numerical Registering Co. v. Sampson*, Sir George Jessel, who has been described as "one of the greatest judges of the nineteenth century", said:

> If there is one thing more than another which public policy requires, it is that men of full age and competent understanding shall have the utmost liberty of contracting and that their contracts, when entered into freely and voluntarily, shall be held sacred and shall be enforced by Courts of justice.[19]

More formally, the law of freedom of contract is comprised of two components, as follows:

1. Each person has a legal right to make such contracts as he desires.

2. The courts will enforce contracts made pursuant to premise (1) and no others.

It can be seen, therefore, that the term "freedom of contract" comprises two aspects, a positive and a negative.

This is expressed in the modern edition of Halsbury's *Laws of England*, as follows:

> Nevertheless it remains generally true that the law of contract does not lay down rights and duties, but rather imposes a number of restrictions subject to which the parties may create by their contract such rights and duties as they wish.[20]

On the one hand, a person is free to obligate himself as he sees fit and, on the other, he will have no other contractual obligations than those which he freely incurs. That negative aspect of the freedom of contract doctrine was expressed in two specific legal rules: (1) that the court would not imply terms into a contract which the parties had left out ,and (2) that there were almost no mandatory contracts, i.e., those where the existence of the contract or its terms are determined by the state, except for those of innkeepers, common carriers, and the like.[21]

C. Contract as Private Legislation

The fact that the power of the state through the medium of the court
system could be invoked by those who were parties to a contract has
been described as the power of the individual to legislate. That is, the
state's power could be invoked to enforce the terms of a private agreement, which is a kind of private lawmaking. It has sometimes been
said that each person writes the law in matters of commercial exchange
for himself. Contracts are not mere promises which are enforced only
by moral suasion; they are enforced by the judicial arm of the state, the
courts.[22]

The notion that the right of individuals to dictate the terms of their
own legal obligations in contractual form constituted a kind of dele-
gation of legislative power was widely held during the nineteenth
century. Kessler and Gilmore developed this theme in their analysis of
nineteenth-century contract law, as follows:

> Freedom of contract thus means that subject to narrow limits the
> law, in the field of contracts, has delegated legislation to the
> contracting parties. As far as the parties are concerned, the law of
> contracts is of their own making; society merely lends its machinery
> of enforcement to the party injured by the breach. To be sure,
> society, in order to accommodate the members of the business
> community, has placed at their disposal a great variety of typical
> transactions whose consequences are regulated in advance; it has
> thus "supplied the shortsightedness of individuals, by doing for
> them what they would have done for themselves, if their
> imagination had anticipated the march of nature." Bentham, *A
> General View of a Complete Code of Laws*, 3 *Works* 191
> (Bowring ed. 1843). Bentham's statement does not do justice to the
> significance of statutory provisions. They often reflect existing
> patterns of behavior. But these statutory provisions come into
> operation only in the absence of an agreement to the contrary.[23]

This private lawmaking aspect of the law of freedom of contract
may be briefly related to the Marxist distinction between civil society
and the state. It presents an interesting question in the context of the
Marxist analysis of capitalist society because it represents a nexus
between the individual's private organization of his life and the power
of this state. Marx portrays the state as leaving the individual to his
own devices in civil society, which includes commercial transactions.[24]
Yet, in distinction to this image, in the area of contracts, the state
actively involved itself in the individual's private lawmaking at his
request. By bringing suit, the individual called upon the corecive forces

of the state to compel compliance with the privately decided upon terms of his contract or to protect him from the onerous terms of a coercively obtained contract. Except in areas of conduct regulated by the government, the terms and existence of the obligation were privately set, but enforcement of those terms largely lay with the state at the individual's request.

D. Specific Content of the Freedom to Contract - The Right to Enter Contracts and the Right to Determine the Terms of Contracts

The doctrine of freedom of contract included both freedom to decide whether to enter a contract at all and freedom to determine its terms.

The legal right to determine whether one would or would not enter a contract was expressed, among other examples, by two legal rules. First, there were in general no obligatory contracts. That is, there were no contracts which an individual was obliged to enter.

Even the practice of a profession, such as medicine, did not entail an obligation to enter contracts for the practice of that profession. For example, in a 1901 case, *Hurley v. Eddingfield,* a physician refused to treat a man who had previously been his patient and who had suffered an accident.[25] No other patients required the doctor's attention, he knew the patient relied upon him and that no other doctor was available, and he was offered his fee in cash. The would-be patient died, and his heirs sued the doctor. The court held that the heirs had no right to sue the doctor because he was under no obligation to render treatment to the man. This continues to be the law.[26]

Thus, one has a right to refuse to enter a contract even where the refusal will cause serious harm. For example, a contractor is under no obligation to embark on a construction contract, and a supplier is under no obligation to supply materials desperately needed for the construction project.

The second half of the content of this freedom is the right to bargain as to terms. It was clear in the nineteenth century that this was considered an indispensable part of the doctrine of freedom of contract. With the exception of the usury laws, relatively few terms of contracts were set by statute or by the courts. As noted above, the courts would enforce contracts where the exchange was unequal, provided that there was no coercion or fraud and that both parties gave up something, no matter how small.

Atiyah maintains that the eighteenth-century courts looked to the fairness of the exchange and the good faith of the parties in deciding whether or not to enforce a contract, even to the point of being paternalistic, but this point is subject to debate.[27]

Morton Horowitz has argued that this rule reflected a subjective theory of value.[28] That is, Horowitz argued essentially that courts permitted parties to write their own ticket because it was generally thought that the items of exchange have no intrinsic, ascertainable value. It is perhaps more plausible to say - and certainly more easily supported by the cases - that the courts believed that each person was the best judge of the worth of an item to him. Sir Frederick Pollock stated that the idea of each man being the best judge of value occurred not only in English positive law but in the English school of theoretical jurisprudence and politics. For example, Hobbes said: "The value of all things contracted for is measured by the appetite of the contractors, and therefore the just value is that which they be contented to give."[29] That remark could be taken as a statement of a subjective theory of value, but it can also be taken as simply saying that in sales, it is fair to hold one to that value which he agreed to give at the time that the bargain was struck.

Regardless of the theory of value involved, it is clear that the courts felt that the state, in the person of judges enforcing contracts, would be tyrannical if it were to impose the judge's values upon the parties to the contracts. "Every man is presumed to be capable of managing his own affairs, and whether his bargains are wise or unwise, is not ordinarily a legitimate subject of inquiry in a court of either legal or equitable juris-diction."[30] For this reason, Anglo-American courts rejected the rule of *laesio enormis*; English courts as early as 1587 held that even an insig-nificant consideration would validate a contract, as Holdsworth observed:

> The law has never attempted to adjudicate upon the adequacy of a consideration. That is a matter for the parties to the contract. If a person chooses to make an extravagant promise for an inadequate consideration it is his own affair. Thus in 1587, in the case of *Sturlyn v. Albany*, it was said that "when a thing is to be done by the plaintiff, be it never so small, this is a sufficient consideration to ground an action"; and this principle is an accepted doctrine of our modern law.[31]

Continental courts, on the other hand, reserved the right to invalidate contracts where the value given by one party was grossly disproportionate to that given by the other. Although English and American courts rejected this doctrine very clearly, the facts of such disproportionate exchange figured in the duress cases as one indication that a free person would not have entered the transaction, as will be discussed further later.[32]

The fact that the courts did not deny a judge's ability to perceive that the terms of a contract were grossly unfair to one party or the other (although the rules of law precluded invalidating the contract on that ground alone) tends to show that the courts, contrary to Horowitz, did not adopt a relativistic or subjective theory of value but rather adopted an affirmative rule of refusing to meddle in contracts which were otherwise valid, regardless of the values exchanged.

It should be noted that the model of social interaction with regard to contracts was that of two individuals engaged in face-to-face bargaining. In general, these individuals were presumed in a paradigmatic contract situation to be rational, adult, free, and generally not oppressed by pressing need.

Another aspect of the party's right to choose the terms upon which he would contract was the well-established rule of law that a court would not imply a missing term in a contract. Today, under the Uniform Commercial Code, a court may imply various terms, including a reasonable price where the parties have failed to specify the exact price. In the nineteenth century, however, the court would simply refuse to enforce a contract which was too vague. Holdsworth has noted that as early as 1553, a court said, "[I]f I bargain with you that I will give you for your land as much as it is reasonably worth, this is void for default of certainty...". The court, it was said, would not undertake to make the parties' bargain for them. If they had failed to specify a crucial term, one which would be necessary to a court's meaningful decree, the court would simply refuse to enforce the contract and leave the parties to their own devices. This also tends to support the argument that, far from adopting a subjective theory of value, the courts were affirmatively abstaining from interference with the parties' determination of their obligations.

E. Exceptions to the General Doctrine of Freedom of Contract

Even during the nineteenth century when many commentators consider freedom of contract to have been at its peak, numerous exceptions to the doctrine were recognized by the courts. As Holdsworth has noted:

> No doubt, in its application to the law of contract, we must remember the epigram of Jessel, M.R., to the effect that not lightly to interfere with freedom of contract is paramount public policy. (Quotation and citation omitted) But that was said in the days when freedom of contract was supposed to be the panacea for all the ills of the body politic. Historically, complete freedom of contract was never regarded as "paramount public policy". If the common law had ever taken this view it would, in effect, have abandoned its

valuable concept of public policy, and have thereby lost much of its power of shaping the legal and political ideas of the many races which acknowledge its sway; for, as Bowen, L.J., truly said: "The interests of contracting parties are not necessarily the same as the interests of the commonwealth".[33]

Four categories of exceptions deserve mention: persons incapable of contracting; contracts with an immoral object; contracts in restraint of trade; and regulation of contracts.

In connection with the category of persons incapable of contracting, there is the historical curiosity of the protection accorded to the expectant heir.[34] Both in Britain and in the United States, eighteenth- and nineteenth-century courts essentially precluded an heir from selling his expected inheritance, although the rule had been considerably weakened in favor of enforcing the sale, by the end of the nineteenth century. Many of these transactions took the form of a sale of the projected inheritance for ready cash, a practice which one court succinctly noted would "tend to the ruination of families". Although in Britain, as one would expect, most of the cases concerned scions of the aristocracy, the doctrine was also applied to ordinary middle-class individuals in the United States. For example, in the case of *Dunn v. Chambers*, the court saw fit to discuss whether the doctrine, then still considered to be good law, would prevent a young man from selling his life estate, worth about $1400, to his brother.[35]

In addition, other classes of persons were precluded from contracting, and their contracts were either voidable, i.e., susceptible to being repudiated by the incapacitated party, or void, i.e., without legal effect. These included imbeciles, married women, and children. An imbecile lacked the ability to form the requisite intention to contract, as did a child, and therefore a child or imbecile could repudiate any contract which was not for the necessities of life. A married woman, on the other hand, was largely without legal status, and her apparent contracts were unenforceable except that she could to some extent deal with her separate property, provided that the technical forms of law necessary to create an equitable separate estate were followed. Except with regard to the necessities of life, husband and wife were regarded as literally one, and "that one was the husband". This doctrine, however, was modified to a large degree in the mid-nineteenth century by the passage of the Married Women's Property Acts, which generally gave a *feme covert* (married woman) the same right of contract as a *feme sole*.

Second, the courts also restricted the content of contracts on the ground of general perceptions of social policy. Contracts to commit a crime or in furtherance of an illegal or patently immoral purpose were universally rejected. For example, a contract tending to promote divorce was void, as was a contract where the consideration was immoral, such as a contract with a prostitute. Similarly, a contract where the consideration consisted in a promise not to prosecute a crime was considered to be against public policy as tending to conceal the commission of crimes. This doctrine has some effect in the duress area, since the force which was brought to bear on the unfortunate victim was often a threat of criminal prosecution.

Despite the great emphasis on freedom of contract, it also should be noted that in certain specific instances the terms of contracts and the obligation to enter them were prescribed. Chief among these instances, and in contrast to *Hurley v. Eddingfield,* discussed above, were the laws governing common carriers. At common law, innkeepers were regarded as common carriers and were required to offer their services to all peaceable comers. Later the doctrine was extended to utilities, railroads, and other like entities.[36] The terms upon which these entities could contract with individuals and the fact that they were required to extend their services to all were subjects of regulation. In addition, as is discussed below, the particular powers which their monopoly position gave these entities were recognized in the law of duress, so that some coercive contracts involving these carriers were set aside.

Third, the rule against contracts in restraint of trade continued through the nineteenth century, although not with complete rigor. By the end of the century, the courts would not enforce a contract in restraint of trade by enjoining a person from the following of his trade but if one party in fact refrained from a particular trade as he had promised to do, the court would order the other party to pay the agreed-upon consideration.[37]

Fourth, certain regulatory statutes were in force. Two of these were the statute of frauds and the usury statutes. The statute of frauds provided that certain oral contracts were not valid. This statute, which is still generally in force, specified that contracts to answer for the debt of another, contracts which cannot be performed within a year, and contracts for the sale of property worth more than a specified amount were not binding unless they were in writing. Usury statutes continued to be enforced throughout most of the nineteenth century. It is interesting to note that the great legal scholar John Chipman Gray felt that the widespread repeal of the usury statutes toward the end of the nineteenth century represented the fullest development of the desirable doctrine of freedom of contract, since the repeal of such statutes naturally permitted individuals to contract for the borrowing of money on any terms which they saw fit.

F. Continuing Paradoxes in the Law of Contracts

A particular paradox has recurred both in the law of contracts and in philosophical discussions of the social contract. This is the paradox of agreeing to restrict one's freedom of action. There are three examples which come to mind in the law: restrictions on the alienation of property, slavery, and restrictive covenants.

The common law has long frowned on restrictions on the alienation of property. These generally occurred in deeds where the seller would provide that the buyer could not sell the property for certain uses. In general, the courts refused to enforce such restrictions on alienation, except under certain circumstances where they occurred in deeds and were of a kind to "run with the property". The paradox is that the seller was free to dispose of his property on such terms as he saw fit, but if he were permitted to impose any terms which he desired, the buyer would never acquire that same freedom with regard to the property. In the sense of having unfettered rights *utendi et abutendi,* the buyer would not acquire the property at all.

Another example of this paradox in the law of contracts is the laws concerning slavery or peonage. The law of contracts did not prohibit, for example, the contract by which one became a bondservant, but some commentators felt that a person could not sell himself into absolute slavery. For example, Locke said: "For a Man, not having the Power of his own Life, cannot by Compact, or his own Consent, enslave himself to any one."[38] Late in the nineteenth century, of course, the institution of slavery was permanently outlawed in the United States by virtue of the Thirteenth, Fourteenth, and Fifteenth Amendments to the United States Constitution. In a sense, the inability to sell oneself into slavery restricts one's rights to enter contracts; yet, the "contract" of slavery would itself be a prohibition of other contracts.

The third example of this paradox has to do with so-called "restrictive covenants". Unlike restrictions on alienation, restrictive covenants affect both property and labor and concern not the disposition of the property or labor but rather the manner of its disposition. A restrictive covenant, for example, in the sale of a business would include a covenant not to compete within a certain area. The courts have enforced these provisions, but only where the provision was reasonable. That is, the courts would not allow a workman to promise never to ply his trade. Similarly, they would not permit a business person to agree never to compete. They would, however, enforce covenants that were limited in geographical and temporal scope.

III.   THE HISTORICAL CONTEXT

In this section, I will briefly review the perceived relationship of freedom of contract to other philosophical and economic theories. The doctrine of freedom of contract formed an integral part of certain widely held views about society, and the concept of contract itself played a key role in widely held views about the nature and history of industrial society.

A.   The General Historical Context of Contract Law

a.   *Status and Contract*

Many historians have noted that the law of contract flourished in the eighteenth and nineteenth centuries, replacing other types of social relationships. In the famous phrase of the great legal historian Maine, this was a period of progress "from status to contract". That is, according to Maine, the individual's relationships during the eighteenth and nineteenth centuries progressed from those which he had as a matter of status to those which he had as a matter of will. Maine himself in *Ancient Law*, published in the early 1860's, expressed the proposition in the following way:

> The movement of the progressive societies has been uniform in one respect. Through all its course it has been distinguished by the gradual dissolution of family dependency, and the growth of individual obligation in its place. The Individual is steadily substituted for the Family, as the unit of which civil laws take account. The advance has been accomplished at varying rates of celerity, and there are societies not absolutely stationary in which the collapse of the ancient organisation can only be perceived by carefuly [sic] study of the phenomena they present. But, whatever its pace, the change has not been subject to reaction or recoil, and apparent retardations will be found to have been occasioned through the absorption of archaic ideas and customs from some entirely foreign source. *Nor is it difficult to see what is the tie between man and man which replaces by degrees those forms of reciprocity in rights and duties which have their origin in the Family. It is Contract.* Starting, as from one terminus of history, from a condition of society in which all the relations of Persons are summed up in the relations of Family, we seem to have steadily moved towards a phase of social order in which all these relations

arise from the free agreement of Individuals. In Western Europe the progress achieved in this direction has been considerable.

The word Status may be usefully employed to construct a formula expressing the law of progress thus indicated, which, whatever be its value, seems to me to be sufficiently ascertained. All the forms of Status taken notice of in the Law of Persons were derived from, and to some extent are still coloured by, the powers and privileges anciently residing in the Family. If then we employ Status, agreeably with the usage of the best writers, to signify these personal conditions only, and avoid applying the term to such conditions as are the immediate or remote result of agreement, we may say that the movement of the progressive societies has hitherto been a movement *from Status to Contract.*[39]

Despite his emphasis on the growth of contract as a social relationship in the nineteenth century, Maine did not underestimate the importance of contract in feudal society. Indeed, in feudal society, more extensive contracts concerning personal liberty were lawful than would now be enforced; for example, the feudal relationship of vassalage was a matter of contract.[40]

Interestingly, Williston argues that the growth of regulatory laws from 1908 to 1921 can be interpreted in part as a return to a status theory of social relationships: "One may freely enter into a certain relation, as that of employer and employee, ...but once having entered the relationship the rights and duties of the parties are fixed by rules and laws independent of the parties."[41] This theory was advanced by Felix Frankfurter in a case which he argued in 1921.[42]

That distinction between status and contract calls to mind at once Marx' analysis of the progress from feudal society to capitalism. Marx claimed that under feudalism, the individual's role in civil society was largely coextensive with his position vis-à-vis the state, whereas under capitalism there was a breakdown between his role in civil commercial · society and his role in public life. Those claims resemble Maine's analysis in some obvious respects.

b. *The Relationship of Freedom of Contract as a Legal Doctrine to Prior Legal Doctrines*

Prior law differed from the law of freedom of contract both as to the parties who could enter certain contracts and as to the terms of those contracts. With regard to the parties who could enter the contract, serious restrictions previously had been raised by statute and other exercises of state power. First, the royal monopolies severely limited the persons who could engage in a particular trade. Second, the guilds controlled both who could sell a particular item and the price at which it could be sold.[43] Finally, the statutes of Edward IV seriously limited the freedom of employees to change their employment.[44] These statutes, which were enacted in the wake of the Black Death in the fifteenth century, were designed to counter the widespread shortage of laborers caused by the plague. They forbade a worker to leave his employment, except with the permission of the employer, and imposed *maximum* wages to prevent greedy servants from extorting unconscionable salaries from their noble masters.

Second, the terms of many contracts had been regulated by statute, a phenomenon which was noted in more than one case as well as by historians.[45] Wages, prices, and conditions of trade were all regulated both in Britain and in the United States. Rather than being determined by the parties themselves or by market forces, fair prices and wages were set by statute.

Courts and commentators of the nineteenth century were very conscious of the transition from state regulation of commercial trans- actions to regulation by the parties through individual contracts. Indeed, in the case of *Carew v. Rutherford*, the court catalogued the previous restrictions and celebrated the change to freedom of contract, saying:

> This freedom of labor and business has not always existed. When our ancestors came here, many branches of labor and business were hampered by legal restrictions created by English statutes; and it was a long time before the community fully understood the importance of freedom in this respect. Some of our early legislation is of this character. One of the colonial acts, entitled "An act against oppression", punished by fine and imprisonment such indisposed persons as may take the liberty to oppress and wrong their neighbors by taking excessive wages for their work, or unreasonable prices for merchandises or other necessary com- modities as may pass from man to man. Another required arti- ficers, or handicraftmen meet to labor, to work by the day for their neighbors, in mowing, reaping of corn and the inning thereof. Another act regulated the price of bread. Some of our town records show that, under the power to make by-laws, the towns fixed the prices of labor, provisions and several articles of merchandise, as late as the time of the Revolutionary War. But experience and increasing intelligence led to the abolition of all such restrictions, and to the establishment of freedom for all branches of labor and business; ... .[46]

As assent came to be regarded as the exclusive basis of contractual obligation, the courts also began to permit the will the widest range of action. As Williston said:

> As theories of individual freedom thus seemed to require that no obligations or defences to obligations should be allowed unless willed by the parties, so on the other hand the same theories led to opposition to restrictions being placed on the kind of contracts which they [the parties] did will.[47]

During the nineteenth century, certain old limitations on the subject matter or terms of contracts were lessened. In general, eighteenth-century courts felt freer than those of the following century to refuse to enforce a contract which the judge felt to be against public policy or immoral.[48] These contracts included those in restraint of trade and contracts where an exorbitant penalty, such as a forfeiture of property, was provided for. An example of the latter would be a debtor who mortgaged his property and agreed to forfeit the entire ownership in the property if he failed to pay the mortgage, as opposed to merely giving the creditor the right to sell the property for payment of the debt.[49]

B. Relationship of Freedom of Contract to Other Social Ideas Entrenched in the Mid-Nineteenth Century

a. Contract as Social Cement

The law of contract - that is, the law of rights dependent upon agreement - is considered by modern common law commentators to be almost an essential feature of any system of law. As P. S. Atiyah says in *An Introduction to the Law of Contract:*

> Every system of law has found it necessary to devise, to a greater or lesser extent, machinery for the enforcement of contractual rights, that is to say, of rights which depend ultimately on the agreement of the parties concerned.[50]

The importance of the law of contract since the seventeenth century is made clear by Atiyah when he notes:

> A person's bank account, his right to occupy his house if rented or mortgaged, his employment, his insurance, his shareholdings, and

many other matters of vital importance to him, all depend for their value on the fact that, in the last analysis, the law of contract will enable him to realize his rights. In the striking phrase of Roscoe Pound: "Wealth, in a commercial age, is made up largely of promises."[51]

In the mid- to late- nineteenth century, contract was considered to be the glue that held the best and most modern societies together, as well as the best and most just system for the distribution of social resources and the highest form of freedom. Freedom of contract was linked with the political doctrines of civil liberty and with the economic doctrine of *laissez faire*. Kessler and Gilmore's text on contracts presents an excellent assortment of examples of this historical phenomenon, from which the following quotations are taken:

> It is through contract that man attains freedom. Although it appears to be the subordination of one man's will to another, the former gains more than he loses. And since contract as a social pheno-menon is the result of a "coincidence of free choices" on the part of the members of the community, merging their egoistical and altruistic tendencies, a contractual society safeguards its own stability. Contract is an instrument of peace in society. It reconciles freedom with order, particularly since with increasing rationality man becomes less rather than more egoistical.[52]

The high hopes with regard to the potentialities inherent in the contractual mechanism found admirable expression in Sidgwick's *Elements of Politics*:

> In a summary view of the civil order of society, as constituted in accordance with the individualistic ideal, performance of contract presents itself as the chief *positive* element, protection of life and property being the chief *negative* element. Withdraw contract - suppose that no one can count upon the fulfillment of any engagement - and the members of a human community are atoms that cannot effectively combine; the complex co-operation and division of employments that are the essential characteristics of modern industry cannot be introduced among such beings. Suppose contracts freely made and effectively sanctioned, and the most elaborate social organisation becomes possible, at least in a society of such human beings as the individualistic theory contemplates - gifted with mature reason, and governed by enlightened self-interest. Of such beings it is prima facie plausible to say that, when once their respective relations to the surrounding

> material world have been determined so as to prevent mutual encroachment and secure to each the fruits of his industry, the remainder of their positive mutual rights and obligations ought to depend entirely on that coincidence of their free choices, which we call contract. Thorough-going individuals would even include the rights corresponding to governmental services, and the obligations to render services to government, which we shall have to consider later; only in this latter case the contract is tacit.[53]

Contract, in this view, is the principle of order par excellence and the only legitimate means of social integration in a free society. Translated into legal language, this means that in a progressive society all law is ultimately based on contract. In the nineteenth century, law enforcement rested on private action to a degree astonishing to modern eyes; even the enforcement of criminal law depended to a considerable degree upon a reward system, which was, of course, a contract-based system.[54]

One can see in Sidgwick's words the view that Marx described in 'On the Jewish Question' as the nature of civil capitalist society, viz., that the law draws boundary lines between the domains of isolated individuals.

b. Contract and Laissez Faire

A system of free contract did not recommend itself solely for reasons of sheer expediency and utilitarianism; it was deeply rooted in the moral sentiments of the period in which it found strongest expression. The dominant current of belief inspiring nineteenth-century industrial society - an open society - was the deep-felt conviction that individual and co-operative action should be left unrestrained in family, church, and market and that such a system of laissez-faire would not lessen the freedom and dignity of the individual but would secure the highest possible social justice.[55] The representatives of this school of thought were firmly convinced, to state it somewhat roughly, of the existence of a natural law according to which, if not in the short run then at least in the long run, the individual serving his own interest was also serving the interest of the community.[56]

The eminent legal scholar Williston in a 1921 article linked the rise in the importance of contract law in the nineteenth century to the dominance of *laissez faire* economic theory. Williston argued that the economic theorists, such as John Stuart Mill, had exceptional success in obtaining popular support for their theories:

The theorizing in metaphysics, politics and economics, could not fail to have its effect on the law, and the law of contracts was a field in which its application was not difficult. Indeed it was a corollary of the philosophy of freedom and individualism that the law ought to extend the sphere and enforce the obligation of contract.[57]

Since *laissez faire* economics consists in the social doctrine that the distribution of goods and services should be left to private decision-making, it can be seen that the legal realization of this scheme would be freedom of contract. That is, the private decisions of individuals would be given legal efficacy, as opposed to a social or state decision-making process or to a system based upon status rather than choice.

Indeed, the doctrine of *laissez faire* as a matter of social justice was expressly adopted by various courts, as where the court in *Carew v. Rutherford* said:

[A]nd all persons who have been born and educated here, and are obliged to begin life without property, know that freedom to choose their own occupation and to make their own contracts not only elevates their condition, but secures to skill and industry and economy their appropriate advantages.[58]

Other historians have echoed Williston's sentiments. For example, Atiyah has said:

It is imperative, at the outset, to recall that the eighteenth and nineteenth century were the heyday of theories of natural law and the philosophy of laissez faire, and the judges, who were largely responsible for the law of contract during this period, were, like most educated men of the time, very considerably influenced by current thought. To the judges of the eighteenth century, theories of natural law meant that men had an inalienable right to make their own contracts for themselves, and to the judges of the nineteenth century, the philosophy of laissez faire similarly meant that the law should interfere with people as little as possible... . As applied to the law of contract, these ideas meant encouraging almost unlimited freedom of contracting, and thus the shibboleths "freedom of contract" and "sanctity of contract" became the foundation on which the whole law of contract was built.[59]

c. *Freedom of Contract and Civil Liberty*

It has been noted above that freedom of contract has been linked by political theorists to general concepts of freedom in society, and historically the idea of freedom of contract has been closely linked to other ideas of social freedom. The stability of contractual relations was considered so important by the framers of the Constitution that they adopted a provision prohibiting the states from impairing the obligations of contract. Similarly, Max Radin has noted that the hatred of monopolies, which restrained freedom of contract, was the essence of liberty as far as the framers of the Constitution were concerned.[60] The fullest expression of this view can be seen in the cases on economic regulation which were decided around the turn of the century and which were not overruled until the end of the 1930s.

In 1915, a court expressed the concept of freedom of contract as part of the individual's civil liberty in the following way:

> We had supposed that it was elementary law that a trader could buy from whom he pleased and sell to whom he pleased, and that his selection of seller and buyer was wholly his own concern. *"It is a part of a man's civil rights that he be at liberty to refuse business relations with any person whomsoever, whether the refusal rests upon reason, or is the result of whim, caprice, prejudice, or malice."* Cooley on Torts, p. 278. See, also, our own opinion in *Greater New York Film Co. v. Biograph Co.*, 203 Fed. 39, 121 C.C.A. 375.
>
> Before the Sherman Act it was the law that a trader might reject the offer of a proposing buyer, for any reason that appealed to him; it might be because he did not like the other's business methods, or because he had some personal difference with him, political, racial, or social. That was purely his own affair, with which nobody else had any concern. Neither the Sherman Act, nor any decision of the Supreme Court construing the same, nor the Clayton Act, has changed the law in this particular. We have not yet reached the stage where the selection of a trader's customers is made for him by the government.[61]

Many regulatory laws enacted about the turn of the century were challenged on the ground that these laws inhibited the freedom of contract of the workers whom they were intended to protect. Among these cases is *Lochner v. New York*.[62] The state legislature of New York enacted a statute which limited the hours of bakery workers to ten hours per day. The Supreme Court of the United States held as follows:

The general right to make a contract in relation to his business is part of the liberty of the individual protected by the Fourteenth Amendment of the Federal Constitution. Under that provision no state can deprive any person of life, liberty or property without due process of law. The right to purchase or to sell labor is part of the liberty protected by this amendment, unless there are circumstances which exclude the right.[63]

The court acknowledged that the states had the power to make laws which would promote the "safety, health, morals and general welfare of the public" and that "both property and liberty are held on such reasonable conditions as may be imposed by the governing power of the State in the exercise of those powers...".[64] In the judgment of the court, however, these police powers did not include the power to outlaw employment contracts requiring more than ten hours work per day, and the statute was declared unconstitutional.

Marx' description of the appalling working conditions in English bakeries may be of some interest in this connection.[65] Assuming that Marx was even partially accurate in his description and that those conditions also prevailed in the United States, it can be seen that the justices were willing to permit a substantial amount of human suffering in the promotion of freedom of contract.

Many other reform statutes were struck down in the early years of the twentieth century on the ground that they unduly infringed on freedom of contract. Williston listed fourteen cases decided from 1903 to 1915 as examples.[66] These cases included laws dealing with the working conditions of firemen, bakery workers, railway workers, women, etc. Gradually, the courts relaxed this prohibition, beginning with a case upholding restriction on the working hours of women in factories, laundries, and "mechanical establishments".[67] The doctrine that freedom of contract was embodied in the Constitution was radically eroded by the Supreme Court during the New Deal and is now generally regarded as not being the law.

d. Freedom of Contract and Capitalism

It is a common point of view today among Marxist, as well as non-Marxist, legal scholars that freedom of contract necessarily accompanied the burgeoning growth of capitalism. Kessler and Gilmore express this popular sentiment well:

The predominance of individualism in one sector of the law of contracts may be explained by the fact that this part of contract law is the counterpart, if not the product, of free-enterprise capitalism. Contract, in this point of view, is the legal machinery appropriate to an economic system which relies on free exchange rather than tradition and custom or command for the distribution of resources.

The triumph of capitalism during the eighteenth and nineteenth centuries, with its spectacular increase in the productivity of labor, was possible only because of a constant refinement of the division of labor. This development in turn presupposed that enterprises could depend on a continuous flow of goods and services exchanged in a free market. And to be able to exploit the factors of production in the most efficient way, enterprisers had (and still have) to be able to bargain for goods and services to be delivered in the future and to rely on promises for future delivery. Thus, it became one of the main functions of our law of contracts to keep this flow running smoothly, making certain that bargains would be kept and that legitimate expectations created by contractual promises would be honored.[68]

Citing Max Weber's *Wirtschaft und Gesellschaft,* Kessler and Gilmore observed that "[c]ontract, to be really useful to the business enterpriser within the setting of a free-enterprise economy, must be a tool of almost unlimited pliability." Kessler or Gilmore further reasoned that entrepreneurs in a free enterprise society needed maximum flexibility in economic arrangement in order to enhance the Weberian rationality of those arrangements, noting that "contract, then, in the sense of a system of free contract, enhances the mobility of factors of production in the interest of the enterpriser who wishes to secure them in the most efficient way, so as to be able rationally to experiment with new methods of satisfying wants." Thus, Kessler and Gilmore believed that freedom of contract followed from the economic structure and needs of the time, saying as follows:

Within the framework of a free-enterprise system the essential prerequisite of contractual liability is volition, that is, consent freely given, and not coercion or status. Contract, in this view, is the "meeting place of the ideas of agreement and obligation".[69]

The causal and logical relationships postulated by their lengthy discussion are outside the scope of this book. It is worth noting, though, that while it is undeniable that freedom of contract was an accepted legal doctrine when industrial capitalism was in progress, yet limitations on contractual freedom were and are being developed in ostensibly capitalist countries.

IV. SURVEY OF THE LAW OF DURESS
AND UNDUE INFLUENCE

A. Duress and Undue Influence

Duress and undue influence, the two areas of law to be considered here, have certain characteristics in common and certain differences.

a. Duress and Undue Influence - The Similarities

First, these kinds of cases arise where one party is attempting to invalidate an apparent contractual obligation. That is, the formal requisites of a contract have been satisfied. There is an apparent meeting of the minds on the terms of the contract, and value has been exchanged. Further, the terms of the contract are not in dispute; in that sense, these cases are not like those of mistake or misrepresentation, where the case may concern what exactly has been agreed to. The duress cases generally arise after a contract has been signed or a deed handed over, while the undue influence cases characteristically concern a will which has been made.

If a contract had not apparently been entered, there could probably be no lawsuit for duress or undue influence itself. There was no cause of action, in general, for "attempted duress", although some components of the law of duress might themselves provide an action for tort. For example, if an over-eager heir browbeat and nagged his aged relative to make a will in his favor and the aged relative resisted this pressure, there was no available remedy at law against the immoral relative.

A second shared feature of these areas of law is that both are common-law doctrines. That means, of course, that they arose by virtue of the decisions of the court and not by statute.[70] Contracts are a matter of civil law, and although the courts might look to the criminal law of extortion as a guide in determining what constituted a wrongful threat, these statutes were not the basis of their decision.[71]

b. Differences Between Undue Influence and Duress

Duress may be distinguished from undue influence. First, the law of duress requires that the pressure be exercised by means of threats, whereas undue influence consists in the destruction of free will by other means, usually by overbearing persuasion and psychological pressure.

Second, the nineteenth-century law of duress required that the pressure be such as would overcome a hypothetical person of ordinary firmness. On the other hand, the courts in undue influence cases expressly took into account individual characteristics. Therefore, a court considering the issue of undue influence, for example, with regard to a will, would expressly consider the age, sophistication, business acumen, need, and dependence of the person whose bequest was challenged. In the duress cases, however, the courts applied what was considered to be an objective standard, that is, the standard of a person of ordinary firmness, rather than expressly considering the individual characteristics of the individual involved. This objective standard was in the process of change, however, and by the end of the nineteenth century the courts had expressly adopted the view that a subjective standard should be adopted for both classes of cases.

The doctrine of duress in a contractual context differs technically from the doctrine of *laesio enormis*, which in the mid-nineteenth century the courts in England and America had clearly rejected. Therefore, as a matter of doctrine, the English courts distinguished between pressures which overcame a person's free will and the mere injustice of the situation.[72]

The two doctrines, however, were not totally unrelated. The gross disproportion of the terms of a contract was considered to be one of the indicia of duress; the unfairness of the exchange was not the basis upon which the court grounded its invalidation of the obligation, but rather, the unfairness was only evidence of the fact that the person entering the contract had not been free in doing so.

In the case of *Dunn v. Chambers*, argued by John Van Buren in the Supreme Court of New York in Equity in 1848, the court said:

> Every man is presumed to be capable of managing his own affairs; and whether his bargains are wise or unwise is not ordinarily a legi- timate subject of inquiry in a court either of legal or equitable juris- diction. No principle is better settled than that mere inadequacy does not form a distinct ground of equitable relief. And yet there are cases where there is no positive evidence of fraud, in which the inequality of the bargain is so gross, that the mind cannot resist the inference, that though there be no direct evidence of fraud, such a bar- gain must have been in some way improperly obtained.[73]

The court quoted from Lord Hardwicke as describing these as "such bargains as no man in his senses and not under a delusion would make on the one hand, and as no honest and fair man would accept on the other."[74]

c. Procedural Setting

1. Duress - Procedural Setting

In the typical case involving the doctrine of duress, A threatens B with dire consequences if B does not convey his property to A for a small sum. B gives A the deed and then sues to recover his property. In an alternative, but equally typical, case, A threatens B with dire consequences if B refuses to enter a contract with A. B signs the contract, and then either A sues to force B to perform or B sues, asking the court to release him from the contractual obligation. In essence, duress arises either as a defense to a suit seeking to enforce the contract or as a basis for an affirmative action to get back the property conveyed or to avoid the contract. Duress, therefore, may arise in a defensive situation or in an offensive one.

Because the doctrine of duress arises in cases where one party is attempting to invalidate an apparently valid contract, however, the burden of proof is upon the party asserting the duress.[75] This means that the victim has to convince the court that he did not freely consent to the contract. If he fails to convince the court on this point, then his alleged oppressor wins on the strength of the objective evidence, i.e., the fact that the deed was transferred to A, who paid a price for it, or that B signed the contract. The oppressor is not required to prove as part of his case that the victim subjectively wanted to enter the contract. It is up to the victim to prove that he did not freely enter the contractual situation.

2. Undue Influence - Procedural Setting

In a typical undue influence case, A and B share the same household. B is old, foolish, and rich. A is young, smart, and poor. A browbeats and terrorizes B, but B trusts A. B suffers various delusions as to the rest of the world, including his or her own children, which the courts are fond of calling "the natural objects of his bounty". B puts his affairs in A's hands, and A profits immensely. In the truly typical case, B leaves a great deal of money to A in his will. After B dies, A attempts to collect under the will, and B's would-be heirs (those who would have inherited had B died without a will) contest the will upon the ground that B was unduly influenced by A.

Like duress, undue influence can be asserted either defensively or offensively. That is, a party, who has been sued on a contract, can attempt to escape the contractual obligation by asserting the doctrine of undue influence, or a party can base an action to recover property or to invalidate a will on the ground of undue influence.

Unlike duress, however, undue influence is characterized by the abuse of a relationship of trust, rather than by an openly adversarial and hostile bargaining situation. In the typical duress case, the parties are unrelated except by their commercial relationship, but in the typical undue influence case, some form of personal interrelationship has developed.[76]

No specific relationship is required by the law, but relationships of lawyer and client, steward and owner, guardian and ward were considered to be relationships particularly *likely* to abuse, as was the relationship of religious adviser and believer. Curiously, the relationship of parent and child was sometimes held not to create a special fiduciary duty to the other party, nor would a husband's brutality toward a wife suffice to invalidate the transaction at issue.[77] There are, however, cases finding that undue influence was exercised by a parent on a child or vice versa.[78]

The ultimate question to be answered by the court in both instances was the same: Was the transaction the product of the individual's free will?

C. Court Systems in Which the Doctrine Arose

Cases involving duress or undue influence arose both in the courts of law and the courts of equity. The significance of the distinction in general is that the courts of equity historically had been freer in doing justice and, in the course of centuries, had developed certain doctrines assertedly based on concepts of fairness, rather than technical rules of law. In theory, the courts of equity were freer to do equity, but in fact, by the nineteenth century they had become bound by their own established and detailed rules. In part, courts of law were bound to a greater degree by the formalities of the contract, and it was difficult to invalidate at law a contract which had actually been signed and sealed, regardless of the conditions under which those actions were done. A court of equity afforded various remedies unavailable in the law court and could refuse to give the aid of those remedies to an unjust situation. The court in which an action was brought, naturally, frequently affected the outcome of cases in the nineteenth century, although its effect on duress cases is not as great as in some other areas of the law.

Since the courts remained heavily fettered with procedural rules even in the nineteenth century, lawsuits had to fall within certain procedural bounds, or the person suing had no remedy. By the nineteenth century, however, the previously rigid forms had considerably expanded and were sufficiently flexible to accommodate most forms of contractual disputes.[79]

Cases generally would arise at law where the oppressor sued the victim for breach of the contract and sought money damages. In that case, the victim would raise the issue of duress as a defense.[80] On the other hand, the victim could bring an action at law for money had and received on the ground that his oppressor was wrongfully in the possession of the money, since it had not in fact been given or transferred legally to him, since the victim had never really willed the transfer.

A person seeking to receive the money owed on a debt sued in the courts of law in an action of debt, provided that the amount owed was a "sum certain", i.e., a definite amount.[81] This action or form of proceeding did not lie only for loans but could be used to recover money in a variety of circumstances. A sum of money might be owed, for example, on a contract of sale, and this money would be sought in court by an action in debt. Similarly, money might be owed on a note. The contract might be represented by a sealed instrument, called a "specialty", or by a written, but unsealed, contract, or by an oral promise. A special action in debt, called "*debet et detinet*", was available for the recovery of goods, as well as money.[82]

At one time, the only suits about contracts which could effectively be pursued were those where the contract was represented by a sealed writing, which were called actions upon a "covenant".[83] By 1596, a suit called "action upon the case upon assumpsit" was becoming available. The courts of law gradually came to recognize lawsuits for breach of an agreement. A sealed instrument could be sued upon, but an oral contract could also form the basis for a lawsuit if the plaintiff could prove that there was an agreement and that there was consideration for the agreement. Actions for breach of contract were often technically based either on deceit or on a trespass, both of which were categories of lawsuits dealing with personal injuries.[84]

The development of assumpsit as a form of proceeding in the courts of law, as opposed to the remedies then available in the Chancellor's courts of equity, is complex, and the procedural nuances which arose from the elaborate forms of lawsuits are almost impenetrable at this distance. The significance to this work of the procedural forms and the separation of the two bodies of law lies in the impact of these forms upon the law of duress. Duress was available as a defense to contract under any of the forms of proceeding; indeed, it was one of the few defenses that could be legally offered in a suit upon a document bearing a seal. If the forms of action were based upon the concept that the party not performing the contract was committing a moral wrong, the defense of duress in turn accused the other party of wrong-doing.

On the other hand, the action might be brought in a court of equity. Only courts of equity had the power to order a person to perform a contract; courts of law could grant only money damages. The oppressor could sue the victim seeking specific performance of the contract, or the victim might sue the oppressor seeking to have the contract set aside or the deed returned. For example, the case of *Earle v. The Norfolk & New Brunswick Hosiery Co.* was an action brought in the Chancery Court of New Jersey to invalidate a deed. The victim of duress who had deeded over his property could not bring an action *at law* to get his property back because the oppressor was rightfully in possession of the deed, but he could sue *in equity* to rescind the deed.[85]

The equity court thus continued to have the power to refuse to be involved in unfairness. It could refuse to enforce a contract because specific performance was an equitable remedy, literally a remedy not to be granted except when it was fair. It could also order the rescission of a deed, the undoing of a transaction, and the repayment of money that had been paid.

Part of the power of the equity court lay precisely in its ability to refuse to act. Where one person had secured an unequal bargain, he desired to have the specific performance, not the damages; he wanted to receive the land for which he had paid a grossly inadequate price, not to receive back the amount he had paid. Therefore, a court of equity could refuse to enforce the contract, i.e., decline to order the oppressed party to perform and leave the oppressor to his (from his point of view) inadequate remedy in the courts of law. The case of *Green v. Wood* is described as follows:

> Where an agreement for a purchase was obtained from a woman of nineteen years of age, and several suspicious circumstances appeared, the court would neither decree it to be carried into execution...nor to be delivered up...but left the parties to their remedy at law.[86]

The courts of equity, although they were bound by their own rules as to what constituted fraud and duress and although they frequently borrowed such concepts as that of capacity to contract from the courts of law, were nonetheless freer to act to redress injustice, at least in theory, because of their greater discretion in awarding a remedy. For example, Bacon's *Abridgement of the Laws*, published in 1854, gave the following rules of equity:

A court of equity will relieve against an unequal contract entered into by a person in embarrassed circumstances; for to avail oneself of the distress of another carries somewhat of fraud in it [citations omitted]. It will relieve, too, where there is a manifest inequality between parties arising from the relation in which they stand to each other. Such is the relation of guardian and ward; and therefore a court of equity will not allow any gift or release to a guardian from his ward on his coming of age, or give validity to any contract the terms of which are not perfectly fair and equal, made by persons in that situation, or between whom, a similar confidence hath existed. Such also is the relation of parent and child, attorney and client, and steward or agent and his principal.[87]

An earlier edition of Bacon's *Abridgement of the Laws*, published in 1844, noted that "agreements, out of which an equity can be raised for a decree in specie, ought to be obtained with all imaginable fairness, and without any mixture tending to surprise or circumvention; and that they be not unreasonable in themselves".[83]

The rule of the equity court was well expressed, at least in theory, in the case of *Bosanquett v. Dashwood*, where the court said this:

In matters within the jurisdiction of the court it will relieve, though nothing appears which, strictly speaking, to be called illegal. The reason is: because all of those cases [of extortionate interest rates] carry somewhat of fraud with them. I do not mean such a fraud as is properly deceit; but such proceedings as lay a particular burden or hardship upon any man; it being the business of this court to relieve against all offenses against the law of nature and reason; and if it be so in cases which, strictly speaking, may be called legal, how much shall it be so where the covenant or agreement is against an expressed law (as in this case) [the usury laws] against the statute of usury, though the party may have submitted for a time to the terms imposed on him.[89]

Yet the courts of equity, at least by the nineteenth century, technically did not have the power to relieve against any contract merely on grounds of unfairness. As was said in the case of *Heathcote v. Paignon*:

Courts of equity have no jurisdiction to enforce common honesty; their jurisdiction is confined to cases where fraud is an ingredient.[90]

The court went on, however, to define fraud as including actual fraud or deceit, fraud "apparent from the intrinsic nature and subject of the bargain", and fraud arising from the weakness of one of the parties.

V. OUTLINE OF THE LAW OF DURESS AND UNDUE INFLUENCE FROM 1820 TO 1870

In discussing the law of the applicable period, I intend to depart from the standard form pursued in law review articles. In much legal writing today, the applicable principles of law are discussed in the text, while the references and much of the factual development are relegated to the footnotes. As a compromise, in view of the importance of both quotations from the opinions and of the factual backgrounds of these cases, the remaining text of this chapter discusses the rules of law, while detailed discussions of the facts of each case have been relegated to appendices.

A. Elements of the Law of Duress

The law of duress as a defense to a contract has existed for many centuries and was clearly expressed in Roman law. It was, however, much more limited in the original common-law form and has been in a process of continual expansion from its origins to the present day.

The Year Books reveal that in the fourteenth century duress was mentioned frequently in lawyers' discussions of voidable transactions. For example, in 1308 a court sustained a plea of duress in an action concerning a debt.[91]

The five major elements of the law of duress are as follows:

    a. The nature of the threat
    b. The nature of the harm threatened
    c. The effect of the threat upon the weaker party
    d. The imminence of the harm
    e. The person making the threat

Although these elements are closely related and interdependent, for the sake of clarity they will be discussed separately to the extent possible.

a. The Nature of the Threat

The key element is that the threat must be of a wrongful action, that is, an action which the oppressor does not have a legal right to take. For example, a person who was acting in self-defense would not be making a wrongful threat if he said: "If you come one step closer, I'll kill you." This is because, in that factual context, the threatened act is one which the person has a right to take; that is, where a person has a right to kill in his own self-defense, he obviously has a right to threaten to do that. Shylock, it may be assumed, had a perfect right to threaten to collect his pound of flesh because he had a right to collect it.

An element of the duress doctrine which is not often commented upon by legal scholars is that a mere threat of harm is not the determining factor. A threat of damage to reputation did not constitute duress, and even today, a threat to ruin someone's credit or blacken someone's reputation does not necessarily constitute duress.[92] It should be noted, however, that certain forms of these threats constitute the crimes of extortion or blackmail.[93]

The issue is the wrongfulness of the action to be taken. There are many sorts of harm which we in Anglo-American society have the legal right to inflict upon one another. I may, within the bounds now of the antitrust and civil rights laws, threaten not to do business with you, even though that will cause you grave financial harm, because I have the right to do business with whom I choose. I may threaten not to marry you, even though that will cause you grave emotional suffering, because I have the right to marry whom I choose. Thus, for example, a widow who threatened to bury her husband's body in a distant part of the country where his grieving mother would never be able to visit the grave was held not to have inflicted any duress upon the mother sufficient to invalidate the mother's assignment of a life insurance policy on the son to his widow. The wife had, after all, the right to have her husband buried where she chose.

An often overlooked point is that there must be a threat, as will be seen in the cases discussed below; neither predictions of dire harm, advice, nor persuasion would constitute duress, even if in fact the weaker person were persuaded to act by such means.

b. The Nature of the Harm Threatened

Since not every threat of harm constituted duress sufficient to set aside a contract, it may be useful to examine a catalogue of the kinds of harm which were frequently the issues of these cases.

1. Threats of Death or Physical Injury

Threats of physical harm had long been a basis for invalidating a contract and, indeed, had been the only kind of pressure recognized as sufficiently coercive to invalidate a contract. Centuries earlier, Bracton, in *De Legibus,* had stated that "the threat must include the peril of death or bodily torture". The thirteenth-century cases collected in Bracton's *Notebook,* however, generally refused to award relief for duress, since, in light of the essentially criminal and violent nature of the alleged threats, several actions were required of the alleged victim. For example, the coerced act must have been promptly disaffirmed, the hue and cry must have been raised, and the violence shown to the king's coroner and later to the county court.[94]

In the mid-seventeenth century, the great legal authority Coke somewhat confirmed the older restriction on the defense, which limited the concept of duress to coercion exerted by threats of physical harm.[95] This restriction persisted into nineteenth-century treatises on the law and was perpetuated in an edition of Blackstone's *Commentaries,* published in 1859.[96] Blackstone stated that only threats of immediate loss of life or limb could constitute such duress as would invalidate a contract. The reason given by Blackstone was that all other harms could be redressed by a suit for damages.[97]

During the period from 1820 to 1870, it was clear that a threatened battery would suffice to invalidate a contract - one did not have to be in fear of imminent death to escape from one's contractual obligations, and "such menaces of serious bodily harm as would overcome the will of a man of ordinary firmness" would suffice.[98] The rule, thus, had expanded from recognizing only threats of death or maiming as sufficiently fearsome to constitute duress to setting aside contracts induced by threats of mere pain.[99]

2. Imprisonment

Actual imprisonment, or at least unjust imprisonment, would invalidate a contract.[100]

The question of whether actual imprisonment or the threat of imprisonment would constitute such duress as to invalidate a contract was particularly important in mid-nineteenth-century Britain because of the law that one could be imprisoned not only for a proven, existing crime or debt, but - until the Civil Procedure Act of 1838 - by process issued by the court prior to judicial determination of the existence of a debt. Thus, a court might issue a writ for a person's arrest upon the application of the alleged creditor. It frequently followed that, although the supposed debtor might deny the existence of the debt, he would be compelled to sign a "new" note or to pay over money as the price of being released from prison. It might then follow that either the would-be creditor would sue on the new document and the coerced debtor would defend on the grounds of duress, or the debtor would seek to recover the money paid as being paid under duress.[101]

In English common law, an agreement executed while in prison might be voidable for duress, although the courts sometimes required that the imprisonment be unlawful. This latter requirement was not uniformly imposed, however.[102]

In 1899, *The American and English Encyclopedia of Law* summarized the doctrine with regard to imprisonment as follows:

> The imprisonment is such duress as will avoid any contract made under it, first, where there is an arrest for improper purpose without just cause, second, where there is an arrest whether for a just cause or not; or, third, where there is an arrest for a just cause, but for an unlawful purpose, even though under proper process. It must, however, appear that the act sought to be avoided must have been induced by the custody. The existence of duress is generally a question of fact and will not be assumed because of the restraint, if the contract sought to be avoided is a just one.[103]

In *Williams v. Bayley*, a contract was held to be unenforceable when a father agreed to sign a note under the threat that his son otherwise would be prosecuted for forgery.[104]

The holding in *Williams v. Bayley* was repeated in several later cases.[105] A case interestingly similar to *Williams v. Bayley* was decided in 1843, when a court sitting in equity ordered the return of certain securities which had been given to pay a gambling debt under threat of a prosecution for cheating at cards.[106]

The difficulty in the *Williams* case and similar cases was that the result of the contract was the concealment of a crime, and that concealment was immoral and itself a crime. Thus, the contract was technically unlawful, but the threat (prosecution) was to be encouraged. The threatened parent was technically a conspirator and, therefore, should not have been able to invoke equitable doctrines. Thus, curiously, under almost precisely identical facts as those in *Williams v. Bayley*, an Arkansas court refused to invalidate the father's signature on the ground that a felony was being concealed ("compounded"), and therefore, no relief would be granted.[107]

Indeed, the policy of the law against relieving parties who were both participants in an illegal transaction was so strong that at one time it was doubted whether a person who had paid usurious interest could recover it. After all, usury was against the law and the debtor was as much a party to the usurious contract as was the creditor.[108]

3. Privileged Harms

The courts in the mid-nineteenth century, however, consistently continued to refuse to consider certain forms of pressure as sufficiently coercive to invalidate a contract. For example, as noted above, a threat to ruin someone's credit or standing in the community had been held not to be such a threat as would invalidate a contract. Similarly, a threat to have someone confined to an asylum has been held not to be sufficient, nor was a general threat to make a person sorry if he did not enter the contract.[109]

4. Financial Need

Generally speaking, English and American courts refused to consider mere financial pressure, whether arising from the general economic circumstances or harsh measures imposed by the other party, as duress. In other words, the pressure of need for the goods to be exchanged in the contract did not constitute duress.

The prevalence of this rule can be seen by the absence of cases ever mentioning the needs of the parties. For example, there were many cases concerning injuries to factory workers, and the employer often defended on the ground that the employee had assumed the risk of working in a dangerous environment. The courts seldom discussed the worker's need for employment as a response to that essentially con-tractual argument.

Some cases which arose during the period from 1820 to 1870, however, permitted recovery where a known desperate need was particularly ruthlessly exploited. Other courts permitted recovery on the ground of duress only where the person exploiting the duress was also somehow responsible for the need, as where the exploiter had pushed the weaker individual into a position of dependency.

Judges were not unaware, however, of the force which economic necessity exerted upon individuals, and the effect of this force upon the cherished idea of free will was also sometimes recognized. In 1762, Lord Northington wrote in the case of *Vernon v. Pethell* that "necessitous men are not, truly speaking, free men."[110] Similarly, Chief Justice Abbott said in 1824: "If one party has the power of saying to the other, 'That which you require shall not be done except upon the conditions which I choose to impose,' no person can contend that they stand upon anything like an equal footing."[111] The use of the term "require" in this context deserves mention; clearly, Justice Abbott was referring to conditions of need, rather than of preference. Second, this quotation reveals an early instance of the concept of bargaining power; that is, of the concept that where one person has the economic power to dictate the terms of the transaction, the parties are not in a process of mutual negotiation in arriving at the terms of the contract, so that the parties cannot in a true sense be said to have reached voluntarily a free accommodation of their varying interests.

5. Detention of Goods

One way of applying economic pressure was to seize the other party's property. This differs, of course, from a mere threat of an action. The pressure exerted, however, was economic, rather than physical.

Dawson noted that duress by threats of economic harm was a recognized concept in the fourteenth century and that several cases are recorded where a transaction was sought to be voided on the ground that it had been induced by the wrongful seizure and detention of the victim's beasts. One eminent attorney, Littleton, is known to have argued eloquently that it was "all the same to a man to be beaten and to lose all his goods or have his buildings destroyed".[112]

Dawson argued that the extension of duress into the field of economic pressure began in the eighteenth century. The situation which inspired this development involved a relatively simple and clear-cut type of oppression - the wrongful seizure or detention of personal property.[113] Dawson argued that this extension was consistent with the underlying principles of the law of duress to that date: The seizure or detention was "an actual invasion of chattel ownership independently wrongful by the common law of tort. Restitution of payments made or property transferred under such pressure provided a sanction which merely supplemented the damage remedy already available."[114]

This doctrine was called duress of goods, where the oppressor lawfully had possession of the victim's property but wrongfully refused to give it up unless the victim paid an exorbitant price for its return. The fact that the person making the threat *lawfully* had the goods in his possession distinguishes these cases from those where a threat of unlawful destruction of property, such as arson, was made.

The victim of duress of goods had the option of paying the price and then trying to recover the money. For example, in the famous case of *Astley v. Reynolds*, decided in 1732, a pawnshop owner refused to return a pawned item except upon the payment of additional illegal interest. The victim paid the illegal interest and then sued to get his money back. The court held that he had a cause of action because he might have needed the goods and "a lawsuit might not do his business".[115]

The doctrine of duress of goods, as noted, was relatively limited and was not consistently adopted. *The American and English Encyclopedia of Law* noted that duress of goods, in the sense of an unlawful detention or seizure of the goods, would not "constitute duress sufficient to avoid a contract".[116] The authors, however, also observed that such an illegal holding of goods would invalidate a contract where the property was threatened with destruction as, for example, where the goods were oysters and subject to spoilage.

In contrast to other contract cases, in cases dealing with utilities, the concepts of need and lack of an acceptable alternative were clearly in focus. The courts were well aware that a shipper might have no other way of getting his goods to market or wherever they were required except by rail. In *C.& A. R.R. Co. v. Chicago, etc., Coal Co.*, the court said:

> It can hardly be said that these enhanced charges were voluntarily paid by [the coal company to the railroad]. It was a case of "life or death" with them, as they had no other means of conveying their coal to the markets offered by the Illinois Central, they were bound to accede to any terms [the railroad] might impose. They were under a sort of moral duress, by submitting to which [the railroad] has received money from them which in equity and good conscience they ought not to retain.[117]

There is one curiosity of English law which requires some explanation. This is the fact that apparently while duress of goods would suffice as a ground for the recovery of money actually paid over, it would not suffice as a ground to avoid an executory (regarding actions yet to be performed) contract, such as a note. For example, the court in *Astley v. Reynolds* permitted recovery of the money.[118] Equally clearly, however, the English courts held that where the debtor had not actually paid the money but had merely *agreed* to pay it *at some time in the future*, the court would enforce the transaction. In *Summer v. Ferryman*, the court held that a bond given to secure release of a barge which had been seized by a bailiff was not given under duress.[119] In 1838, Justice Parke said in *Atlee v. Blackhouse* : "I think the law is clear, that in order to avoid a contract by reason of duress, it must be duress of a man's person, not of his goods."[120] In 1851, Justice Parke repeated this doctrine in the case of *Parker v. Bristol & Exeter Ry. Co.*[121]

In the case of *Skeate v. Beale*, the landlord seized his tenant's belongings and threatened to sell them unless the tenant agreed to pay the back rent and an additional sum, which the tenant claimed was not owed. Under threat of suit, the tenant executed a note for the amount claimed. The tenant subsequently paid part of the note and refused to pay more, whereupon the landlord sued on the note. The jury found that the tenant had acted under duress, but the appellate court granted judgment for the landlord (thereby requiring the tenant to pay), holding that duress of goods would not invalidate an agreement to pay.[122]

Whatever the actual rule in the above English cases may have been, the American rule appears to have been that money paid to obtain goods which had been attached by a creditor for good cause could not be recovered on the ground of duress, and the American courts did not always follow the English eccentricities in this regard.[123] In the American case of *Chase v. Dwinal*, the court held that money paid for an *illegal* toll in order to get possession of a raft of lumber could be recovered back as paid under duress.[124]

A threat of a civil lawsuit was not such a threat as would invalidate a contract because the threat must be of an unlawful action and, obviously, invoking a legal remedy is not unlawful.[125] Interestingly, this remains the general rule to this day, although some courts have limited it by stating that the proceedings must be such as could be brought in good faith. Therefore, even though the courts recognized that litigation could be ruinously expensive, they did not consider such a threat grounds for invalidating a contract.

In the 1851 case of *Powell v. Hoylund*, the court found that duress had not been shown. In that case, the plaintiff held certain bills of exchange which had been given to him by a trader.[126] The trader had become bankrupt, and a representative of some of his creditors called on the plaintiff and demanded that the plaintiff hand over the bills of exchange to the creditors, which essentially would have deprived the plaintiff of the ability to claim the amount due to him under those documents. The creditors' representative claimed that if the plaintiff, who was ill at the time, did not give up the bills, the entire expense of the bankruptcy proceeding would fall on him and he, too, would be ruined. The plaintiff gave up the documents, and then he sued to recover them. The court found that the bills were voluntarily handed over, since these dire predictions did not constitute duress.

A threat of a breach of a contract, although technically wrongful, was not considered to be an action which would invalidate a contract.[127]

Even more clearly, a threatened refusal to contract was not the sort of threat which would invalidate a contract, regardless of the kind of harm which it inflicted, provided, of course, that the threat was not otherwise unlawful. That is, the courts held that a threatened refusal to contract could be wrongful where a group of people combined to make that threat, as where a group of workmen threatened to boycott an employer in order to exact an illegal payment.[128] A combination of workers for the purpose of raising wages was lawful at common law and, therefore, did not constitute duress of the employer because the self-interest of the workmen was a legitimate end. An association for the purpose of extorting money which was not owed was unlawful and therefore constituted duress.

An interesting aspect of the law of duress arose with regard to monopolies, such as public utilities or railroads. Such common carriers could not legally refuse service to anyone, nor could they charge unequal rates.[129] Therefore, a threat to refuse to contract, which would perhaps not normally have been duress, was held to be duress where the person making the threat was a public utility or a common carrier, such as the two railroads in the *Parker* case. In fact, the *Parker* case cited the case of *Ashmole v. Wainwright*, which in turn relied upon the doctrine established in *Astley v. Reynolds*.[130] The reason was that the threat was wrongful, one which the utility or carrier had no right to make. Moreover, the victim of the threat literally had no choice in the matter, since there was no other source of rail transportation, light, power, or water.[131]

c. Effect of the Threat upon the Weaker Party

The law of duress mingled subjective and objective factors in the determination of whether or not a person had been coerced. On the one hand, as noted above, it was a necessary element of the law that a threat be wrongful. In addition, however, the courts took into account the effect of the threat on the person threatened and required that the threat have actually overcome the will of that person. Clearly, that is a subjective matter. Yet, the determination was not wholly subjective. Indeed, the courts originally required a certain level of courage or fortitude on the part of the victim.

1. Common Firmness and Constancy of Mind

The nature of the threats was important irrespective of the effect of the threats upon the victim; a simple threat of adverse or unpleasant consequences was not sufficient, even if it in fact induced the other party of act. For example, in the case of *Cooper v. Crane*, decided in 1891, a lady was invited by a male acquaintance to attend a church service at St. Paul's Cathedral.[132] On the way to the church, he informed her that if she did not marry him immediately, he would blow his brains out. They went through the form of a marriage ceremony, which she later attempted to invalidate on the ground that she acted under duress. The court rejected her claim, feeling that the facts did not reveal the existence of duress.

This aspect of the law of duress has been changing in a constant and consistent manner. In the early law, it was required that the threats be such as would frighten a man of reasonable courage. Gradually, this standard was broadened to a less judgmental standard of requiring only ordinary firmness, and during the period which is under study, even this standard was weakening.[133] By 1899, *The American and English Encyclopedia of Law* reported that the standard was clearly changing to consideration of the effect of the threats upon the particular individual threatened.[134]

It seems, however, to have fairly well still been the law at mid-century that the individual characteristics of the person threatened were not the paramount consideration, which was, rather, whether the threats were such as would intimidate a person of ordinary courage. In addition to this requirement, the threats must have actually intimidated the person before the court. In short, it may be said that it was a necessary but not sufficient condition for duress that the individual be actually frightened and a necessary but not sufficient condition that the threat be of sufficiently grave harm as to influence a person of ordinary firmness.[135]

The proposition that a threat must be such as to strike with fear "a person of common firmness and constancy of mind" was the basis for one court's holding that duress by "mere advice, direction, influence, and persuasion" was unknown to the law.[136] Significantly, though, an inordinate amount of influence, such as from a confidential relationship, might be sufficient to avoid a deed on the ground of undue influence.

Even in the law of undue influence, however, mere advice was not sufficient to invalidate the deed; the psychological force of the pressure exerted had to be such as to overcome the will of the other person. The difference, therefore, between undue influence and duress lay partly in the psychological effect required by the law as a basis for setting aside the transaction.

An interesting aspect of the law is that some protection was granted a wife from threats by her husband. For example, where the husband threatened the wife with physical violence unless she joined him in the conveyance of property, the deed would be set aside by a court of equity, although mere angry words and looks from a paralytic husband were held not to amount to coercion of the wife.[137] An Illinois court held that a husband who used undue influence and abusive treatment to compel his sick wife to accept a separation and a certain amount in alimony had coerced her, and the agreement was void.[138] Similarly, threats by the husband to take the children away from the wife, to abandon the wife, or to separate from her and refuse to support her have been held to be duress.[139] It was not sufficient, however, that the husband was a violent, turbulent, and intemperate man, that he dominated his wife, and that he was prone to violence. Rather, the wife had to show that she was coerced in that particular transaction, as opposed to being generally under his domination.[140] Again, mere threats of emotional stress were not sufficient, as where the husband threatened that if the wife did not convey her dower interest in the property, she would never live with him in peace.[141]

2. Fact and Law

Closely related to the notion that the threats must be sufficient to intimidate a person of ordinary firmness is the requirement that the threats have actually produced the challenged action. The mere presence of threats or even of imprisonment would not suffice to invalidate a contract unless accompanied by an actual destruction of the victim's free agency; that is, no matter how wrongful the threat was and how clearly the oppressor had the power to inflict the threatened harm, if in fact the victim was not motivated by fear, then the victim did not act under duress.[142]

The issue of whether the will was overcome was consistently held to be one of fact for the jury. In the law courts, the judge, naturally, ruled on issues of law, while the jury decided the application of the general rules of law to the particular facts of the case at hand. Of course, this division arose only in courts of law because courts of equity sat without a jury. Even in courts of equity, however, the issue of the effect of the coercive conduct on the victim was considered one of fact, although the judge determined it.

Whether the threat was wrongful, on the other hand, was evaluated as an issue of law. That is, was the threat against the law? Similarly, the issue of whether there was an adequate remedy at law was a question of law; a threat to breach a contract did not constitute duress because it was clear as a matter of law that a person could sue and recover damages for the breach of the contract. The significant point of an issue's being one of law is that, in theory, no factual evidence is admitted on that issue. The judge does not decide that a threat is wrongful based on the evidence in the individual situation. The evidence tends to prove whether a particular threat was made or not; the rules of law establish whether that threat was wrongful or not.

3. What Constitutes Lack of Free Will

Courts sometimes described the requirement that the will actually be overcome by saying that the threats must be the effective cause of the decision. It was, therefore, not sufficient to invalidate a contract when the victim had been threatened; the threats must have caused the victim to elect the choice which he finally made.

The "civilians," as Holmes referred to those who followed the civil law of continental Europe rather than the common law of England and the United States, held that an act done under compulsion "is not an act in a legal sense".[143] Some courts in England and the United States also expressed their rulings on the existence of duress in this way, i.e., that where a person was subject to coercion, his apparent acts in entering a contract were not acts at all - not, in other words, the expressions of his will. In 1875, Judge Folger distinguished fraud from duress by arguing that in the case of fraud,

> [T]here is a voluntary parting with possession of the property and there is an uncontrolled volition to pass the title. But where there exist coercion, threats, compulsion and undue influence, there is no volition. There is no intention nor purpose but to yield to moral pressure, for relief from it. A case is presented more analogous to a parting with property by robbery.[144]

Some commentators have improperly equated such statements about the overcoming of the will with statements about the total absence of will. In fact, there is some confusion in the language and probably in the metaphysics of the cases; some courts, however, at least distinguished between the extreme case where even the manifestation of consent, such as a signature, is literally not voluntarily performed and those where that act may be willed but the agreement evidenced by that signature did not exist. For example, Hale somewhat misleadingly interpreted Justice Black's statement in the *Bethlehem Steel* case that "there is no evidence of that state of overcome will which is the major premise of the [government's] argument of duress" as being equivalent to the idea that "coercion necessarily implies that the party to whom it is applied has no volition ..."[145] As Hale himself points out, Justice Holmes clearly distinguished the two concepts of coercion in 1887 in the case of *Fairbanks v. Snow,* where he said:

> No doubt if the defendant's hand had been forcibly taken and compelled to hold the pen and write her name and the note had been carried off and delivered, the signature and delivery would not have been her acts; and *if the signature and delivery* [the prerequisites

for a valid transfer of property] *had not been her acts, for whatever reasons, no contract would have been made*, whether the plaintiff knew the facts or not.   There is still sometimes shown an inclination to put all cases of duress upon this ground. *Barry v. Equitable Life Assurance Society*, 59 N.Y. 587, 591. *But duress, like fraud, rarely, if ever, becomes material as such, except on the footing that a contract or conveyance has been made which the party wishes to avoid. It is well settled that where, as usual, the so-called duress consists only of threats, the contract is only voidable.*[146]

The distinction between contracts which were voidable and those which were absolutely void is a technical rule of law which reflects the substantive concept of the will held by the judges of the period here under study. *The American and English Encyclopedia of Law* expressed the distinction as follows:

As has been seen, where the consent of one party to a contract is obtained by the other under such circumstances that the consent is not free, the contract is voidable at the option of the party coerced. If, however, there was no consent whatever, as if the party's hand was forcibly guided to sign his name, or perhaps if he was so prostrated by fear as not to know what he was doing, the contract is absolutely null and void.[147]

That same authority expressed the rule again as follows:

There are cases, however, in which the severity of the duress is such that the person on whom it is imposed is converted into a mere automaton for the purpose of obeying the command and registering the will of the person who imposes it; in such cases the formal contraction is simply null and of no effect.[148]

The substantive distinction which is revealed here is between the concept of a will overborne and forced to counterfeit its true appearance and the mere illusion even of the appearance of an act of will. In the former case, those actions which normally signify voluntary assent to the transaction which they symbolize are in fact a sham; the will may direct the fingers to write a signature, but the signature evinces no consent on the part of the mind. In the latter case, the fingers are literally moved at the direction of another.

Yet the above distinction does not fully resolve the actual ambiguity in the cases, which amounts to an ambiguity in the term "unwillingly." Some courts, as, for example, in *Barry v. Equitable Life Assurance*

Society, held that consent under pressure was not consent at all, because it was literally not an act of will, and the distinction between void and voidable contracts appears to recognize the idea of a fear so great that the victim literally did not act. On the other hand, some judges, such as Holmes, held that the victim of coercion had in fact made a choice, i.e., had elected or willed a particular result, but that, under the circumstances, that person would be permitted by the court to rescind the forced consent. This ambiguity is between "unwillingly" as meaning "without an act of will" and "unwillingly" as meaning "reluctantly."

In most nineteenth-century cases, this ambiguity had little effect on either doctrine or decision, and it seems to have been largely unrecognized at the time. Regardless of the precise metaphysics of the issue, the courts recognized a causal relationship between a wrongful threat by one person and an action by another.

4. Definition and Evidence of Free Will

Since the courts sometimes rejected a plea of duress, the judges obviously believed that one could differentiate a coerced action from one taken freely. Free will is never clearly defined in the cases, however, although certain synonyms are given for it. The evidence needed to establish a lack of free will was likewise never clearly delineated, although many factors were listed in the reports of the cases. For example, the courts considered the following factors: whether a person had an alternative, whether the person later affirmed the contract, the totally subjective reports of the alleged victim, the presence of other people who might have been able to help or counsel the alleged victim, and the presence or lack of protest on the victim's part.

Two of these evidentiary matters were codified to some extent as rules of law. For example, when a person who claimed that he had been coerced into agreeing to a contract later behaved as if he intended to perform the contract and did not object to it, he was considered to have ratified the contract.[149] Once the duress was removed, therefore, the victim was not allowed to continue to go forward with performance and still set the contract aside later. In particular, the alleged victim could not accept payment for his part in the contract after the threatened harm had been relieved.

Similarly, for a time the courts toyed with the idea of incorporating a requirement that the coerced party protest the alleged contract. For example, an Indiana court in 1874 required that where a payment had been compelled by a threatened prosecution, the payment must have been made under protest.[150] In 1872 and 1873, the Michigan courts clearly held, however, that no protest was necessary where money was paid under demand by an officer who had legal process which reportedly authorized the arrest or seizure of property.[151] A California court in 1875 said that where an officer of the law knows that a payment is being illegally required, no protest is necessary, but that where the officer does not know that the payment is illegal, the protest is necessary.[152]

This was never clearly adopted, though, as a rule of law, and the lack of protest remains more an evidentiary matter than one with precise legal significance. By the turn of the century, it was clear that protest was not required.

There are cases requiring a similar condition for the recovery of money paid under a mistake of fact; some courts held that the person who was mistaken was required to give prompt notice of his discovery of the error to the other party, while other courts rejected this condition.[153]

d. The Imminence of the Harm

It was not enough to invalidate a contract that the threatened action be one which the oppressor had no right to take and one which frightened the victim. Rather, it was also required that the harm which would ensue from the threatened action have certain characteristics.

The harm had to be imminent, that is, it had to be one which could not be avoided except by entering the contract. This is sometimes expressed as the party's having no alternative, that is, no alternative but to suffer the harm or sign the contract.

Similarly, the harm must be one which could not be adequately redressed at law. As suggested by the case of *Astley v. Reynolds*, *supra*, this requirement caused some trouble in the courts. There was often in theory a remedy available in court, and yet the courts were not unaware of the immense expense and delay which might be caused. Therefore, some courts required that the harm be one which could not be adequately redressed, meaning that the party could claim duress successfully if, although he had a basis for a lawsuit, he would have been bankrupt in the meantime.

Finally, the harm must be one which the oppressor had the apparent power to inflict. Outlandish threats which it is clear that the oppressor cannot carry out will not suffice to invalidate a contract, no matter how honestly the victim believes in those threats.

e. The Person Making the Threat

Finally, the other party to the challenged contract must have been a party to the coercion. For example, where the grantor of a deed had been whipped by a mob but the grantee was not implicated in the mob's action *and* paid the requested price, the deed was not given under duress.[154]

Where the dominant party did not create the coercion, particularly where the weaker party's compulsion arose from need, the transaction would not be set aside unless the dominant party knew of the need and used it to extort an unconscionable bargain.[155]

B. Elements of the Law of Undue Influence from 1820 to 1870

Undue influence consists in pressures by which the will of one person is overborne by the will of another. Unlike duress, no specific list of the elements of undue influence can easily be given, because the concept was more equitable and less rigid; however, a catalogue of the characteristic components can be drawn up.

The first of these components is the exertion of overbearing influence by one party on another. Usually the victim of this influence was the weaker party. A court of law did not consider matters of diminished intellectual capacity; a person either had the capacity to contract or did not. In equity, the courts felt that as a matter of law they also could not consider diminished capacity per se as a defense to a contract, but they could consider the effect which a given pressure would have on a person of weak intellect even if such pressure would not have the same effect on a person of normal capacities.[156] Similarly, a person might be advanced in years and yet be capable in law of disposing of his property. Such an aged person, while having the legal capacity to devise or make other transactions, would be especially susceptible to influence by a stronger, more forceful personality.

Another factor was the existence of confidence reposed in the other party. Certain relationships were considered to give rise especially to this confidence and, therefore, to the obligation not to abuse the confidence. The courts recognized that certain relationships tended to abuse and undue influence.[157] A special relationship such as that of guardian and ward was not necessary if there were a factual finding by the court that trust had been reposed by one party in the other.

The confidence reposed must have been abused. In general, such abuse consisted in the fact that the grant was beneficial to the stronger party and unfair to the weaker. For example, property might be transferred for a grossly inadequate consideration. Further, unlike the

law of duress, the law of undue influence required that the transaction
be substantively unfair in order to be set aside. Usually, the unfairness
consisted in an inadequate price.[158]

Like the law of duress, though, the central issue in the undue
influence cases was the destruction of the will. Again, this issue was
decided as a matter of fact; many cases of undue influence arose in
equity and, therefore, the judge made the requisite determination of fact.
Again, no definitive list of the determinative facts can be given, but
those which were often considered may be listed. These included the
unfairness of the transaction; the fact that no reasonable person would
make such a transaction; the fact that the transaction was kept secret
from members of the family who might have dissuaded the weaker
party; whether the transaction was freely lived up to by the allegedly
influenced party; and the subjective testimony of the victim.

Like duress, no definition of free will was given, but there were a
few synonymous descriptions. One court picturesquely said that "the
will of another was substituted for her own". Another description was
that it was not an act which the alleged victim would do in the absence
of the alleged influence.

The illegality of the pressure exerted was not a factor in undue
influence cases, unlike the duress cases where, the unlawfulness of the
threat was a key element. The central elements in the undue influence
cases were the existence and effect of the pressure.

In order to constitute undue influence, the pressure must have
overcome the will of the victim. As in the law of duress, influence,
even if it achieved the possessor's desired end, would not be grounds
to set aside the transaction unless it overbore the will of the weaker
party. Both proper influences, such as those exercised by a dutiful
child on an aged parent, and also improper influences, such as threats,
could invalidate a contract where such influence gave rise to control of
the will of the other party.[159] Thus, the influence which a dutiful child
exercises over an aged parent by acts of filial duty will not invalidate a
deed from the parent to the child where the parent's will was not
dominated.[160] For example, where an old man of feeble mind was
improperly influenced to execute a deed but executed it with the
knowledge and without the objections of competent members of his
family, the court held that there was no undue influence.[161]

Moreover, the court held in the case of *Sturtevant v. Sturtevant* that
the exercise of an influence fairly and honestly acquired was not an
undue influence even though it succeeded in convincing the person
making the deed of the wisdom of his actions.[162]

A Massachusetts court clearly stated that an improper influence
used for a selfish purpose to obtain an unjust advantage still would not
avoid a deed unless it amounted to fraud or duress, or the influence was

exerted by a stronger mind over a weaker one to such a degree "as to substitute the will of the person exerting the influence for that upon whom it is exerted, so that the latter is no longer a free agent."[163] Similarly, a Maine court held that the party unduly influenced must have done what he would not have done other than for such influence.[164]

Unlike the laws of duress, the law of undue influence recognized the particular weaknesses of the individual and did not require resistance of the kind capable of being offered by a man of ordinary firmness. For example, where a son was reckless, intemperate, and had little business capacity, a deed to his mother, in whom he trusted, was set aside for undue influence.[165] The courts did not require that the person be so insane as to be incompetent, but would grant relief to someone who was so weak in body and mind as to be susceptible to being influenced.[166] It was clear that the courts thought that such mental weakness was a factor in determining whether the free will required by contract law had been overborne. For example, in the case of *Guest v. Beson*, the court required that the victim's mind be so weak as to render him incapable of resisting the influence and asserting his independent will.[167] Similarly, in 1869 an Indiana court required that in order to set aside a deed for undue influence, where the grantor was influenced by a stronger party, the deed must be such as would not have been made by the grantor in the free use and exercise of his deliberate judgment.[168]

VI. CONTRACT LAW AND WILL THEORY

The law of contracts embodies many aspects of the will theory of law. First, the conceptual relationship involves both the descriptive recognition theory (contract law in fact expresses human will) and the normative recognition theory (law ought not to interfere with the free exercise of will). Both theories can be seen in the general doctrine of freedom of contract and in the specific doctrines of duress and undue influence. In the discussions of Savigny and Hegel above, for example, the emphasis placed upon the role of will in contract is apparent. Second, to the extent that in a basis will theory, law itself is considered to arise from human will, it is natural to suppose that private lawmaking, as in the area of contracts, is also a matter of human will, that is, the will of the individual becomes a legally relevant fact in the adjudication of disputes between individuals. Third, the doctrine of freedom of contract expresses a normative recognition will theory. In fact, the general concept that the law ought to respect and enforce consensual arrangements, rather than the courts establishing general rules of fairness or the legislature setting rules of exchange, expresses the essence of freedom of contract. Fourth, the law of duress and undue influence explicitly contains various other aspects of the recognition will theory. Fifth, the factual groundwork of the cases on duress reveals some of the factual premises underlying the recognition theory.

A. The Concept of Will in Contract Law

As noted above, the doctrine of freedom of contract as expressed in the rules of law contains the essence of the normative recognition will theory. The judges' remarks about the existence of freedom of contract express a descriptive recognition will theory.

That relationship is more than mere historical accident. Although Savigny is perhaps not as well known today, his works on contract influenced notable English and American legal writers, including, for example, Oliver Wendell Holmes.

The will theory of law had a practical influence upon the rules of law current in the nineteenth century. Prior to the latter part of the eighteenth century, indeed, the main theory of contract law had rested on the idea of consideration; where one party had given up something of value or relied upon a promise, the bargain morally ought to be enforced.[169] In the late eighteenth and early nineteenth centuries, the rules of law adopted by the courts were more concerned with the will of the parties as the basis for decision than with the ideas of reliance and exchange.

As Williston says:

> It was a consequence of the emphasis laid on the ego and the individual will that the formation of a contract should seem impossible unless the wills of the parties concurred. Accordingly we find at the end of the eighteenth century, and the beginning of the nineteenth century, the prevalent idea that there must be a "meeting of the minds" (a new phrase) in order to form a contract; that is, mental assent as distinguished from an expression of mutual assent was required.[170]

It might be useful here to explore briefly the specific ways in which the idea of freedom of contract includes aspects of a recognition theory of law.

Some of the links specifically relate to the normative form of the theory. That normative aspect is complicated, however, by the additional moral notion that the will ought to be free. Thus, some aspects of the doctrine of freedom of contract relate more to the idea of preserving freedom of the will, rather than simply to the idea of recognizing acts of will.

On the other hand, this is one point at which the distinction in the duress cases between lack of true consent and the appearance of consent may become important. By making that distinction, one is able to stress the rule that a contract does not exist unless there is a meeting of the minds (two acts of will), as opposed to requiring an entirely unfettered will. The force of the distinction can be stated as being that the courts simply looked for a way to give force to ("recognize") true acts of will and to avoid giving force to contracts where there was actually no meeting of the minds. The focus, therefore, was on the existence of an act of will and, semantically at least, some of the metaphysical problems associated with the concept of free will were thereby avoided. The courts spoke less of a free will than of an individual so oppressed that he or she did not actually will the resulting contract at all.

Not only did the judges consider it morally good to give force to consensual arrangements, but they considered that that good outweighed any social desirability of a judicially established standard of fair transactions. This, of course, is the effect of the rejection of the doctrine of *laesio enormis*. In refusing to adopt that doctrine, Anglo-American courts said in effect that the value of giving expression to what two mature individuals have decided upon as a desirable transaction was higher than any uniform system of fair exchange, even if the bargain was unfair.

The existence of the undue influence doctrine and the discretion of the courts of equity in awarding such remedies as specific performance, however, permitted the judges to avoid enforcing truly outrageous bargains. This available detour, however, should not be regarded cynically as a subterfuge by which the judges were able to give lip service to the doctrine of freedom of contract, while covertly but effectively giving voice to their views on justice. If that were so, the courts would always have availed themselves of the option, and there would be few if any reported cases denying relief from burdensome and harsh contracts on a plea of undue influence. In fact, of course, such cases do occur in the reports, so the judges did not simply indulge their own predilections. While it may well be that some courts simply refused to enforce truly outrageous contracts, there is no reason not to take the stated doctrine that an outrageous bargain (such that no free man would offer or honest man accept) might be a sign of duress or fraud as being in fact the rule; even if the judges believed that courts should enforce freely arrived at contracts even if those contracts subsequently proved disadvantageous to one party, they were not oblivious to the fact that many, if not most, harsh and inequitable contracts were entered into by the losing party under some form of coercion by the dominant party. Most sensible, ordinary people do not have widely disparate views about the value of what they are exchanging in the absence of mistake; common sense suggests that a great disproportion in value indicates either fraud or oppression or mistake.[171]

Another aspect of the recognition theory found in the freedom of contract area is the refusal of the courts to imply a term into a contract. If the primary value is the recognition of what the parties agreed upon, then there is no obvious basis for holding them to a term upon which they in fact reached no agreement; there is no act of will to recognize. Here again the moral and metaphysical aspects are blended. On the one hand, the courts may have felt that it would be oppressive to compel someone to comply with a contractual provision which he did not in fact undertake of his own free will. Equally, however, one may justify the doctrine on the ground that there simply was no meeting of the minds or other act of will to which the courts could properly give force, whether or not to do so would be oppressive or unfair in the case at hand.

The more theoretical aspects of the recognition will theory can be seen in the general view that contract determined the relationships of obligation between people. With the many exceptions noted above (which were themselves sometimes justified on social contract grounds), the courts generally held that the obligations of one otherwise unrelated individual to another were set by their agreement, rather than by their respective *status* or other factor. The boundaries between individuals were set by their property rights and their arrangements with regard to those rights. Thus, the doctor had no obligation to treat a former patient, and the seller of a particular item had no obligation to make it available at a price within the means of one who needed.

The doctrines of duress and undue influence, however, most clearly reveal the recognition will theory by virtue of their very existence; they are doctrines about the presence or absence of an act of will, and the decisions discuss the evidence which tends to be probative on that question, that is, in order to give effect to an act of will, one must first determine if the requisite act took place. Where one who has apparently given his or her consent to a contract repudiates that act, the courts perforce had to consider what facts tended to bear on the issue of actual consent.

The duress and undue influence cases, therefore, concern the recognition of when acts of will occurred. The fact that those cases discussed in detail the kind of evidence which would tend to show that a given consent was or was not an actual act of will shows that the judges thought of acts of will as actual psychological phenomena. The concept of a meeting of the minds, therefore, consisted in a concept of an actual event, which could be shown or proven like other events. A decision about a contract, therefore, recognized the component acts of will in the most literal sense, as giving effect to an actual, proven event.

Interestingly, French and German courts tended to adopt a purely subjective concept of the will in the context of contracts, whereas the Anglo-American courts adopted an objective concept of will.[172] That is, continental courts stressed the notion that the contract consisted in a meeting of the minds, which they interpreted to mean that the subjective perception of the individuals must agree in all particulars. Conversely, English courts followed the rule that the objective expression of a person's intent governed the contract. Thus, for example, continental courts adopted the rather metaphysical rule that agreement to a contract was effective at the moment that the person subjectively agreed. Thus, if A extends an offer to B, who subjectively decides to accept but delays in forwarding his acceptance to A, a binding contract between A and B is nonetheless formed, even though A does not know of B's acceptance. English courts, on the other hand, adopted the rule that A is not bound by his offer until B has objectively manifested his assent.

That subjective/objective distinction, however, is primarily an evidentiary matter. That can be seen from the fact that in the duress and undue influence cases, the courts concerned themselves with subjective matters, viz., what really went on in the person's mind. Those cases arose, of course, when a person was attempting to refute the binding effect of objectively manifested indications of consent.

The cases dealing with the doctrines of duress and undue influence expressly refer to the issue of free will, which was linked to the concept of actual consent, and the courts considered this issue to be the crucial one in these cases. The concept of actual consent was that a forced or coerced assent was not a real assent at all, and the paradigm duress case was one where the wrongdoer physically compelled the victim's signature, creating only the merest semblance of consent.

Certain commentators on the law, however, have questioned whether these cases are truly about free will in the sense that the usual concept of a free choice involved real consent as opposed to a coerced or apparent consent.[173] These commentators - including Dawson, Hobbes, and Atiyah[174] - have pointed out that a person who makes a choice under immense pressure may be very glad to accept the alternative offered by his oppressor, and the choice may be in that sense a true assent. These commentators acknowledge that in some of the cases, for example, a person had not truly willed the contractual obligation (i.e., that there was not a true meeting of the minds but only the semblance of a meeting of the minds on one side), but they argue that consent under pressure may be a very real consent. As Justice

Holmes said in the case of *Union Pacific R.R. Co. v. Public Service Comm. of Mo.*, where a railroad company argued that it had been coerced into applying for a state certificate:

> Of course, it was for the interest of the Company to get the certificate. It always is for the interest of a party under duress to choose the lesser of two evils. But the fact that a choice was made according to interest does not exclude duress. It is the characteristic of duress properly so called.[175]

Savigny argued that the true issue in a duress case was the wrongfulness of the threatening party's conduct and that the courts were essentially punishing this wrongdoing by invalidating the advantageous contract. This argument has been made in modern form by Dalzel also.

That the law of duress was actually concerned with issues of free will and not wholly with the culpability of one of the parties to the contract can be seen by the fact that the law of duress developed along the same lines as other doctrines explained in terms of will or assent. For example, fraud cases also concern the absence of actual assent, since there is no knowing consent when the one party is deceived about the object of the contract. Similarly, in mistake cases, mutual assent is lacking because the parties do not subjectively have the same object in mind:

> In 1869 [the mistake rule] was applied to a case where a man was induced to indorse a bill of exchange by the fraudulent representation of the acceptor that he was signing a guarantee; and other modern cases afford illustrations of different varieties of this fundamental error or common mistake, which, because it excludes consent, prevents the conclusion of any contract. Similarly, there was authority in the Year Books that an agreement induced by threats or violence could be avoided, because in such a case consent was not freely given ... . It was, however, very early recognized that the effect of duress was different from the effect of a common mistake. Inasmuch as consent had been given, though not freely given, the effect was to render the deed not void but voidable.[176]

These arguments, however, are not of central importance for our discussion because at the time these cases were written, the judges and most students of the law regarded the duress cases as being about free will, that is, for example, judges decided cases based upon a jury's finding about the presence or absence of actual consent, and thus, the ideology of the time included the concept of acts of will. The scholarly argument by Dawson *et al.* really is a proposal for a purportedly sounder conceptual basis for the law, rather than a description of existing doctrine. It is discussed at somewhat greater length in Appendix A.

Moreover, these scholarly arguments have a certain metaphysical aspect in that they are claims as to what the law is *really* about as opposed to what it *appears* to be about or was thought to be about. As a phenomenon at the time, the law took the issue of free will as a legally relevant fact. The best, or most logical, or even the true psychological basis for these early decisions is not immediately before us.[178]

One key aspect of the doctrines of freedom of contract, duress, and undue influence bears further elucidation here. A review of these cases shows that the courts did not look to the total absence of any influence on the weaker party as the appropriate indicia of true consent. Rather, the courts looked for the absence of personal oppression by another individual. For example, mere economic need would not suffice to invalidate a contract on the grounds of duress, but rather the contract could be set aside only if another created the need and then ruthlessly exploited it.

Further, and consistently, freedom of contract consisted in a right to have one's contracts enforced as written, untampered with by the state. Thus, one did not have a right to a fair contract; a contract was voidable if procured by coercion but not solely on grounds of unfairness. Similarly, the reluctance of the courts to imply terms in a contract shows that the content of the contract was considered to rest entirely on the will of the contracting parties. The rejection of *laesio enormis* tends to show the same attitude on the part of the Anglo-American court system. Again, the absence of factors, even coercive factors, which might have influenced strongly the parties' choices was not the determining test; to the contrary, the absence of coercion or limitation of choice by another entity or individual, such as the state in the person of the judge or a stronger individual threatening physical harm, theoretically decided the outcome.

Although the earlier discussion tends to show that the nineteenth-century law embodied some aspects of the will theories, it may be worthwhile to review briefly the extent to which the specific premises attributed to that theory by Marx are found in the cases. The extent to which these elements entail the results ascribed to them by Marx is discussed below in Chapter Four. Generally speaking, the doctrines of freedom of contract, undue influence, and duress did contain the ideas that contract could be entered into or not at will, even while recognizing the potential existence of coercion or pressure sufficient to overcome the will. Indeed, the existence of an act of will was the determining factor in those cases. If a contract could not be entered into or not at will (in other words, if coercion had been brought to bear), then the fundamental requirements for a contract did not exist.

CHAPTER FOUR

An Examination of the Accuracy of
Marx' Description of the Law

This chapter deals with the accuracy of Marx' description of the law of contracts, including the following premises:

1. It is altogether accidental that individuals enter into contracts.

2. Contracts can be entered into or not at will.

3. The terms of the contract rest entirely on the individual free wills of the contracting parties.

In summary, these remarks are generally accurate as a description of certain aspects of contract law in the nineteenth century, but they also represent a substantial distortion and simplification of those aspects of the law.

Earlier in this account, I developed the idea that the above premises could represent either statements about the world or rules of law. The relevant questions with regard to the accuracy of Marx' description of the law contracts are, therefore, first, whether nineteenth-century judges and legal scholars believed that those statements expressed facts about the world and, second, whether those statements actually expressed rules of law.

The specific criterion used here to answer those questions will be whether the above premises actually occur in the case law; that is, whether the actual nineteenth-century judges stated in their opinions that individuals in society were fundamentally unrelated to each other; that contracts are entered into as the result of an act of will; and that the terms of those contracts likewise result from an act of will. If these premises appear in nineteenth-century opinions as statements of fact, then it would seem that we may assume that the judges believed them to be true. Similarly, if the statements appear in the decisions as statements of law, that would seem to establish, obviously, that they were rules of law. To distinguish these two sorts of statements is to pose the questions of how these two sorts of statements are related and what the truth conditions are of each of them. For example, as discussed elsewhere, a given sentence can express both a rule of law and a factual proposition.

I. CONTRACTS AS ACCIDENTAL

The concept of "accidental" renders the first premise difficult to analyze, since it does not translate readily into ordinary descriptive terms except, as discussed below, as an absence of external pressures. The concept of "relatedness" which I have used earlier as explicating that idea is rather too metaphysical to be sought with any confidence in case law.

Nevertheless, there is material in the case reports which suggests that in fact judges did hold to some form of the view that individuals in society were in a basically atomic, unrelated state. This point must be examined with care, however; for, I submit, the courts held that the law viewed individuals as fundamentally unrelated, while at the same time the judges were well aware of the social ties that bind.

Judges apparently believed that persons were unrelated in the sense that the individual's selection of an occupation and status in life was not a matter of his social identity but was a matter of choice - of, therefore, contract.[1] For example, the court in *Carew v. Rutherford*, said "all persons who have been born and educated here, who are obligated to begin life without property, know that freedom to choose their own occupation and to make their contracts...secures to skill and industry and economy their appropriate advantages." The judge who wrote that opinion spoke of freedom of contract as a social fact, having direct economic consequences; in making the quoted remark, he did not simply state a rule of law.

The rules of law which embodied this perceived legal separation of one individual from another form the basis of freedom of contract. The great authority *Cooley on Torts* listed among one's civil liberties the right to refuse to do business with anyone that one chose.[2] Similarly, in the case of *Hurley v. Eddingfield*, *supra*, the court held that a doctor was not legally obligated to treat a patient. One construal of that holding is that the status of patient and doctor did not create an obligation of continued treatment - rather that obligation or relationship was an accidental (non-necessary) addendum to their both existing in the same society.

Further, under the law of the nineteenth century as revealed by such cases as *Hurley v. Eddingfield*, people did not have reciprocal relationships with each other, such as master and servant, until they had entered into a contract establishing that relationship. Therefore, it may be said that the courts did indeed regard the contract as "accidental" to the individual in the sense that the mutual obligations linking two people were not grounded in social status or a pre-existing social relationship but arose from their agreement.

In this sense of the word "accidental", one may contrast the obligations of contract with the obligations of status, following the feudal society/civil society distinction discussed in 'On the Jewish Question'. Both Marx and Sir Henry Maine, as discussed above, compared the nature and source of the individual's obligations in feudal society with those binding the individual under capitalism. Maine characterized the distinction as that between contract and status, and of that same distinction Marx said:

> The character of the old civil society was directly political, that is to say, the elements of civil life, for example, property, or the family, or the mode of labour, were raised to the level of elements of political life in the form of seigniory, estates and corporations. In this form they determined the relation of the particular individual to the state as a whole, i.e., his political relation, his relation of separation and exclusion from the other components of society.[3]

Marx also said that in civil society (nineteenth-century capitalism), "a person's distinct activity and distinct situation in life were reduced into a merely individual significance. They no longer formed the general relation of the individual to the state as a whole".[4]

On the other hand, while judges may have believed that individuals were fundamentally unrelated to each other and their decisions may have stated the legal rule that few legal obligations bound individuals together, they were not oblivious to the ebb and flow of society outside the courtroom. Although the courts were clear that an employment relationship did not exist until the contract was entered into, for example, they were not unaware of the real economic relationships of employer and employee, which were characterized at times as mutual dependency of the parties. In *Carew v. Rutherford*, for example, the court discussed extensively the freedom to associate together in a form of union. That case, however, concerned the pressure that the necessary employees could exert by a threatened strike upon their employer. The court recognized that the force of that pressure came from the economic interdependence of the contractor and the stone-masons.

The same recognition of economic or social dependence, as opposed to legal separability, occurs in a number of the cases on duress, because these cases deal with the exertion of force of one sort or another upon individuals to coerce them into a particular legal relationship. In *Skeate v. Beall,* the court was well aware of the power which a landlord had when he seized a defaulting tenant's furniture, for the judge clearly understood that the tenant desperately needed his furniture. The fact that the exercise of power by the landlord did not constitute duress in the eyes of the court does not show that the court was unaware of the persuasive power of such pressure; the holding of the case was not that the tenant was free from any pressure but that the tenant did not act under any unlawful pressure which would constitute duress.

Nineteenth-century judges recognized the differences in various individuals which might render them more or less susceptible to various kinds of mental pressure, as can be seen in the doctrine of undue influence, which permitted the consideration of the age, sex, infirmity, and other characteristics of the individual in determining whether that individual had freely entered a contract. Among the characteristics which the courts considered in determining whether there had been undue influence was the relationship of the parties, as where, for example, an elderly person had become dependent upon a caretaker, particularly where the caretaker was the child of the older person.[5]

While it is true that one's status as a litigant in the nineteenth century did not depend upon one's social status (that is, in theory, every individual had resort to the courts), it is nonetheless true that the parties' social status and personal relationships figured in the courts' decisions. When the state was called upon to meddle in the relationship of private citizens, as when a contract, a will, or other disposition of property was challenged as having been involuntarily done, the courts considered in detail the relative situations of the parties, as can be seen by the detail contained in the cases discussed in Appendix B.

The fact that the judges noted that the beneficiary of a will or contract stood in a position of confidence and influence over an older person, for example, demonstrates that they were aware that such contracts were not entered into "accidentally" in the sense that the weaker party simply happened to bestow his bounty on the stronger. The relationship of dependency existed prior to the formation of any contract whatsoever, as the courts recognized in their depiction of the facts leading up to the purported contract. Thus, the nineteenth-century judges recognized in their opinions that people existed in a web of social relationships which influenced the contracts into which they entered.

The nature of any legal "unrelatedness" needs, therefore, some clarification in order to form an accurate description of the case law. The judges did not believe, as can be seen from the earlier discussion, that people existed in nineteenth-century England as isolated savages occasionally venturing forth from some Lockean jungle fringe timidly to trade with another tribe. The question dealt with by the courts was not whether individuals were wholly unrelated to one another, but rather, whether a particular form of legally enforceable relationship of obligation existed. In other words, the courts were deciding whether under the circumstances of the particular social interaction of Smith and Jones, Smith could use the mechanism of the judicial system to force Jones to give him something of value with which Jones did not wish to part. If Jones wanted to raise money and voluntarily sold his house to his neighbor Smith, and both were satisfied with their bargain, the courts heard nothing of it. In that situation, it was indifferent to the legal system whether Smith or Jones were pauper or prince, aged father and greedy son, or husband and estranged wife. If, on the other hand, Smith and Jones subsequently disagreed about the transaction, then the courts would inquire into the circumstances and determine whether the legal indicia of ownership would pass to Smith or to Jones. In that case, the relationship of dependent parent and grasping child might determine the question of whether the relationship of willing buyer and seller existed, and that in turn would answer the question of whether a binding contract of sale existed which the courts would enforce.

Several points may be gleaned from the above discussion. First, the courts held that many reciprocal duties arose only by an act of will; many, if not most, legally enforceable relationships of obligation existed only if voluntarily assumed. In that sense, the relationship of being obligated to work exists for a stonemason only if he is employed. Second, the courts did observe that economic and social relationships existed independently of the legal relationship; the contractor needed the stonemason. Third, not all relationships of economic or social dependency constituted pressure of a sort which impeached the free consent necessary to a valid contract. The landlord might lawfully exert his economic influence to coerce payment, but the lawyer might not unduly exploit the confidence reposed in him. To deny that pressure constitutes duress does not entail a denial of the reality of the force exerted. It is not accurate to say, therefore, that nineteenth-century judges considered contracts accidental if that means that they regarded contractual obligations as arising altogether independently of the parties' social and economic position.

II. CONTRACTS AS ACTS OF FREE WILL

The above discussion has dealt with the "accidental" nature of contracts; the question presented in this subsection is, then, whether the courts believed that contracts resulted from an act of free will and whether the rules of law also embodied that premise. This issue represents perhaps the greatest difficulty in analysis because the factual or descriptive statements are so closely linked with the legal definition of a contract; that definition is and was, of course, that contracts consisted in a meeting of the minds, that is, in two mutual acts of will. One must distinguish in this regard, then, the legal rule "contract requires assent" from the factual idea of a psychological act called "assent".

A. Assent and Will

The courts' beliefs about the factual existence of acts of will can be seen, first, by reasoning backwards from the fact that they did find enforceable contracts in some cases where the existence of free consent was challenged and, second, by analyzing the procedural status of some of the cases.

Obviously, courts sometimes found that there were enforceable contracts and sometimes found that there were not. Given that the legal definition of a contract required an assent by both parties, when a court found that there was in fact an enforceable contract, it necessarily found that there had been an act of will, an act of assent.[6] Indeed, the duress and undue influence cases delineate the factual conditions under which the requisite act of will can be said to have occurred.

It is necessary here to distinguish those aspects of the duress cases which deal with the wrongfulness of the threat from those which deal with the actual effect of the threat upon the will. Whether or not one agrees with Dawson and Savigny that the real purpose of the law of duress was to punish those who made wrongful threats (by refusing to enforce the contracts that conveyed their ill-gotten gain), the doctrine of duress nonetheless required that the will of the victim must be shown to have been overcome for the contract to be refused enforcement. That is, a contract could not be repudiated simply because a wrongful threat had been made. Rather, that illegal threat must also have *caused* the act of apparent consent; it is sometimes said that the wrongful threat destroyed the will of the weaker party or substituted one will for another. As one court said: "The extent or degree of the influence is quite immaterial, for the test is, was the influence, whether slight or powerful, sufficient to destroy free agency and render the act brought in judgment rather the result of the determination of the mind of another than the expression of the mind of the actor?"[7]

The extent to which the courts believed that one could examine or even quantify various aspects of others' subjective will is shown by the fact that the legal standard of resistance varied with time. In the older cases, a person threatened was required to resist with courage, while by 1850 it was the general rule that duress was measured by its effect upon the will of the particular person threatened, regardless of that person's courage or hardihood.[8]

Clearly, since the applicable law required assent for a valid contract, judges believed that they could tell whether the required act of will had actually occurred.[9] The *sine qua non* of the duress and undue influence cases was the determination of when an apparent consent did not actually reflect the individual's will but consisted only in a forced mouthing of the words of consent.[10]

The second aspect of the courts' decisions in these cases is the procedural point that the existence of the necessary assent was considered a question of fact for the jury. Thus, the existence of an act of will was considered a matter of perceivable fact, not a determination of a legal rule. The legal rules to be determined by the judge in the duress cases concerned the illegality of the threatened harm, the standard of resistance, etc.; the actual effect of these on the particular person involved was left to be determined by the jury. The significance of this procedural point, of course, is that the courts therefore considered the existence of an act of will to be a perceptible, real, aspect of the world, not an abstract, metaphysical Hegelian issue.

In the detailed discussions of these cases, we see the courts' descriptions of the empirical conditions which bore on the determination of the existence of actual consent. The courts used such words as "overcome", "substituting the will of one for another", "destruction of the will", etc., suggesting that the concept of the individual will was a concept of a perceptible, psychological faculty, subject to various causal influences. It may be worthwhile, in this context, to hark back to Justice Holmes' remarks in 1887 in *Fairbanks v. Snow*, supra, where he distinguished between the physical substitution of one will for another, as where the party's hand had been forcibly guided in a facsimile of her signature, from the situation where the party's will had been overcome by means of threats. *The American and English Encyclopedia of Law* spoke of the conversion of one person into a mere automaton registering the will of the person who imposed the duress.[11]

Such legal requirements as that the alleged victim have protested an invalid contract were really requirements that certain factual conditions which were believed to be associated with true unwillingness be established as part of the case. For example, it is a matter of common experience that when one is forced unwillingly to do something, one customarily protests it when one has the opportunity to do so.

In summary, it is abundantly clear that the courts believed in the existence of acts of will (in the context at least of the entry into contracts) as a matter of perceptible, psychological fact.[12]

B. Social Constraint - Marx and the Judges

The above premises may occur as descriptions of individual actions or as descriptions of the larger economic or social conditions under which contracts are entered into.

In the preceding sections, the concept of something being accidental was analyzed as being one of unrelatedness, so that contractual obligations could be considered accidental in the sense of being voluntarily assumed. Here, however, the concept of something being accidental is applied to the decision to enter into the relationship. In a useful sense, the term "accidental" in that context may be somewhat synonomous with "arbitrary", so that Marx' first premise would refer to the idea that a person is not required by any external force to enter into contracts but arbitrarily does so. Similarly, the other two premises would express the concept that contracts were entered into as a matter of arbitrary choice.

On this reading, then, Marx' premises may be taken as expressing either the absence of legal constraint on a person entering into a contract or the factual proposition that contracts are entered *purely* as a matter of individual, arbitrary whims. To put it another way, his premises may be taken as either referring to the legal limits of the pressure which Smith may exert upon Jones or they may be taken as statements about the constraints which the economic structure of society 'places upon Jones. Case law by its very nature looks to specific, individual situations: what does it reveal about what the judges thought about the individual's free will as a member of society, as opposed to his relationship, or lack of it, with a specific neighbor?

While the courts did believe that, as a matter of fact, contracts were entered into as an act of will and that they always represented a choice between alternatives (if, that is, they were valid contracts), the judges were not unaware of the social and economic pressures which effectively compelled people to enter into contracts. They did not believe in the existence of unfettered choice as a factual aspect of society, nor did they hold that the law required such choice.

The very existence of areas of contract law such as duress and undue influence indicates that the judges knew of the pressures which could be exerted upon people and that their choices were not unfettered. The fact, however, that not all types of coercion invalidated a contract establishes that the courts did not require a completely unfettered choice;

that is, the courts sometimes recognized that a person had very little choice but still held that the unwilling consent was binding.

Perhaps the clearest illustration of that point is the case of *French v. Shoemaker*. In that case, the court said as follows:

> Enough appears in the record to convince the Court that the respondent was in straitened circumstances, that his business affairs had become complicated, that he was greatly embarrassed with litigations, and that he was in pressing want of pecuniary means, but the Court is wholly unable to see that the complainant [the other party to the contract] is responsible for those circumstances or that he did any unlawful act to deprive the respondent of his property, or to create those necessities or embarrassments, or to compel him *to do what he acknowledges he did do*, which was to yield to the *pressure of the circumstances surrounding him, and as a choice of evils* accept the advance of $5,000 ... and *voluntarily signed both the agreement* and the assignment.[13]

French's "reluctant" consent, therefore, was nonetheless consent. In a case which recognized the extreme pressure which financial circumstance could exert (so as to be sufficient indeed to overcome the will), the court in *Hough v. Hunt*, held that financial distress could render a person "incompetent to act freely". Again, in *Wilkerson v. Bishop*, the court dealt frankly with the pressure of public opinion and public reprisal during and after the Civil War.

A central fact about the above cases, however, is that the one factor which almost never would suffice to invalidate a contract was financial need. This is not to say that the judges did not explicitly recognize that financial need could effectively compel a person to enter into a contract which he did not particularly like; it is to say rather that the courts did not recognize that particular coercion as sufficient in itself to render the contract invalid.

That rule, however, was not without one exception, which was that where the oppressive party acted illegally or the oppressing party created the circumstances of financial need, the contract would be invalid.

It is tempting to conclude that the courts simply perversely refused to recognize one particular kind of pressure as sufficient to invalidate a contract. Numerous hypothetical reasons could be advanced for this apparent shortsightedness, such as that the judges were seeking to advance economic free trade at the cost of a modest inconsistency in their thought, and indeed, some decisions expressly advanced the free trade rationale.

Another explanation is possible, however, which is that the courts sought to protect the individual from the coercive acts of another individual and not to create an implausible Utopia in which contracts were entered into wholly free of any motive, except perhaps pleasure. The point is that the duress and undue influence cases focus upon the coercive actions of others, not upon their exploitative effect alone. For example, it would presumably be legal to deal with a helpless old lady who came into one's shop, regardless of how much she looked to the shopkeeper for advice on her purchases. It would not be legal, however, to assume a position of trust and authority over her and then to bully her into an unfavorable contract, nor would it be lawful deliberately and illegally to reduce her to economic dependency and then to extort an unconscionable bargain.

Thus, the law treated individuals as unrelated in the sense that one had no obligation to deal fairly with each other, but it also prohibited the deliberate creation of a coercive relationship, at least to the extent that the end result of that relationship took the form of a contract or other legal instrument.

The holdings of these cases insofar as they reflect the judges' view of societal and economic conditions may be stated as follows: People enter into contracts for a variety of reasons, including pressing financial need, but those reasons do not constitute such duress as will invalidate the questioned contract - rather, duress in the eyes of the law consists in the imposition of direct and illegal pressure by another person so as to overcome the will of the individual. The key element in the duress and undue influence cases is not the presence or absence of unfettered choice, nor is it the presence or absence of compelling reasons for a person to act, but it is the presence or absence of psychological pressure exerted by another individual, so that the stronger individual acts to dominate the weaker party. In this sense, the law did require the existence of a choice; that is, the will must still be functional to create a valid contract. It need not, however, be uninfluenced by circumstances. Therefore, it cannot be said that the nineteenth-century judges believed in the availability of unfettered, arbitrary decision-making, nor was such a factual belief necessary to their concept of contract.

To that extent, then, Marx' remarks are false as a social and economic description. Those premises do not describe views held by nineteenth-century judges, if the statements are taken to mean that an individual acts wholly free from external constraint in entering a contract.

At this point, it may be worthwhile to digress momentarily to consider the description of individuals in 'On the Jewish Question'. In that essay, Marx argued that under capitalism, each individual regarded other individuals as the limitation of his own freedom. Marx said: "The right of man to private property is, therefore, the right to enjoy one's property and dispose of it at one's discretion, without regard for other men, independently of society, the right of self-interest."[14] Marx also said:

> The limits within which each can act without harming others is determined by law just as the boundary between two fields is marked by a stake. This is the liberty of man viewed as an isolated monad, withdrawn into himself ... liberty as a right of man is not based on the association of man with man, but rather on the separation of man from man. It is the right of this separation ... .[15]

Further, in the *Grundrisse*, Marx dismissed that concept of freedom as an illusion. He characterized it as the subjugation of individuality to social conditions and as being only a freedom to enjoy the accidents of society.[16]

That analysis (in contrast to the broad social and economic descriptive interpretation of the three premises discussed immediately above) is parallel to the concept of the free will in the economic duress and undue influence cases. The will can be considered, according to the courts, to act without undue influence or without being under duress even when it acts under the overwhelming pressure of material circumstances, provided that no other individual unduly exploits that pressure. To act without duress then, according to the law, is to act without the undue influence of another individual, but it is not necessarily to act under social circumstances in which one has an unbounded choice of unlimited alternatives; free will in contract law consists in being separated from the personal influence of others but not in being free of the economic conditions of social life.

III. PRINCIPLES OF CONTRACT LAW

In general, the legal interpretations given of the three result premises above do reflect principles of nineteenth-century (and indeed twentieth-century) contract law. They do, therefore, state rules of law.

It may, however, be worthwhile to mention that there were certain limitations upon these statements. For example, a person might not stand in any contractual relationship with another individual, but certain rights and duties, such as the duty to drive with due care, remain.

Similarly, while there was no general obligation to enter into contracts, certain persons and businesses such as innkeepers, public utilities, railroads, etc., were required to offer their services to all peaceable comers. Finally, of course, there were limitations upon the content of contracts, so that contracts tending to promote divorce or other immorality were unlawful.

A few samples of the relevant legal principles may be helpful.

The first of these is the concept of *laesio enormis*. That principle is that the courts will refuse to enforce a contract simply because the consideration exchanged appears to them to be unfair; it was rejected, at least in principle, in Anglo-American law, but accepted on the continent. The English and American courts would not interfere, therefore, to restate the parties' contracts; contracts and their terms are not created by the courts but by the individual parties. The terms of the contract were clearly left to the parties, as discussed in *Carew v. Rutherford*, where the court celebrated the absence of restrictions upon terms of employment and sale.

Similarly, a party was under no obligation to enter into any contract, as in the famous statement that "it is a part of a man's civil rights that he be at liberty to refuse business relations with any person whomsoever ... ."[17] Another example of this, of course, is *Hurley v. Eddingfield*. That case, in turn, also expresses the general proposition that one is not obligated to act positively toward any other individual, such as to save a person from drowning. In the absence of some already existing relationship, as where one person encourages another to go swimming in a dangerous area, there is no obligation to save a drowning individual. In that sense, it may be said that people are legally unrelated prior to entering into some form of contract.

IV. NORMATIVE STATEMENTS IN THE CASE LAW

The chief difficulty in discussing whether the normative interpretations of the above three result premises can be found in the case law is the crucial ambiguity of the term "right", which can refer both to a moral right which people have, as a natural right, and also to the concept of a legal entitlement. Nonetheless, the tone of approval and the language of the decisions suggests that the courts did feel that it was morally right and proper that people determine the terms of their own social obligations. First, the language in the cases suggests that the courts felt that it was part of a person's natural civil rights that each individual be left to form such contracts as he or she desires. The famous passage from *Cooley on Torts* which has been quoted several times strongly suggests that the courts simply considered that a person had a moral, as well as legal, right not to contract with another individual unless both parties were willing.

Second, the courts, at least in *Carew v. Rutherford,* felt that it was also good policy for the individual to have great freedom of contract. According to that court, such freedom "would secure to industry ... their appropriate advantages". The doctrine of *laissez faire* was, of course, widely accepted in the nineteenth century. The court in *Carew v. Rutherford,* however, suggests not only that industry and thrift will be encouraged to the general good of society by allowing people to choose their contracts, but that those desirable traits will be justly or fairly rewarded. In this sense, then, the rules governing contracts were considered to promote the general welfare of society and also a fair and just society.

Third, there was a general perception by the courts that not only was it a person's right to make such contracts as he chose but also that people should be free from the interference of the state. It was generally held to be preferable that people should be allowed to choose the terms of their contracts as opposed to having those contracts dictated by the state. Such dictation by the state was regarded as tyrannical. That feeling, of course, persisted into the twentieth century with such decisions as *Lochner v. New York,* which held that the right to enter into certain contracts was a property right which could not be infringed by the state without due process of law, as required by the Constitution.

V. CONCLUSION

In summary, the mid-nineteenth-century courts generally accepted the legal rules and normative claims stated in the listed result premises. They also accepted a descriptive version of those premises where that version was a description of acts of the will. However, broad claims about the unfettered nature of choice in society were not generally accepted by the courts, whether as rules of law or as empirical statements.

It can be seen that these conclusions will bear on the kind of criticism which Marx can levy against the actual ideology of the time. In particular, the two ambiguous descriptive interpretations will figure largely in the concept of illusion. The reason for this is that the simplest and most straightforward attack which Marx could make on this aspect of capitalist ideology would be to show that necessary underlying factual claims were false and to explain the reasons why they appeared to be true. Given, however, that the cases do not state a belief in arbitrary or unfettered choice, any criticism based on a lack of actual choice or the presence of coercive forces in capitalist society must be carefully directed. In other words, it will not suffice for Marx simply to show that there are coercive forces acting upon the individual in capitalist society; rather Marx must show (in order to criticize on factual grounds the actual views held) that the individual is not free of other people's coercion.

CHAPTER FIVE

An Analysis of Marx' Criticism of
Nineteenth-Century Commercial Law

I. INTRODUCTION

It is impossible to evaluate in any reasonable space more than a small fraction of Marx' attacks on capitalism, in part because of the deep ambiguity of those attacks, which requires that an undue amount of time be devoted simply to elucidating the structure of Marx' arguments. One must narrow one's approach to a small number of objectives, and the objective selected here is an analysis of Marx' rejection of the capitalistic ideal of economic freedom, as reflected in his attempted refutation of the will theories of law.

His criticism of the will theories involved two parts: an attack on the economic premises of the will theory and an attack on the concept of individual choice as the basis of freedom. The objective truth or falsity of Marx' historical and economic theories is outside the scope of this paper. Similarly, it is beyond the scope of this paper to attempt fully to analyze the justification, if any, which Marx advanced for his theory of freedom.

Between these two camps, however, lies the no man's land of illusion, because it not only suggests a content of objective falsity but also occurs in discussions of normative claims. Therefore, Marx' characterization of the will theory as an illusion will be the subject of the concluding portion of this thesis.

Marx' critique of the capitalist concept of economic freedom as an illusion had two fronts. On the one hand, based upon his economic and historical theories, Marx launched a broad-brush attack on the factual components of the will theory of law. On the normative front, Marx launched an equally broad attack on the concept of freedom under capitalism, suggesting that that concept be replaced with a concept that freedom lay in association with one's fellows and co-operation rather than in separation and competition. As Shlomo Avineri has pointed out, this concept derives from the Hegelian notion of freedom as the appreciation of necessity.[1]

Marx described various tenets of nineteenth-century property and contract law as illusions and called certain jurisprudential theories the "juridical illusion".[2] Given Marx' ostensible commitment to empiricism, the central element of his repudiation of these so-called "illusions" is his attempt to prove their factual untruth. I believe that Marx primarily sought to reject the legal theories of the nineteenth century, including their normative aspects, by means of a "scientific" attack on their factual premises.

It is here that the tedious exposition of the multiple ambiguities inherent in the key paragraph, it is hoped, will become of useful significance, for as an empiricist Marx must impeach the will theory of law on factual grounds and then, if he is to utilize the normative theories, he must bridge the gap between his empirical evidence, if any, and the normative claims ambiguously mingled with his statements of the will theory and the law.

In developing his criticism, Marx must avoid three major pitfalls: the genetic fallacy, the is/ought problem, and the problems of relativism and criticism.

The potential of a genetic fallacy in Marx' argument arises from his attempt to impeach certain views on the ground that those views are caused by social conditions. In the following material I will suggest an exegesis of Marx' argument which does not contain that fallacy, being an explanation of apparent self-evidentness, rather than an attempted refutation. On my analysis, Marx first tries to demonstrate that certain views are false and then attempts to explain away the persistent feeling that those views are self-evident.

The problem of deriving normative claims from factual claims is potentially present in Marx' arguments because of his attempt to impeach certain ethical views based upon other factual claims. While this remains a serious problem for Marx, I shall argue that the structure of his argument can obviate the problem, since the argument can be taken as directed separately at the falsity of factual claims and at apparent ethical perceptions. In any event, it appears that Marx has no more problem with this transition than do at least some of the philosophers whom he attacked.

Finally, it has been argued above that Marx wished to adopt a purely empirical philosophy and to limit his evidence to actual historical fact, while preserving his ability to criticize existing views. In other words, Marx may be said to have tried to adopt simultaneously the historicism of Savigny and the transcendence of Hegel. This presents the most serious difficulty for Marx' theory of law, because he wanted to criticize existent social philosophy on some ground other than a universal transcendent trans-historical truth and, at the same time, he sought to construct a theoretical description of the contemporary society which included the facts of its ideology. The difficulty presented by the Savigny/Hegel dilemma is actually twofold. First, as noted, Marx wanted to refute both nineteenth-century views of such moral matters as rights and freedom. He sought simply to demonstrate what he felt was the factual and moral superiority of Communism. Yet, to be consistent with his emphasis on empirically observable evidence, he needed to demonstrate that alleged superiority without reference to some intuitively known universal truth of political philosophy.[3] Second, there is the simple question of whether the ideology of a given period truly depicts the society of the time. On the one hand, Marx rigorously denounced certain ideological components of capitalism; specifically, he rejected, for example, the will theory of law. Therefore, one may expect that he would say something like: "It is believed by capitalists that contract law reflects arrangements entered into at will, but that is false." On the other hand, he is confronted by his desire to argue that people are alienated under capitalism; that they regard themselves as at the mercy of social and economic forces *and that they are* so dominated; that they believe their exchanges to be guided by self-interest and *that they are*; that property as objectified labor is regarded as an alien object in itself *and that it is* such an object under capitalism.[4]

The concept of illusion, however, contains more than merely the concept of a false statement; rather, it includes the idea of a false belief or a mistaken perception. Therefore, Marx' remarks concerning the "juridical illusion" comprise epistemological claims, as well as statements of historical and sociological theory.

Thus I construe Marx' argument as an attempt to show that certain components of capitalist ideology are false and to explain why those false statements appear to be true. More specifically, with regard to the normative content of those components, Marx' argument may be read as an attempt to show that the apparent perception of certain natural rights of man, particularly in the imagination of a state of nature in which those rights are intuitively clear, is neither a perception of empirical fact nor a self-evident moral principle, but rather an illusion generated by certain social conditions. For example, Marx said: "Incidently, when things are seen in this way, as they really are and happened, every profound philosophical problem is resolved, as will be seen even more clearly later, quite simply into an empirical fact."[5]

Prior to beginning the full-scale analysis of Marx' critique of contract law, several underlying assumptions of this section should be made clear. First, this section assumes that Marx has accurately described some portion of capitalist ideology, despite the difficulties which his description contains; in other words, the problems described above are assumed not to exist. Second, this work does not contain an analysis of the Marxist theory of political freedom or the morality of exchange under Communism or the general normative theory which Marx proposed. It is limited to his criticism and does not cover his proposed replacement theory. Third, this part tends away from an exegesis of Marx' precise remarks and toward the construction of an argument which is consistent with his statements but which may or may not be reflected in literal terms anywhere in the classical Marx texts. The detailed work in the preceding chapters was to examine the complexity of the will theory and the ambiguity of Marx' descriptions; here, however, the purpose is to synthesize a clear argument distilled from Marx' several disparate and unclear remarks; the structure of his argument is, if possible, more ambiguous than his empirical statements. Finally, this part focuses on Marx' criticism of economic and philosophical reasoning based upon the hypothetical state of nature. The reason for that focus is threefold: first, simplicity; second, that reasoning was a prime target for Marx' charges of "illusoriness"; and third, reasoning from such a state is still widely used in some political philosophy, such as the work of John Rawls and Robert Nozick.[6]

The structure of this last section will be as follows: first, I will discuss Marx' attack on the basis will theory; second, I will review his criticism of the recognition will theory; and, finally, I will address a few brief remarks to his attack on the specific idea of freedom of contract.

II.   CRITICISM OF THE BASIS WILL THEORY

The central tenets of Marx' theories of history and society suggest that he rejected a basis will theory.   Marx believed that such social institutions as law and such components of the superstructure as legal theory were caused by economic conditions, and that changes in the superstructure were brought about by changes in the means of production. Among the many statements by Marx on that point are the following:

> The fact is, therefore, that definite individuals who are productively active in a definite way enter into these definite social and political relations.   Empirical observation must in each separate instance bring out empirically, and without any mystification and speculation, *the connection of the social and political structure with production. The social structure and the state are continually evolving out of the life-process of definite individuals*, however, of these individuals not as they may appear in their own or other people's imagination, but as they actually are, i.e., as they act, produce materially, and hence as they work under definite material limits, presuppositions, and conditions *independent of their will* ... .

> *Conceiving, thinking, and the mental intercourse of men at this stage appear here as the direct efflux of their material behaviour* ... .

Men are the producers of their conceptions, ideas, etc., that is, real,
active men, as they are conditioned by a definite development of
their productive forces and of the intercourse corresponding to
these, up to its furthest forms.[7]

Thus, according to Marx, man does not choose the form of his social
institutions; rather those are caused by the economic and historical
forces which shaped the means of production, which in turn caused
certain ideas to be formed in the minds of men. The characteristics of
society are not brought about by an arbitrary act of will but by the
molding pressure of economic forces; indeed, society may be reduced
on the Marxist view to the ideas produced in consciousness by life
under certain material conditions.[8]

That claim by Marx constitutes a rejection of the basis will theory as
held by all three of the philosophers discussed earlier. First, Marx
expressly, of course, rejected the Hegelian primacy of Spirit in favor of
a materialistic view.[9]

Marx' rejection of Hegel was far more explicit than his criticism of
Savigny or Locke. Indeed, Marx characterized the philosophical
underpinnings of his theory as "turning Hegel on his head". So Marx'
rejection of a Hegelian version of the basis will theory consists in
reversing the order; if Hegel says that society is a moment in the
actualization of pure Spirit, Marx responds that, to the contrary, the idea
of pure Spirit is caused by the evolution of the material means of
production.

Second, it may seem that the Marxist theory implicitly rejects
Savigny's idea that the law arises from the common will, at least to the
extent that that will is considered as shaping society, rather than itself
being shaped by the material conditions of society.

Actually, that brief comparison may be an unfair statement of both
Savigny's and Marx' views. It is not at all clear that Savigny felt that
the general will had an unconstrained choice among possible societies;
indeed, Savigny's remarks suggest a view that the legal systems of
different societies develop in certain forms as a matter of historical necessity. To that extent, Savigny's theories are not wholly inconsistent
with Marx', although the two positions might differ to some degree in
the amount of effective force that was attributed to the will; in fact, it
appears that Marx' theory coincides strikingly with Savigny's.[10]
Earlier, the following remark by Savigny was briefly discussed:

In the earliest times to which authentic history extends, the law will
be found to have already attained a fixed character, peculiar to the
people, like their language, manners and constitution. Nay, these
phenomena have no separate existence, they are but the particular

facilities and tendencies of an individual people, inseparably united
in nature, and only wearing the semblance of distinct attributes to
one view. That which binds them into one whole is the common
conviction of the people, the kindred consciousness of an inward
necessity, excluding all notion of an accidental and arbitrary origin.[11]

That quotation contains many of the same elements found in Marx'
theory, viz., the concept that law varies systematically with the
historical situation of people, that law and other social phenomena do
not have an existence of their own but are only the tendencies of a
particular people under actual historical conditions, that law does not
have an accidental or arbitrary origin (i.e., that law does not arise from
arbitrary choice), and that the binding effect of law consists in the
awareness of necessity.

The parallels are not exact, largely because of Savigny's rather
racist conception of a "people" as opposed to Marx' conception of a
historical period in the development of the means of production.
Nonetheless, given these many similarities, it remains to be seen
whether Marx can also avoid the ethical relativism that he abhorred in
the historical school of law.

Although Marx' theory of law is not inconsistent with the idea that
the law consists in the common perception of social order (and, indeed,
that may well be exactly Marx' view), it is inconsistent with the idea
that the reason why society has its present form is that its denizens have
consciously willed it to be so as a matter of election among alternatives.
Third, therefore, Marx' view is at odds with that of Locke, who held
that society was founded on the individual consents of its members.

Locke described the origin of society as a group of previously
isolated individuals joining together by agreement. Marx denied the
historical fact of such an occurrence and also denied the historical
possibility of any such analogous occurrence happening in any existent
society. In this regard, Marx' comments on the Utopian socialists such
as Owen are interesting.[12] To be consistent, Marx had to deny the
possibility of persons starting a perfect communist society by agreement
because the creation of such small, isolated, futuristic societies would
imply that individuals could decide to become communists and to live in
a communist society and could then create such a society, regardless of
the historical stage of the larger community. That possibility would be
inconsistent with Marx' generally deterministic view of society and its
superstructure.

As Avineri noted:

Marx cannot accept on principle any economic theory that starts with individualistic modes of human existence or behaviour. Such a model starts from the individual producer who produces for his own needs. Ideally his production is autarchic and Robinsonesque... . Marx' objection to this theory is not limited to refuting as an historical explanation... . Marx argues that as an explicatory model the "Robinsonade" is fallacious and misleading for it presupposes the existence of private property prior to the existence of any human relationship, whereas property is obviously a mode of inter-human relationship.[13]

As Avineri interpreted Marx, Marx not only rejected the historical accuracy of the state of nature, but he also rejected that hypothetical state as a model of human behavior.

There are, then, two major aspects of Marx' remarks in the context of the basis will theory of law. First, Marx generally rejected the premise that the will, whether individual or collective, is the effective cause of social institutions.[14] Second, he rejected specifically the individualistic model of human behavior which underlies the social contract model of the origin or nature of society. The details of these two aspects will be discussed separately.

A. REJECTION OF THE EFFICACY OF WILL

As noted earlier, the basis will theory technically has two forms: one which deals with the origin of society, as in the Lockean concept of the state of nature, and one which deals with the origin of specific laws in a given society. Marx rejected both versions.

In regard to the origins of society, for example, he stated in *The German Ideology* that the social structure and the state "continually evolve out of the life-process of definite individuals".[15] At a later point in that work, Marx rejected the basis will theory as applied to the origin of particular laws in the capitalist state, saying:

Since the state is the form in which the individuals of a ruling class assert their common interests, and in which the whole civil society of an epoch is epitomised, it follows that all common institutions are set up with the help of the state and are given a political form. Hence, the illusion that law is based on the will, and indeed on the will divorced from its real basis - on free will... .[16]

In this passage, Marx incorporates the concept of political society which he proposed in 'On the Jewish Question', i.e., that in the political sphere of society, man regards himself as acting in a universal or general way and loses there his individual identity.   Marx, then, argued that, under capitalism, the law appears to result from a general will; thus, Marx offered an account of the perception by members of a capitalistic society that they are creating laws by their choice, their vote. To the contrary, Marx maintained, the state actually expressed the interest of the ruling class, and its role as intermediary creates an illusion that a general will is involved. Marx maintained, of course, that the law does not result from an act of will but is only the reflection of economic forces.

Assuming that that brief explication is correct, the argument in the above paragraph can be set out more fully as follows:

1. The ruling class asserts its common interests through the social institution of the state (as opposed, perhaps, to direct physical domination).

2. Social institutions, such as laws, are formed through the medium of the state, as by voting rather than, for example, by direct interaction among the members of society.

3. Since social institutions are created thus through the medium of the state, they become political, i.e., the act of voting appears to the individual citizen as the act of an abstract, universal kind of citizen, of his act in a role distinct from his everyday identity and, therefore, universal.

4. Thus, the social mechanism of the vote appears to the voter to create laws through the medium of the state as a matter of the will of the citizens.

5. Since, however, the state and its laws actually express the interests of the ruling class, the state mechanism does not actually express a general will and the perception of the citizen is false and, therefore, an illusion.

The above argument presents several problems. On one level of analysis, it levels a fairly simple charge at capitalist democracy; the laws appear to be the result of the will of all the citizens, but in fact represent the interests of only a minority. Even if that were correct as a matter of fact, that simple claim presents difficulties. First, the connection between the existence of a state and the claimed perception of universality is left vague and unsupported; indeed, it seems to run directly contrary to the perception of many people that it is futile to vote, because the influence of powerful people ultimately determines the outcome anyway. Second, even if it were true that the state expressed the interests of the ruling class, that would not impugn the democratic system unless it were impossible that it do otherwise. That is, a belief that the present state only advances the interests of a wealthy few may simply function as a cry for reform of the system, rather than as a repudiation of the entire will theory.

The idea that laws are formed by a consensus of wills would be impeached by the claim that laws express the interests of a few, only if (a) the many have not chosen to advance the interests of a few, and it is not possible for the system to do otherwise. It seems clear that if the general population agreed that society would be better off if the interests of the wealthy were promoted, then the fact that the laws adopted did so would not show that the laws were not the choice of everyone.

It is interesting that Marx' argument seems to assume that people are greedy; that is, of course, Marx assumes that each member of society votes in his own self-interest and that the interests of one class are irretrievably opposed to those of the others.

More fundamentally, it does not follow from the idea that the state does not express a general will to the idea that laws are not caused by acts of will. That is why, I believe, Marx felt compelled to add the additional phrase "on the will divorced from its real basis, on free will". By adding that phrase, Marx has shifted his focus and, on one level, introduced an inconsistency in his position. The first sentence says that through the laws, the "individuals of a ruling class assert their common interests"; and the word "assert", of course, suggests that those individuals act to bring about the advancement of their interests; in other words, that they decide what laws will benefit themselves and cause those laws to be in force. That theory, obviously, itself supposes that the will of certain individuals is effective in creating laws, which in turn is a form of will theory. Marx attempted to avoid that problem by adding the phrase referring to free will, suggesting perhaps that even the ruling individuals were not free to choose which laws would be enacted.

That addition, however, closes the circle on Marx' argument and renders it invalid. If Marx argues that the capitalist democratic state only appears to embody the will of all its citizens but actually is controlled by the wealthy, then his position is not only unoriginal but is limited to a plea for reform. If, on the other hand, Marx argues that the state only appears to embody the free will of all its citizens because states necessarily express the economic interests of the ruling class (and therefore are not affected by their (or anyone else's) will), he has assumed his conclusion; that is, that argument contains as a premise the proposition that states and their laws are not the result of acts of will, which is the desired conclusion. Therefore, the argument will not suffice as a refutation of the basis will theory.

Here also, Marx is in danger of running into the proposed psycho-historical genetic fallacy. His explanation of why laws appear to be the result of acts of will (as opposed to his assumption that it is not so) could be correct, whether or not laws actually were created by acts of will. In other words, Marx cannot, without additional premises, reason backwards from the proposed mechanism, which causes a given belief to the falsity of the belief thus generated.

It can be seen that the above problems are likely to be found in any attempt by Marx to link the actual functioning of the capitalist state to the will theory. Even if no actual historical state ever expressed the general will of its members, that only proves that states have not so done. Marx does not make an inductive argument on this point, and it is not clear what form such an argument would take. Marx needs to argue that states simply do not (or cannot) express *anyone's* will in order to reject all forms of the basis will theory, and that position, of course, would directly contradict the Marxian argument that laws promote the interests of the ruling class. The latter contradiction can be resolved by Marx' denying that the ruling class' will is what *causes* the laws to take a certain shape, even if the law reflects their decision.

On the other hand, in fairness to Marx, it may be responded that the earlier argument, if true, at least would show that the capitalist democratic state as it existed in nineteenth-century Britain and America was not the expression of the general will. It is interesting to note an almost Rawlsian notion in that claim; Marx seems to assume that the voters would not create such a society if their will were in fact being realized - that is, that the citizens would choose differently if they were truly choosing. That perhaps is part of the force of Marx' use of the concept of illusion, that if citizens understood that the existing system of property was neither natural nor necessary, they would revolt. Yet, that appeal itself assumes the efficacy of the will, since it is an appeal to action and, indeed, to action in one's own self-interest.

An effort will be made now to comb out specific premises which Marx held and which he asserted against a basis will theory, as follows:

1. Economic forces cause or shape society.

2. Man's perception of the world, including his perception of the will, is shaped by economic forces and social conditions.

3. It is not true that society resulted from a group of solitary individuals who banded together by choice.

4. It is not true that present-day society is shaped by the will of its

members; property relationships have their present form, for example, because of the form of the economic structure of society, not because the will of the people has created them in this fashion.

5. It is historically necessary that society be as it is; i.e., society did not acquire its present form by virtue of a choice among alternative forms.

Even this clarified list of claims leaves Marx with several problems. Since the purpose of this study is to focus on Marx' critical remarks and not upon his own alternative theory, let us turn first to his argument against the basis will theory which these premises were used to support. The force of these factual claims against the basis will theory, in any of its descriptive forms, is fairly obvious; the two factual accounts are inconsistent, and if one is true, then the other is false.

The interesting question, then, is what effect these premises have upon the normative versions of the will. What is the relationship between the claim that the will of the members of society (whether in the sense of a general will or the common will of a group of individuals) does not in fact determine the rules of society and the claim that the law should be determined by the will? Then what is the logical relationship between the denial on factual grounds of the basis will theory and the normative view that law should be willed?

The answer is that Marx' theory of society, if it is true, appears to disprove that normative claim in two ways: it makes it both false and impossible. If Marx' account is true, it makes the normative basis theory impossible because, on Marx' view, the will of people simply does not determine the nature of the social structure or rules and therefore, there *cannot* be a society in which the social rules are *determined* by the will of the individuals. Rather, the social structure precedes and determines the decisions which the members of society seem to make. Therefore, Marx' theory of history makes the normative version of the basis will theory false because it precludes the causative element. In Marx' theory, in other words, the concept of the desirable society cannot precede the social conditions which make that society possible (and which will bring that society about); and, in addition, the desire for a given society is not the cause of its coming into being, its existence being rather determined by the economic forces already in motion which have created the very idea of that society.

The ideas of the above paragraph are, of course, the basis of Marx' vitriolic attacks on what he called "utopian socialism".[17]

There is yet another sense in which Marx' denial of the basis will theories is inconsistent with its normative form. That sense is that Marx did not believe in the existence of a range of choices as to the form of society. Therefore, the will cannot freely choose and create a society in the sense of being able to elect what form of society will exist.

Actually, Marx' view contains two senses in which there cannot be a genuine range of choices as to the shape of a desirable society. First, the type of society is determined by the shape of the means of production. That form of society will arise which is appropriate to the means of production, according to Marx. If the underlying concept of the basis will theory is that individuals freely choose among alternative, historically possible, societies, then that concept is false if Marx' theory of history is true.

Second, it may also be that Marx thought that the individual's concept of the desirable society was determined, i.e., that there was no choice in a subjective sense among alternative ideas. On that view, the individual as a matter of psychology can desire or comprehend only those possible societies, for which the economic conditions are already in existence. Marx knew that there had been thinkers who had theorized about political systems which were not then in existence, but he attributed this phenomenon to the existence of the components of those imagined societies in embryonic form in the presently existing society. It is clear that, even if the individual could elect among various images of utopia, only one society is possible as the outcome of history. For Marx, the choice of a society is neither accidental nor arbitrary.

On the above argument, it can be seen that Marx' theory, if true, presents serious difficulties for a basis theory of law. It can be seen, however, that Marx' denial of the factual basis will theory refutes the normative basis will theory *only* if that normative theory contains three premises about the freedom of the will, as follows:

1. The will is the effective cause of the formation of social institutions. Yet it can be seen that that first premise is not a necessary part of the normative basis will theory. If an individual is born into a particular society, he obviously did not create it, but he can, it would seem, effectively consent to being a member of that society, if by good fortune he comes to agree in principle to its institutions.

2. The will is able to choose among various institutions. If an individual or a group of individuals make a particular choice as to the structure of a society where there is no other alternative, is that choice less free?

3. The individual is free to choose that view which most appeals

to him. The question of Marx' psychological determinism raises issues which are also raised by many other versions of that theory; if ideas themselves are not freely chosen on the ground of their perceived truthfulness, then can the will be said to be free?

Criticism of Marx' position in this context must be directed either at his theory of history or at the alternative theory which he proposes. Both of these undertakings are beyond the intended scope of this section, but a few remarks about his version of the ideal society are in order. Basically, one may plausibly say that Marx did accept the idea that a society the structure of which was in accord with individual will was desirable. For him, however, the concept of the individual's relation to that society was not one of an election among alternatives, least of all a free election among alternatives. Rather, under Communism, each individual would will the shape of society to be what it is (because the productive forces will shape the ideology there as effectively as under capitalism) but that willing will be rationally recognized as the acceptance of necessity (because of the communist man's scientific, Marxist understanding of the necessary nature of society).[18] On that theory, however, why should one simply not will the existence of capitalism, surely a necessary phenomenon of its time, and go on with life? Why, in other words, should one become a communist before the revolution?

B. REJECTION OF THE INDIVIDUALISTIC MODEL

As noted above, Marx not only rejected the general proposition that law was based upon acts of will, he also rejected the proposition that the organization of society could be based upon the individual consents of its members. In other words, Marx rejected the social contract theory. That rejection took two forms: first, that the social contract did not exist and, second, that the social contract is not an adequate model for individual choice in society.

We have seen above that Marx provided an alternative historical explanation for the origin of society, in that he argued that societies arise out of and are caused by the form in which their members produce the goods necessary for existence. Marx, however, also rejected the general conceptual framework of the social-contract theory on two grounds: he rejected the individualistic concept of mankind, and he rejected the idea that that concept was universally valid. That is, he rejected the individualistic conception of man as a universal description of man's role in society, and he rejected that description of man's nature as an accurate description at all. In other words, Marx wanted to argue that the concept of the solitary individual entering into a society not only did not describe the relationship of the individual to society in all cultures but did not describe the relationship of the individual to capitalist society. The latter idea is actually inconsistent with some of Marx' other ideas, as will be seen. In the subsequent discussion, I will try to elucidate these related notions and then to analyze the relations of these ideas to the normative version of the basis will theory.

First, Marx argued that the relationship in which the individual stood to society under capitalism was not true of other societies. For example, he argued that in the Teutonic tribes the individual did not own property to the exclusion of the interests of others and of the tribe as a whole. Rather, according to Marx, the individual was allowed to possess temporarily material goods such as land, which were regarded as fundamentally belonging to the tribe as an entity, rather than to the collection of individuals or to any one of them.

Observed cultural variation led Marx, given his commitment to empirical observation and his theory that theoretical social entities are only man's perception of his situation, to reject the idea of property or contract as meaningfully existing in any trans-cultural, trans-historical sense. In other words, Marx argued that the capitalistic concept of a contract would not have the same meaning (or any referent at all) outside capitalist and proto-capitalist societies; in a feudal society, except with regard to the budding bourgeoisie, the individual's relationships were not created by contract but derived from his role in the community. The term "contract" there simply would not have the same meaning as it would under capitalism, and it cannot truthfully be used by later social scientists to describe the social phenomena of the earlier time. Marx said that all that can be observed of each society are the actual relationships in which people stand to each other and to physical things. Those relationships vary from one society to another, and Marx believed that a solid scientific explanation of society did not include a universal concept like property or contract as a description of some underlying, continuing reality. (In a sense, one may argue that Marx may have held to a form of behavioral reductionism; i.e., that social entities may be reduced to observable behavior patterns.)

It is important to distinguish Marx' view from an alternative Rawlsian account. Marx did not believe that other forms of property ownership, such as Communism or tribal ownership, were simply alternative social structures that could be adopted at will by individuals with regard to their own present or future individual ownership of goods. Rather, Marx thought that the individual's perception of his relationship to physical objects fundamentally varied through different historical periods, and from one society to another *and* that an adequate explanation of this historical variation did not rest on a universal trans-cultural concept of property. To put it another way, Marx did not regard Communism as a voluntary sharing of each individual's property. Rather, he believed the whole relationship of man to man and man to thing was malleable, so that the members of a community would stand in different relationships in a different society. Man's perception of his relationship to nature and to his fellow men simply varied from society to society. As will be discussed below, this interpretation of Marx is inconsistent with some of his other positions.

Marx argued that the use of a hypothetical state of nature, either in economics or in political philosophy, as a device to determine the true structure of society in general is fallacious because such a hypothetical state postulates that man is fundamentally egoistic, isolated, complete in his identity, and standing in a certain relationship to his labor and the fruits of it, as well as to any other individuals that he might encounter in that state. In Marx' words, the state of nature presupposes the concepts which it is used to defend; arguments involving that state are not only based upon an historical error but upon a misleading mode of thought.

Marx set out his position as follows:

> The individual and isolated hunter or fisher who forms the starting point with Smith and Ricardo belongs to the insipid illusions of the eighteenth century. They are adventure stories ... . They are no more based on such a naturalism than is Rousseau's *contrat social*, which makes naturally independent individuals come in contact and have mutual intercourse by contract. They are fiction ... . They are, rather, the anticipation of "civil society", which had been in course of development since the sixteenth century and made gigantic strides towards maturity in the eighteenth.[19]

One may respond to the above theory that the hypothetical state of nature may indeed contain in its concept of man the concepts of capitalist property and contract, but that that is precisely the model's virtue. That is, it may be said that the social contract model of the individual with its attendant consequences merely shows that the relations of property and contract described under capitalism are simply the social structures which correspond to man's nature. Here one may see the importance to Marx' position of his general social theory; it is not enough for his argument that the social contract theory presupposes a particular concept of mankind and certain relationships as appropriate to that concept - rather, he needs in addition to have shown that that concept is false as a description of man's nature, both for purposes of the science of economics and for purposes of moral philosophy.

"But", one may say, "that image does appear to me to be an

accurate image of man's nature - I see it in action daily." Indeed, this is the persuasive power of the state of nature model - it appears to elucidate our intuitive perception of man's true nature.

Marx' view that ideas are a product of one's specific situation in life attempts to negate the intuitive force of that perception. Assuming that Marx can establish his own theory, he can then use it to explain why the state of nature with its individualistic inhabitants appears as such a persuasive model of human nature. Indeed, according to Marx, private property as it appears to the observer is the perceptible expression of alienated human nature, not an entity itself.[20] Thus, Marx said:

> Everyone believes his craft to be the true one. Illusions regarding the connection between their craft and reality are more likely to be cherished by them because of the very nature of the craft. In con-sciousness - in jurisprudence, politics, etc. - relations become concepts; since they do not go beyond these relations, the concepts of the relations become fixed concepts in the mind. The judge, for example, applies the code, he therefore regards legislation as the real, active driving force.... . Idea of law. Idea of state. The matter is turned upside down in ordinary consciousness.[21]

In the continuation of Marx' criticism of economic theories based on the hypothetical, isolated individual, Marx attempted to explain away the apparent perception that such a thought experiment reveals man's nature, as follows:

> The individual and isolated hunter or fisher who forms the starting point with Smith and Ricardo belongs to the insipid illusions of the eighteenth century.... . In this society of free competition the indi-vidual appears free from the bonds of nature, etc., which in former epochs of history made him part of a definite, limited human conglomeration ... . Since that individual appeared to be in con-formity with nature and corresponded to their conception of human nature, he was regarded as a product not of history, but of nature.[22]

Indeed, Marx argued that entire theories were generated from their creator's role in a particular society, such as the theory that relationships between people are actually real objects or the manifestations of a larger, transcendent entity as spirit, or an entire historical method.[23] Here, therefore, one may read Marx' argument as proceeding in three steps: the first step was to construct a method ostensibly limited to empirical observation with a minimum of theoretical entities; the second step was to argue that that method applied to society demonstrates that man is fundamentally a social animal, not an isolated, egoistic individual; and the third step was to demonstrate the source of the apparent evidence to the contrary. Thus, in one version of his theory, Marx has apparently avoided the genetic fallacy. The argument given above purports to use the explanation of beliefs not to demonstrate their falsity, but to explain away an apparent perception that would otherwise count as evidence against Marx' own general theory.

The question which must be answered next (assuming that the above construction is plausible) is what the effect of that argument is upon the normative consequences of the concept of the state of nature. To the extent that a concept of political obligation or civil rights is drawn from the concept of a state of nature, according to Marx it is drawn from a conception which is both false historically and false as a portrayal of man's nature. Any "natural" laws which are derived from that theory, in Marx' view, are derived from false concepts of man's nature.

C.   CRITICISM OF THE RECOGNITION WILL THEORY

The recognition will theory as described above is the view that the laws of contract and property recognize or codify the actual relationship of the individual will to objects and other people.

The Marxian criticism of the recognition will theory is parallel to the criticism of the basis will theory. In essence, Marx would say that the relationships supposed by that theory are simply not the relationships which actually obtain as a matter of the facts of the nature of man. The recognition theory postulated that man is fundamentally complete in his individual identity (i.e., that contractual relationships are "accidental" to that identity), that his basic relationship to the world of nature is that of individual domination and exclusive possession, and that his basic relation with other people is that of mutual exchange of desired items, including labor.

On the proposed synthesis of Marx' works, the Marxian response would be that these relationships are not in fact the universal relationships of individuals to nature and others. Thus, the Marxian view is that, as factual claims, the recognition will theory is simply false.

As with the normative version of the basis will theory above, then, a normative version of the recognition will theory ("the law ought to effectuate the natural relationship of contract", for example) would also fail. On the criticism, to the extent that that normative theory was asserted to follow from the assertion of certain will/nature connections, it would be founded upon false premises. To the extent that the normative premises were established on some other ground, the command "The law ought to effectuate the mutual assent to a contract of two free parties" would be impossible to carry out. In both the Marxian criticisms of the recognition will theory and of the basis will theory, the emphasis falls upon the universal aspect of these target theories. Marx felt that the vice of importing the exclusively capitalist concept of man into supposedly universal theories infected both economics and political philosophy. Its alleged specific effect on economics can be seen in the following passage:

> In saying that existing conditions - the relationships of bourgeois production - are natural, the economists want it to be understood that these are the relationships in which wealth is created and productive forces are developed in conformity with laws of nature. Hence, these relationships are themselves natural law, independent of the influence of time. They are eternal laws which must always govern society.[24]

Both with regard to that economic thesis and with regard to political ideas such as natural rights, Marx again said that the individualistic model upon which those ideas was based was simply false as a matter of fact.

The assumption of the necessary universality of these theories is rather troubling and will, I believe, prove the basis for a serious problem in Marx' analysis. In light of that idea, it is appropriate to turn to the concrete, specific premises of the law, especially premises 2, 3, and 4.

D.   CRITIQUE OF THE RESULT PREMISES

The question will be, of course, what the connection is between the above-described arguments and any Marxian rejection of the specific premises of the law. For simplicity's sake, this discussion is limited to the predicate or result premises as they may have occurred in the case law. Again, I believe that the strongest construal of Marx' remarks is as an attack upon the factual underpinnings of those premises. The material below will begin with a discussion of the connection between any falsity of the "juridical illusion" and a rejection of the predicate premises. From there it will proceed to a consideration of the nature of Marx' attack, if any, on the three different interpretations of the three premises.

In Chapter One, three different readings of the connection between a will theory of law and the specific statements were discussed. These were a logical connection, a psychological causal connection, and a purely historical causal connection. It is not at all clear in either of the latter two interpretations what effect the falsity of the "juridical illusion" would have on the truth of the subsequent premises; it would seem that a false view could cause, subjectively or otherwise, a true view or vice versa.

With regard to the logical connection, the situation is more complex. If the logical structure of the capitalist position is, as Marx held, a premise that if law is based upon will, then contract law is based on mutual wills, then the falsity of the antecedent will not, of course, entail the falsity of the subsequent claim. If, on the other hand, Marx wished to say that law is based on will if and only if contract law is based on mutual wills, then the falsity of the former would entail the falsity of the latter. The logical situation is particularly acute with regard to the recognition theory, since it does seem that the specific result premises do entail some form of the recognition theory.

Turning now to the criticism which Marx made of the different interpretations of these premises, it can be seen that the factual interpretation is of the greatest interest. First, it is generally true that these statements basically are accurate reflections of principles of law. Moreover, as noted earlier, a rule *qua* rule cannot in any clear way be said to be true or false. As to the normative interpretations, Marx' more powerful argument against those premises would be based upon a criticism of the factual claims; otherwise, Marx stands to be accused of simply substituting one transcendent moral theory for another and of putting himself on a plane different from other mortals, where he alone could determine a true, universal moral theory.[25]

Let us turn, however, to Marx' criticism of the factual accuracy of the result statements. To understand this portion effectively, it is necessary to return to the distinction developed earlier between reading these statements as propositions about the will and as propositions about economic conditions. When Marx criticizes the descriptive interpretation of the result premises, his remarks therefore may be taken as being directed at either the economic interpretation of those descriptions or at the will interpretation of them.

Marx' remark concerning the economic necessities for the actual use of property and the economic constraints on actually using it as one chose (Theses II, III, and IV), may be read as critical remarks about the fact that certain financial circumstances were necessary to the true enjoyment of one's property. Although those premises may form the ground for another kind of criticism of these views (viz., that a right is not worth much if the economic conditions for its exercise are not present), they do not impinge upon any fundamental factual premise of the legal position. As noted above, the nineteenth-century judges did not believe in the existence of a completely unfettered will insofar as economic and social pressures were considered; those judges did, however, believe in the existence of a will free from the pressures exerted by other individuals in certain proscribed manners, as by threats or undue extortion in times of hardship.

That fact about the actual views of nineteenth-century judges weakens significantly the force of Marx' remarks, which appear to be directed at the factual conditions of free choice and also appear to assume that the concept of will included in contract and property law involved a concept of unlimited choice.

Those factual claims by Marx, to the effect that there was not an unlimited range of choices as to the disposition of property in capitalist society, do not refute the idea that contracts are entered at will for the reason that the judges did not equate the "at will" concept with a concept of wholly arbitrary choice. It is true that the choice of the terms of a contract or the use of property could be arbitrary insofar as the law was concerned, since the law did not prescribe that property be used in a certain way or that people enter into contracts with each other; in other words, the individual had a legal right to dispose of his property as he chose. That legal right, however, was not regarded as equivalent to the economic or social power to do so. The law, as discussed in *Carew v. Rutherford*, did not dictate the terms of employment, such as wages, but that same freedom of contract did not suppose that the contractor and the stonemason had an absolute economic ability to determine wholly arbitrarily upon what conditions they would assume the relationship of employer and employee.

In order for Marx to criticize effectively the factual interpretation of the predicate premises, therefore, he must criticize the will version of the descriptive interpretation. That is, he must do so if he wishes to show that the premises are false; he may utilize, as discussed earlier, the alleged fact of a lack of alternatives in society to show that the legal right is futile or meaningless.

A reading of Marx as rejecting the idea that contracts and property under capitalism represent the realization of the will of particular individuals has serious problems, however. These problems arise primarily, I will argue, from the fundamental difficulty with Marx' concept of ideology; is the ideology of a time an accurate description of the social conditions of the time? If that description is accurate, then Marx can obviously not successfully attack it as false. If it is not accurate, then can such statements as those about the alienation of labor be true, where those statements depend upon the individual's perception of himself within that society?

The first step in analyzing Marx' factual critique of the descriptive premises is to compare that issue with his criticism of the recognition will theory. As noted above, that criticism focused upon the universal nature of the claims involved, i.e., upon the idea that the institutions of property and contract under capitalism somehow were taken to be the universal relationships of individuals to each other and to the physical world. That imputed universality was then attacked on the ground that other societies did not organize themselves so. As an element of that criticism, Marx expanded the concept of property to include the specific concept of exclusive, self-interested possession and the concept of contract to include the concept of two individuals "subtly reckoning with each other's need".

Let us assume that Marx' expansion of the concepts of property and contract under capitalism is correct. When we leave the recognition will theory, however, and turn to the will-descriptive claims, there is no reason to suspect that those claims are being put forward as universal. They are portrayed as statements contained in the ideology of capitalism. If they are limited in their reference to that society, so what? There is no reason to think that when a judge spoke of the freedom of a New England stonemason to enter a contract, he had in mind anything other than the capitalist concept of a contract as a relationship entered into by mutually self-interested, socially separate parties in New England. Even if that judge thought he was speaking of the eternal nature of a contract, if we accept Marx' notion of the term "contract" as socially dependent so that the judge's remarks are properly limited in their reference to one particular economic system, the remarks may still be true of that system, although they might not be true of contracts as a trans-historical entity. Similar reasoning applies to Marx' rejection of the social contract as an actual historical phenomenon. The question as to the truth of the premises here considered is not whether the descendants of Cain and Seth entered into a social contract which thereby formed the first society, but whether the contracts under consideration by the nineteenth-century judges were entered as a matter of will.

If Marx wishes to refute the idea that contracts are entered as a matter of the will of the parties (to show, in other words, that that is an illusion), he must then show that it is an illusion in capitalist society as it then existed, i.e., that those contracts were not entered by the will of the parties.

Yet, Marx cannot consistently show this, except insofar as he replaces one concept of will with another. We can see this impossibility if we examine Marx' concept of ideology and his descriptions of man in capitalist society. First, Marx emphatically rejected the idea that a true social or economic theory included such trans-historical entities as "property" or "contract" as the basic elements of the theory. Such entities only exist in the particular forms in which they occur in actual historical societies, and they do not have more than the most general reference in other societies. Moreover, there is no such entity as society or other apparent social institutions, such as the state (except as a very basic, broadly defined, entity in social theory or perhaps as a component of a given superstructure); rather, there are only actual men and their behavior. Second, Marx described man in capitalist society as alienated, as producing only in order to exchange, and as seeing his labor as producing objects independent of his own relationships with others, etc.

If those latter statements are to be true descriptions of capitalist society and if Marx' expansion of the concept of contract is correct, then it is true that individuals enter contracts as a matter of will.

The idea that contracts are a matter of will is not, therefore, an illusion.

If the descriptive statements of capitalist society had been false, then presumably the normative statements that rest on descriptive versions of the predicate premises would be false, as such: "One has a moral right to choose which contracts one will enter." If the descriptive statements are true, however, then even if such moral claims are not universally true, they may well be true in capitalist society, in whatever sense Marx thought that moral statements were true or false. The absence of acts of will which would have rendered those normative statements false or impossible has not been shown. That situation presents a serious problem for Marx. He can deny that the normative claims are true for any other society and adopt a relativistic theory of ethics, in accordance with Savigny's historicism. But that position leaves him without the ability to reject capitalism on moral grounds. He may, on the other hand, say that while those normative claims were widely believed in capitalist society, they are not true; in that case, however, Marx has abandoned his attempt to limit himself to observable empirical premises and has, on the contrary, adopted a view of ethics which permits of trans-historical, trans-cultural judgments.[26]

There is one last criticism of Marx to be made before our account is complete. If Marx held that contracts were not entered into as a matter of will, that social relationships were, for example, determined by economics, then his position would appear to be inconsistent with his description of the communist society. In *The German Ideology*, Marx said that the proposed "community of revolutionary proletarians" would "take their conditions of existence and those of all members of society under their control.... It is the association of individuals (assuming the advanced stage of modern productive forces, of course) which puts the conditions of the free development and movement of individuals under their control ... ."[27] The term "control" signifies domination and acts of will: how then shall the members of that society take control of the means of production, if the relationship of the individual to nature is not one of the will to the world?   This problem is not helped if Marx substitutes the concept of "appreciation of necessity" for the term "free" above.

E.   CONCLUSION

In summary, therefore, it may be said that Marx' remarks on nine-teenth-century law, including the then-current theories of jurisprudence, are a confused amalgam of attempted refutations of separate and distinct positions.   The strongest aspect of Marx' theory is his attempt to connect the factual aspects of these theories to sociological theory, and thereby also to refute their normative content.   However, his own ambiguous conception of ideology and his own inability to formulate criticisms which did not imply special knowledge of the universal character of human nature have committed him to various paradoxes, which render illusory his perception of his theory as avoiding both relativism and idealism.

APPENDIX A

Discussion of Dawson's Theories

It may be worth responding in some detail to Dawson's arguments concerning the role of free will in this developing area of law. Dawson was concerned to argue in his classic article that the primary function of the law of duress was to prevent unjust enrichment.[1] He therefore dismisses the issue of free will in the first several pages of his essay and likewise discharges the question of the wrongfulness of the threatened act at a later point. These cursory rejections deserve attention because, I believe, the abhorred doctrines form two central elements in the concept of duress developed by these cases.

In rejecting the role of free will, Dawson notes that the concept of a man of reasonable firmness as the standard for determining whether coercion existed was not a major factor in decisions, scornfully noting that "it directly influenced decision at any time is unlikely and for present purposes it can be henceforth ignored. Its chief effect was to preserve emphasis on the misconduct of the coercing party, thus distracting attention from the specific consequences to the party co-erced."[2]

There are several obvious problems with this statement. First, unlike the remainder of this scholarly article, there is absolutely no historical citation given for the alleged fact that the doctrine did not influence decisions. Second, the authorities which Dawson gives, including Coke and Blackstone, included the doctrine as settled law, and the cases consistently mention it as an element of the defense or action of duress. Third, Dawson seems to ignore the plain fact that this standard was not one to be applied by the judge, at least in the law courts, but was a standard for the guidance of the jury. Technically, it was also the standard for the chancellor when he decided the issues of fact, such as the subjective impact of the threat, as opposed to his decisions on the law, such as the wrongfulness of the threat. Therefore, like the standard of reasonable care in actions for personal injury, there was little reason to elaborate upon the standard; whatever may have happened to the doctrines of law concerning which threats could form duress in the eyes of the law, the jury continued to be given the same instruction that it must consider the effect of the threats, not upon the individual before it, but upon a man of reasonable firmness. The expected impact of a standard for the fact-finder is not upon the appellate decisions, but upon the outcome of the trial. Finally,

Dawson's flat remark that "[i]ts chief effect was to preserve emphasis on the misconduct of the coercing party" seems clearly and simply wrong - how can a doctrine which specifically addresses itself to the standard by which the effect of threats is to be measured be considered to direct attention to the wrong-doer as opposed to his victim?

Moreover, Dawson's remark obscures an interesting phenomenon of the law in the mid-nineteenth century: even as the political doctrine of *laissez faire* was making itself felt in the legal doctrine of freedom of contract, the courts were modifying the law from the harsh standard that the threat must be such as to intimidate a man of ordinary firmness to the more lenient standard which considered the infirmities of the individual then standing before the court. While the doctrine was preached and adopted that each man ought to look out for his own self-interest, the courts were turning from a stringent socially absolute standard to a particular and individualized one.

In the second half of his attack on the importance of free will concepts in the law of duress, Dawson states:

> It was at first assumed, as in the English cases, that the wrongfulness of the means used made unnecessary any inquiry into their precise effects on the party coerced. But the need was soon felt for explaining the functions of duress doctrines in terms of a broader objective. The objective...was that of ensuring the freedom of the individual will.

Yet, this statement appears to be wrong as a matter of historic fact. The earliest case on economic pressure which Dawson cites is the classic case of *Astley v. Reynolds*, 2 Strange 915 (1732). In that case, a pawnbroker refused to release an item which had been pledged with him unless the person making the pledge paid an additional price. The victim of this coercion paid the extra money and then sued for its return, claiming that it had been paid involuntarily. The defense of the pawnbroker to the suit was that the money had been freely paid over to him and that, if the plaintiff had not wanted to pay the money, he was free not to pay it and to sue for the return of his property. The courts said (*and Dawson includes this quote*) as follows:

> The plaintiff might have such an immediate want of his goods, that an action of trover [the appropriate action for goods improperly held by another] would not do his business; where the rule *volenti non fit injuria* is applied, it must be where the party had his freedom of exercising his will, which this man had not; we must take it that he paid his money relying on his legal remedy to get it back again.

The point of the case was that the wrongful detention of the goods deprived the man of his free will because of his need for his property. The concept of free will was not invented in the nineteenth century, as Dawson suggests, but was an integral part of the developing eighteenth-century law. While it is true, as Dawson argues, that the concept of threats of economic harm by wrongful actions is like the concept of threats of physical harm by wrongful assault, it is also true that the doctrine of duress of goods resembles the earlier doctrines because it deals with the kinds of threats which may affect the free will.

Dawson's rejection of the importance of the wrongfulness of the threatened action is more prospective than assertedly grounded in historical fact. I believe that it will appear in the following discussion of specific cases that, in the mid-nineteenth century, the concept of the wrongfulness of the action was intimately tied to the concept of free will as freedom from wrongful oppression, not from all coercion.

Facts of Various Cases
(Page references to lengthy quotations are omitted)

MILLER V. MILLER

The case of *Miller v. Miller* presents an interesting development of the facts sufficient to constitute duress. *Miller v. Miller*, 68 Pa. St. (18 P.F. Smith) 486 (1871). In that case, a brother and sister lived together for over twenty years, bickering and quarreling most of that time. The father of this pair had died in 1835, leaving by his will two farms. The brother, who was the defendant in this lawsuit, received one farm, while the other heirs, including Nancy, received the other. The brother, David, agreed to buy the second farm from the other heirs for $30 per acre. The price was later reduced to $20 per acre upon the condition that David provide a home for his sister Nancy for life. David gave Nancy a note for $1200, dated 1847, for her share in the farm. Nancy then began to live on the farm with David; she kept house for him and also managed the books. Every year for several years, David punctually paid the interest on the note, but in 1861, according to Nancy, he began to comment that it was, after all, a sin to take interest. Again, according to Nancy, he persuaded her and her sister to forgive some of the interest on the note, in the amount of $500 then due. The intra-family feud continued with increasing bitterness and increasing financial and legal complexity, as David refused to pay the interest due and Nancy executed releases of a portion of the amount. Finally, under the auspices of the family lawyer, a complete settlement was reached in about 1866. In 1871, Nancy sued David on the original note. David defended on the ground that the note had been endorsed by Nancy "settled in full". Nancy responded that her settlement of the note had been coerced. She testified that David constantly importuned her and her sister, that he called them names, and that he threatened to turn both of them out of the house. The court, summarizing the trial testimony, recorded a portion of her direct testimony as follows:

> He said I had better not say too much, that the carpenter had left a hole, pointing to the door. I could not live there in any kind of peace, unless I had given up. We had no rest, no peace, without doing these things... .

On cross-examination, however, she noted:

I called him a skinner and stripper... . The abuse was, he said a
great deal. He said if we would give it up, we could live and let
live, and such talk. His abuse was all talk. I could have gone
away from the house. I stayed because I thought I had a right. He
never said: "Unless you put a receipt on the note, I will use
violence."
Miller v. Miller, at 488-489.

The trial court found that there was an issue of fact as to whether
the plaintiff had acted under duress in executing the notes.
    In so ruling, the trial court found that there were two essential
questions involved in Nancy's recovery on the loan; the validity of the
initial contract and the invalidity of the settlements, saying:

On the whole we instruct you that the plaintiff is only entitled to
recover, if you should be of opinion, that under a contract with her
brother, based upon a valuable consideration, and fulfilled on her
part, she was entitled to live in his house, the home of her
ancestors, as long as she chose; and that under threats to drive her
out and other ill usage, the defendant exploited and forced the
receipts and settlements from the [sic], without a full valuable
consideration for them. Such receipts and settlements as he
extorted from her in this wrongful way, she may avoid, and only
such. And you must find that such threats were the operative
reason and cause of her action, and that without them, she would
not have signed them. Her freedom in this regard must have been
destroyed by the oppression of the defendant exercised upon her by
means of these threats.

The case of *Miller v. Miller* clearly lists all of the elements in a defense
of duress, but its discussion of two of these is of particular interest: the
nature of the threats and the nature of free will as a matter of fact.
    The trial court, in its instructions to the jury, clearly distinguished
between threats and what may be loosely termed 'persuasion', saying
as follows:

All his importunity, however urgent, or any religious scruples
attempted to be excited about taking interest--the plaintiff not being
shown to be of weak mind--nor alleging that the defendant
succeeded in arousing her religious scruples--will not avoid the
receipts. Only the threats to turn the plaintiff out of the home to
which she was entitled, where she had lived for many years, and
where her sister was, compelling an unwilling and forced action on

her part, will have that effect.

If you find that what the plaintiff did before 1864, was done only in consequence of the defendant's promptings and importunity, and not upon a well-founded fear of being turned out of plaintiff's house, she cannot be relieved as to those things.

The effect of this discussion is two-fold. First, it continues a distinction clearly made in the undue influence cases between persuasion, argumentation, or importunity, and threats or undue influence. Significantly, the court does not say that such actions by one person are not sufficient to overcome the free will of another, but simply that they are not sufficient to avoid a contract. That is, it seems implicit in what the court says that this plaintiff may well have been unwilling to deed over the note to her brother. It may be that she very much desired not to endorse the note but did so under the pressure of the constant bickering and the psychological harassment practiced upon her by her brother.

Several bases can be advanced for the court's policy in this regard, which was clearly the law. It may be, as Dawson suggests, that the court wished to focus the attention on the wrongfulness of the action of the brother; it is not generally considered legally wrongful to persuade or argue in the same way that it is wrongful to threaten bodily harm. Second, the court may have feared the flood of litigation that would result about otherwise valid contracts if they could be called in question upon the statement of one party that he or she had been unwillingly persuaded into entering into the contract, although not threatened or otherwise forced. Finally, it may be that the courts felt that there was an obligation on each individual's part to withstand such pleadings.

The second interesting aspect of this trial court's instructions referred to above is the description of free will.

Before that she only speaks of his pointing to the door, saying the carpenter had left a hole, and that she ought to be kicked out, and seems to have been said in reference to her recriminations upon him. But she says that in 1864, he said: "You (her sister and herself) must give up the $1,000 or leave the house." If you believe the plaintiff it would seem that the last $500, at least, was surrendered in fear of being turned out. It is for you to say, but the impression left upon us by the plaintiff herself was that the threats made before 1866, were not sufficient to excite a well-founded fear of being turned out of home and house, and that she did what she did for the sake of peace.

She can recover only on the ground that the unjustifiable oppression of her brother, in threatening to turn her out of the house, where he had solemnly engaged she should remain as long as she lived, destroyed her freedom, and that she was virtually not assenting to the receipts and settlements. The plaintiff must have had a right to remain in the house under the agreement alleged. The threats of the defendant to turn her out, and his conduct (but without the threats to turn her out the other conduct would not be sufficient), must have so operated on the mind of the plaintiff as to destroy her freedom in the signing of the receipts and making of the settlements. That is, she must have been so constrained by the threats and other conduct that no matter how much she desired to avoid signing the receipts and settlements, and how she strove against it with herself, she was unable to resist the influence of the constraint, and was forced to yield to it. Where one is in prison, or labors under threats of great bodily harm, there is still and always is a possibility of resisting and of suffering the imprisonment or great harm, rather than yield. But the mind may not be able to resist the desire of freedom, or to escape injury, and to be forced to submit. That is duress. So in this case. It was of course possible that the plaintiff might have resisted the threats and left the house. That would depend upon her firmness of mind and attachment to her home. But if her firmness of purpose and attachments were not in your opinion of sufficient strength to resist the influences of the threats, and they overcame her, strive against them as she would, then they destroyed her freedom, and the receipts are not truly her receipts. The threats must have been to exclude her from the house unless she yielded her money. If they were, unless she ceased her charges and recriminations, they amount to nothing. She was only entitled to remain in the house on condition of quiet and civil behavior.

The significance of this language is the causal psychological description which is given of duress. We note, for example, that the court says, "Such threats were the operative *reason* and the *cause* of her action, and that without them, she would not have signed them." The court goes on to say, "Her freedom in this regard must have been destroyed by the oppression of the defendant exercised upon her by means of these threats." The significance of this is that the court suggests that it would not be enough for the defendant merely to have persuaded the plaintiff to sign the note. Rather, the threats must have caused her action. That is, it appears from this opinion that merely yielding with bad grace to a bad bargain would not constitute duress. Rather, there must be a literal inability to resist the threats.

The faculty of free choice between alternatives is referred to as if it were a physical object; the court three times uses the phrase "destroyed" in one form or another, and this is later defined in the following words:

> That is, she must have been so constrained by the threats and other conduct that no matter how much she desired to avoid signing the receipts and settlements, and how she strove against it with herself, she was unable to resist the influence of the constraint and was forced to yield to it ... But if her firmness of purpose and attachments were not in your opinion of sufficient strength to resist the influence of the threats, and they overcame her, strive against them as she would, then they destroyed her freedom and the receipts are not truly her receipts.

The significance of this is that the court portrays the will, the psychological consent which is given to an action, as being literally destroyed so that the challenged action becomes in a sense the action of another and is not the product of the individual's will. The will is usually associated with desires; here the court characterizes the desire and will of the person as being totally in the opposite direction from the action actually taken; the action, in this case signing a receipt, which should be an expression of her will to release her brother from the obligation, is essentially, under the pressure of the threats, a sham. She wills the actual action of writing the release, but she does not will the act of releasing her brother.

This can be seen from the distinction between cases where absolutely no will was present, as where a person's hand was guided in the semblance of writing by another, and where a semblance of will was apparently present but was in fact only an illusion. The court goes on in this case to contrast the existence of choice from the presence of will saying:

> Where one is in prison, or labors under threat of great bodily harm, there is still and always a possibility of resisting and of suffering the imprisonment or great harm, rather than yield. But the mind may not be able to resist the desire of freedom, or to escape injury, and to be forced to submit. That is duress. So in this case. It was of course possible that she could have resisted the threats and left the house.

Here the court is clearly saying that, as Locke (and perhaps the Stoics) held, there is always an alternative range of choices available; except where physical constraint is applied, as where the hand of a person is physically guided in making his signature, there are always two alternatives from which the person under duress may elect. But, the court argued, the existence of the alternatives does not preclude the fact that in a sense the person had no choice, that is, that the election was not a free one, that the person did not choose but was forced to take one path or the other.

Having submitted the issue to the jury, the verdict was for the plaintiff (Nancy) in the amount of $1,666. David appealed, challenging the instructions to the jury that were given as above and some of the evidence which was admitted.

The appellate court did not challenge the definition of free will as eloquently given by the trial court, but nonetheless reversed the trial judge's decision to permit the jury to decide, on the ground that the threat to turn the plaintiff out of the house was not sufficiently imminent to amount to duress, saying as follows:

> We concur with the counsel of the defendant in error that in civil cases the rule as to duress *per minas* has a broader application at the present day than it formerly had. Where a party has the goods or property of another in his power, so as to enable him to exert his control over it to the prejudice of the other, a threat to use this control may be in the nature of the common law duress *per minas*, and enable the person threatened with this pernicious control to avoid a bond or note obtained without consideration, by means of such threats. See *White v. Heylman*, 10 *Casey* 142, where the authorities are collected. But mere threats of injury, in regard to property, without a power over it also, to enable the party to execute his threats, are not in themselves duress per minas, however otherwise they may enter into questions of fraud or extortion: 2 Greenleaf Ev. §301; *Fulton v. Hood*, 10 *Casey* 372; 2 Inst. 483; 1 Black. Com. 130. The constraint which takes away free agency and destroys the power of withholding assent to a contract, must be one which is imminent, and without immediate means of prevention; and be such as would operate on the mind of a person of a reasonable firmness of purpose. A threat to withhold payment of a debt, or to refuse performance of a contract, or to do an injury which may at once be redressed by legal proceeding, will not amount to duress *per minas*. Nor is there a duress *per minas* in equity, which does not exist at law ... *Stouffer v. Latshaw*, 2 *Watts* 168. The power of mind necessary to give assent to a contract is the same in law and equity. A chancellor, it is true, will refuse his aid to enforce specific performance of a contract, for a reason less than that constituting duress *per minas*, or will set aside a bargain for extortion or undue influence operating upon a weak mind, or under circumstances of a confidential relation; but equity will not set aside an agreement on the ground of duress *per minas* alone where the law will refuse to do so.

The appellate court found first of all that her history of the threats to turn her out of the house apparently were made more than two years before the alleged settlement. Moreover, if David had turned her out of the house, Nancy could have sued him to enforce his contract to support her. It may be also that the court was influenced in its opinion that she was not under imminent fear by her remark that she "could have gone away from the house". The appellate court characterized the lack of free will as the existence of a "constraint which takes away free agency and destroys the power of withholding assent to a contract ...". *Miller v. Miller*, at 493.

FRENCH V. SHOEMAKER

The case of *French v. Shoemaker*, 81 U.S. (14 Wall.) 314 (1871) reveals some interesting aspects of the nineteenth-century law of duress, because it concerned a defense of duress made solely upon the ground that the party entering the contract was coerced by his financial straits. In the case of *French v. Shoemaker*, the transaction at issue arose out of land speculation in the mid-nineteenth century in some of the undeveloped areas of the country. Negotiations had been protracted, and French found himself in desperate need of money. He therefore accepted a transaction, that he had consistently refused over the course of the past year. Later he tried to invalidate the transaction on the ground that he had been acting under duress at the time. (*French v. Shoemaker*, at 332). The court said as follows:

> Much discussion to show that a contract or written obligation procured by means of duress is inoperative and void, both at law and in equity is hardly required, as the proposition is not denied by either party.

In this case, the other parties to the contract may well have taken advantage of French's financial needs in that French found himself unable to refuse the proposal which they had begun to make over a year previously. To put the factual matter more accurately, French would have suffered serious financial losses if he had not obtained a $5000 advance, which was part of the contract that he entered with Shoemaker; without the cash money, French could not keep his other financial transactions going. However, the other parties to the contract did not make any overt threats, nor does the court suggest that the bargain was unconscionable. The court discusses the nature of the pressure required for duress as follows:

> Actual violence, even at common law, is not necessary to establish duress, because consent is the very essence of a contract, and if there be compulsion, there is no actual consent, and moral compulsion, such as that produced by threats to take life or to inflict great bodily harm, as well as that produced by imprisonment, is everywhere regarded as sufficient in law to destroy free agency, without which there can be no contract, because in that state of the case there is no consent. *Brown v. Pierce*, 7 *Wallace*, 214. In its more extended sense duress means that degree of constraint or danger, either actually inflicted, or threatened and impending, which is sufficient in severity or in apprehension, to overcome the mind and will of a person of ordinary firmness.

Chitty on Contracts, 217; 2 *Greenleaf on Evidence*, 283.

It can be seen from this language that the court is referring to the distinction between physical force and threats. This is clear from the reference to actual violence in opposition to moral compulsion, where the latter is defined as threats to "take life or inflict great bodily harm". The court can be seen to be establishing three principles: (1) "If there be compulsion, there is no actual consent"; (2) "Moral compulsion ... is everywhere regarded as sufficient in law to destroy free agency", and (3) a contract cannot exist without free agency, "because in that state of the case there is no consent".

Once again we see the usage of the term "destroy" just as it was used in other duress cases. Again, free will or free agency is regarded almost as a physical entity, which can be in a physical sense destroyed.

We also see the distinction between the appearance of consent, such as signing the contract, and the reality of an actual willing of the contractual obligation.

A second point of interest in this paragraph is the reference to "constraint or danger" since the court's later discussion reveals what is meant by "constraint". Shortly after the paragraph quoted, the court discussed the effect of financial need upon the validity of a contract, saying as follows:

Enough appears in the record to convince the court that the respondent was in straitened circumstances, that his business affairs had become complicated, that he was greatly embarrassed with litigations, and that he was in pressing want of pecuniary means, but the court is wholly unable to see that the complainant is responsible for those circumstances or that he did any unlawful act to deprive the respondent of his property, or to create those necessities or embarrassments, or to compel him to do what he acknowledges he did do, which was to yield to the pressure of the circumstances surrounding him, and as a choice of evils accepted the advance of five thousand dollars and the shares assigned him in the new organization as proposed, and voluntarily signed both the agreement and the assignment. Such an act as that of signing those instruments, under the circumstances disclosed in the record, must be regarded both in equity and at law, as a voluntary act, as it was unattended by any act of violence, or threat of any kind, calculated in any degree to intimidate the party or to force the result, or to compel that consent which is the essence of every valid contract. Suppose he consented reluctantly, as he avers, still the fact is that he did consent when he might have refused to affix his signature to the instruments, as he had repeatedly done for the year preceding;

and having consented to the arrangement and signed the instruments he is bound by their terms, and must abide the consequences of his own voluntary act, unless some of his other defenses set up in the answer have a better formulation.
French v.Shoemaker, at 333.

The court gave a laundry list of the actions which the other parties to the contract might have taken, which would have invalidated the contract, but did not take. One, the other parties to the contract did not cause French to be in financial difficulties. Two, Shoemaker did not deprive French of his property by any unlawful act. Three, Shoemaker did not create French's "necessities or embarrassments". Four, Shoemaker did nothing to compel French to yield to the pressure of the circumstances surrounding him. Next, Shoemaker did not use any physical force toward French. Finally, Shoemaker never threatened French.

The question may be raised as to what the court had in mind when it noted that Shoemaker did nothing to create the plaintiff's needs. In general, the cases tend to suggest that one needs to take affirmative action to constrain the other party financially in order to be guilty of duress. In the fairly recent case of *Slade v. Slade* , 310 Ill. App. 77, 33 N.E.2d 951 (1941), an elderly widow had been left well provided for by her husband's will. Her fortune, however, consisted in stock which was effectively controlled by her brother-in-law. He in turn manipulated her finances so that she received no income at all. The stock being her sole source of income, the widow was reduced to dire poverty, and the brother thereby forced her to accept a low offer for the stock. The court held that she could recover in damages for the duress that had been practiced upon her.

The effect of the doctrine developed in *French v. Shoemaker* is that a party who simply deals with someone who is in distress does not by virtue of that fact take the role of an oppressor. This doctrine is also discussed in the case of *Hackley v. Headley, supra* .

The fact that an *action* by the other party is required, whether it consists in creating the oppressed person's hardship or in exploiting it ruthlessly, is important to the concept of constraint developed by the nineteenth-century courts.

In the absence of such an action, as can be seen in *French v. Shoemaker*, the person in financial need is not considered to be under constraint, which is therefore essentially defined as requiring the affirmative action of the other party, beyond merely dealing with someone in financial need.

Additionally, it can be seen from the above-quoted language of *French v. Shoemaker* that the court does not consider the lack of alternatives or the unappealing nature of the alleged alternative as indicating a lack of free consent. The court does not minimize the effectiveness of financial pressure. Rather, it emphasizes that financial pressure may bring about an agreement. The court is in effect holding, however, that such financial pressure is not constraint. In *French v. Shoemaker* the court is clear that French had the choice of signing or refusing to sign, although it acknowledges that if he had refused to sign, he would have suffered grave financial loss. The court says: "[H]e might have refused to affix his signature to the instruments, as he had repeatedly done for the year preceding...". It refers to French's decision as "a choice of evils", but as a voluntary choice. It is significant that the court characterizes French's action not only as a choice of evil alternatives, and as a reluctant consent, but also says that he "yield[ed] to the pressure of the circumstances surrounding him...". A reluctant choice or a choice among undesirable alternatives is, therefore, as a matter of law, a free choice when it is made in the absence of pressure by another party. Financial stress does not invalidate free will as seen by the law.

The significance of the words "choice", "voluntary", "yield", etc., is that the court viewed the action of French's will, again, as a fact. In the court's viewpoint, French had not been coerced into signing the contract. He had, rather, chosen the lesser evil of two undesirable alternatives. He willed that result. It may be true that the result was not one which he wanted, but his signature in complying with the contract, it may be said, was not a mere appearance as it might have been had he signed the contract under fear of imminent death. In the court's view, French freely elected which course to pursue.

WILLIAMS V. BAYLEY

A very famous case in the area of duress is that of *Williams v. Bayley*, 6 Ruling Cases 455, 148 Rev. Rep., 1 H.L. 200 (S. C. 35 L. J. Ch. 717; 12 Jur. N. S. 875; 14 L. T. 802) (1866). In that case a son and his father were both in business in neighboring towns. The father was a coalmaster and also a farmer. One of the sons went into business as a dealer in coke and coal, and the father and son banked at the same bank, the father often maintaining a large balance. The son began to forge his father's name as an endorsement to some of the son's notes. The bank paid no particular attention to the apparent fact of the father's endorsing his son's notes because the father and son were frequently endorsing notes to each other through the medium of the bank in the course of their business. In April 1863, however, the bank became suspicious and demanded a settlement of the account from the father. This "produced the discovery that William Bayley had, in many instances, forged the endorsements of his father, whose liabilities, so created, had become very large". *Williams v. Bayley*. On the twentieth of April, 1863, the concerned parties and their attorneys met at the bank. The total amount owing was discovered to be six or seven thousand pounds. In the course of the discussion, several methods of resolving the issue were apparently suggested, and at one point it was proposed that William Bayley should pay the bank a thousand pounds a year. The banker, however, responded as follows: "We shall have nothing to do with any 1000 pounds a year. If the bills are yours (addressing the father) we are all right; if they are not, we have only one course to pursue; we cannot be parties to compounding a felony." As the court notes, "There was afterwards a conversation, in the course of which the solicitor for the banker said it was 'a serious matter;' and the [father's] solicitor added, 'a case of transportation for life'." (*Williams v. Bayley*, at 457)

In other words, the bankers made clear to the father that they would not accept any kind of delayed payment plan; that if he did not make good the forged endorsements, they would prosecute the son for forgery; and that the penalty for forgery was transportation for life. There was never any serious allegation that the bankers did not realize that the notes had in fact been forged, nor did the father ever, other than in connection with the forced settlement, acknowledge the notes as his own. The attorney general, Sir R. Palmer, argued for the father by comparing the pressure exerted in this case with an older case where a grant of property was set aside because the maker of the deed had been "compelled to accede to the terms from distress and poverty, occasioned by the party procuring the [deed]". (*Williams v. Bayley,* at 462)

In spite of the analogy, however, the attorney general went on to argue that "the pressure that could be exerted on a father under such circumstances is enormous. It is against public policy to allow such agreement, so obtained, to be valid." (*Williams v. Bayley*, at 462-3)

This case was decided in equity, as it was an action by the father to set aside the agreement. It was therefore debated by the lords' chancellor. Cranworth distinguished a mere threat to exercise legal rights from the threat of criminal prosecution against the victim's son, saying:

> I very much agree with the argument of [the bankers' lawyer] that it is not pressure in the sense in which a court of equity sets aside transactions on account of pressure, if the pressure is merely this: "If you do not do such and such an act, I shall reserve all my legal rights, whether against yourself, or against your son." If it had only been, "if you do not take on yourself the debt of your son, we must sue you for it", I cannot think that that amounts to pressure, when the parties are at arm's length, and particularly when as in this case, the parties supposed to be influenced by pressure had the assistance of a solicitor...

However, Lord Cranworth pointed out that the real pressure was not a threat to sue the father but a threat to prosecute the son criminally and, in view of the plain fact of the forgery, to have him exiled from Britain for life. Two of the lords' chancellors also argued the issue of the existence of free will. Lord Cranworth stated:

> The fears of the father were stimulated and operated on to an extent to deprive him of free agency, and to extort an agreement from him for the benefit of the bankers. It appears to me, therefore, that the case comes within the principle upon which a court of equity proceeds in setting aside an agreement where there is inequality between the parties, and one of them takes unfair advantage of the situation of the other and uses undue influence to force an agreement from him.
> *Williams v. Bayley*, at 470.

Several strands of the concept of duress are visible in this case. First, there is the element, which Dawson stressed, of the inequality of bargaining power between the parties and the essential unfairness of the transaction which is extorted. It may well be asked whether the chancellors would have been so eager to void the transaction if in fact a moderate scheme of repayment had been decided upon, as opposed to the extreme settlement of forcing the father to pay the entire amount by mortgaging most of his property.

The second theme is the concept of the wrongfulness of the action engaged in by the bankers, although it is perhaps unclear whether the father's action was criminal. There was considerable discussion among the lords' chancellors as to whether the transaction was a form of the crime known as misprision of a felony, which consists in concealing the evidence of a crime. Certainly, the court considered, as revealed by the above quotation, that it was against public policy for persons to bargain with the means given to the courts for the enforcement of criminal liability. Nonetheless, the plain language of the opinion suggests that the lack of free will was as much an issue as any of these. The interesting aspect of the case, however, is that it appears in this case that it was the total unacceptability of one of the father's alternative courses of action that was considered to have destroyed his free will. That is, it is clear that the lords' chancellor thought that the father had two possible courses of action: to accede to the demand that he pay the notes or to see his son condemned to life in Botany Bay. Remembering that there is no jury in the courts of chancery, and therefore that the issues of law and fact tend to blend together, it is interesting to note that the presentation of these alternatives itself was considered by the lords' chancellor to destroy the power of freely electing between them.

The lords' chancellor affirmed the decision of the lower court that the agreement was invalid.

SKEATE V. BEALL

In the case of *Skeate v. Beall*, the English appellate court had a chance to consider the effect of duress of goods upon a contract. *Skeate v. Beall*, (XLII 113 Eng. Rep. 688; 11 A.D.&C. 984; 9 L.J.A.B. 233 (1841)). Skeate was Beall's landlord, and Beall fell behind in the rent, owing Skeate about 3 pounds 7s. 6d. In early February 1838, Skeate took possession of Beall's household goods by use of the legal process called "distraint", and refused to release them unless Beall signed an agreement to pay 20 pounds, which was the amount that Skeate claimed to be due. Skeate also threatened to sell the furniture. Beall signed, and Skeate relinquished possession of the furniture. Beall later paid the 3 pounds but refused to pay the remaining 16 pounds 2s. 6d., stating that he did not owe the additional amount, which coincidentally also represented the precise amount that he claimed his furniture, etc., was worth. Skeate sued Beall on the agreement, and Beall defended on the ground that he had signed the memorandum under duress. The jury agreed with Beall, and the verdict was therefore in his favor. Skeate, however, moved that judgment be entered in his favor, despite the jury's finding (*non obstante veredicto*), on the ground that duress of goods could not as a matter of law be sufficient duress to invalidate a contract. The court agreed and entered judgment in Skeate's favor, whereupon Beall appealed.

The question, therefore, in this case is one of law; the issue is not whether lack of his furniture in fact forced Beall to sign the agreement, since the jury has decided that it did so, but whether such pressure will be considered such duress as will invalidate the contract.

The first point to notice is that the contract at issue was valid unless it was entered under duress. Since Beall admitted that he owed something to Skeate, the legal means by which Skeate got possession of the furniture was proper. Therefore, Skeate's relinquishment of his right to possession was adequate consideration for the agreement signed by Beall; having signed the contract, Beall was obligated, if it was valid, to pay the twenty pounds. The amount of rent actually owed was no longer a question when Beall entered the new agreement, since Skeate was not suing for the rent but on the note.

In the appeal, Beall's lawyer argued that if Beall had paid the entire amount, he would have been able to recover the excess back under the rule expressed in *Astley v. Reynolds*: "It is difficult to understand why any distinction should be made, in this respect, between an actual payment and a written engagement to pay; the probability, indeed, is that a party would be more cautious in making a payment than in writing a memorandum." *Skeate v. Beall*, at 689.

Skeate's lawyer relied on the rule that duress of goods would not invalidate a contract, arguing that the authority of *Astley v. Reynolds* had essentially been weakened by intervening decisions. The court agreed with Skeate, arguing as follows:

> We consider the law to be clear, and founded on good reason, that an agreement is not void because made under duress of goods. There is no distinction in this respect between a deed and an agreement not under seal; and, with regard to the former, the law is laid down in 2 Inst. 483, and Sheppard's Touchstone, p. 61, and the distinction pointed out between duress of, or menace to, the person, and duress of goods. The former is a constraining force, which not only takes away the free agency, but may leave no room for appeal to the law for a remedy: a man, therefore, is not bound by the agreement which he enters into under such circumstances; but the fear that goods may be taken or injured does not deprive any one of his free agency who possesses that ordinary degree of firmness which the law requires all to exert. See *The Duke de Cadaval v. Collins* , 4 A. & E. 858. *Wilson v. Ray* , 10 A. & E. 82. It is not necessary now to enter into the consideration of cases in which it has been held that money paid to redeem goods wrongfully seized, or to prevent their wrongful seizure, may be recovered back in an action for money had and received; for the distinction between those cases and the present, which must be taken to be that of an agreement, [991] not compulsorily but voluntarily entered into, is obvious.
> *Skeate v. Beall*, at 690.

There are several points of interest in this argument. The first is contained in the sentence:

> [A threat to one's person] is a constraining force, which not only takes away the free agency, but may leave no room for appeal to the law for a remedy: a man, therefore, is not bound by the agreement which he enters into under such circumstances; but the fear that goods may be taken or injured does not deprive any one of his free agency who possesses that ordinary degree of firmness which the law requires all to exert.

In this sentence, the progression in the law's treatment of threats can be clearly seen. Originally, as the discussion above of earlier authorities shows, only threats of murder or maiming were considered sufficient to overcome a man of reasonable firmness, because a mere beating or other physical harm short of death could be recompensed by a suit for battery. Later, it was decided a person did not have to be willing to withstand any form of physical harm, and if the threatened harm actually caused such fear that he could not resist, a contract signed under such conditions was voidable. The court in *Skeate v. Beall*, however, refused to extend this doctrine to a threatened loss of property, holding that a reasonably firm person *ought* to be required to resist such pressure. The significant point here is that the court did not deny that such a threatened loss might actually as a matter of psychological fact force some people to sign contracts; the court held that *regardless of the reality of such pressure* (evidenced here by the jury's finding of fact, which could not easily be and was not here challenged on appeal), a contract entered under those conditions was still entered voluntarily. The voluntary nature of the contract arises from the fact that the party coerced always had the choice of suffering the destruction and suing for damages, and a reasonably firm man, according to the court, had sufficient presence of mind to elect voluntarily to pay the demanded ransom, rather than to wait for a court to vindicate his rights.

Atiyah interprets *Skeate v. Beall* as mistakenly resting on the notion that some kinds of pressure overcome the will, while others do not. He argues that the rule should rest rather on the kinds of threat. This interpretation seems to me mistaken, although the decision is not without ambiguity. A better reading is that the court did look to the kind of pressure, as well as to its effect. (Atiyah, *Freedom of Contract, supra* at 436)

The second point of interest, however, is the murky way in which the court seeks to distinguish the earlier cases, such as *Astley v. Reynolds*, saying:

> It is not necessary now to enter into the consideration of cases in which it has been held that money paid to redeem goods wrongfully seized, or to prevent their wrongful seizure, may be recovered back in an action for money had and received; for the distinction between those cases and the present, which must be taken to be that of an agreement, not compulsorily but voluntarily entered into, is obvious.

The distinction is not at all obvious, however.

One basis for distinguishing *Astley v. Reynolds*, at least, would be that the pawnbroker's detention of the goods there was clearly wrongful, since the pawnbroker was obligated to give them back upon the payment of the agreed-upon amount. The court in *Skeate v. Beall* appears to be stressing the wrongful nature of the detention in such cases, as opposed to the proper use of distraint in this case. Indeed, the court goes on to say, essentially agreeing with Beall's counsel, that there could be no logical difference between paying money and agreeing to do so, that even if Beall had paid the full amount, he could not sue to recover the excess, since the payment would have been voluntarily made, and therefore the specific legal procedure (action for money had and received) would not be available to Beall, although it was afforded to the plaintiff in *Astley v. Reynolds*.

Yet this distinction seems odd, because the court goes on to suggest that even if the detention was in fact wrongful, Beall's only remedy was to sue for damages. The significance of this specific remark is that the court noted that because some rent was due, Beall could not replevy (obtain immediate possession by court order) his property. The distraint, therefore, was lawful to the extent that it would not be set aside, but might have [been] unlawful so as to permit Beall to be recompensed for the excess value of his goods over the amount actually owed. In other words, if Skeate seized goods worth 20 pounds to secure a debt of three pounds and Beall paid the 20 pounds and sued, Beall he could recover 17 pounds since the distraint was excessive in that amount. Technically, on this analysis, Beall would not be recovering for money had and received, but for excessive use of a legal process.

Given the rigidity of forms of procedure in the English courts at the time, this highly technical distinction is not unusual nor unsupportable. But this discussion is inconsistent with the court's earlier reasoning concerning the consistency of his case and *Astley v. Reynolds*; the *Astley* court had also noted that a legal remedy might be available but had rejected the idea that that was inconsistent with duress because an action "might not do his business" if the coerced person was in desperate need of the property. The *Astley* holding may be stated as being that one is not required to resist an unlawful taking of one's property. Here, if the distraint was proper, the court need not worry about whether there was a remedy at law, because there could be no duress anyway without a wrongful action; but, if the distraint was unlawful, then logically the case fell, as the court recognized, within the rule in *Astley* .

Therefore, the court's holding cannot readily be reconciled with *Astley* .

CAREW V. RUTHERFORD

The Massachussetts case of *Carew v. Rutherford,* 106 Mass. 1 (1870) presents several interesting questions of free will. Carew was a master mechanic, a stonemason, who had a contract to furnish cut stone for the building of the Roman Catholic cathedral in South Boston. The contract price was $80,000. Carew had a large number of stonemasons working for him, but according to his story, the number was not enough to permit the completion of the contract, so he sent some of the stone out of state to be cut in New York. Such subcontracting, however, was a violation of the rules of the Stonemasons' Association. This was an organization of stonemasons, principally workingmen, and an organization to which Carew did not belong. The organization voted, having noticed that Carew had violated their rules by sending the stone out of state, to fine him $500. When he repeatedly refused to pay the $500, the Stonemasons' Association called a strike, and the majority of Carew's workers left his employ. After a week or ten days without any workers, Carew was forced to pay over the $500. He did so and then sued for the return of the money. The trial court found the facts as above described but concluded that no remedy was available. There was no contract between himself and the Association since he was not a member.

Technically, Carew's suit contained two counts, one in tort (that is, for a personal injury), and the other for money had and received.

It is apparent from the beginning that the court was more in sympathy with Carew than with the Stonemasons' Association but faced several problems in deciding the case. There were two major problems entwined in the court's opinion. The first was whether there was a proper legal form for such a lawsuit. No precedent existed which was precisely like this one. The second problem was whether the stonemasons could be liable to return the money when they had done nothing more than that which they had a right to do, which was to refuse to work. After noting the greater power possessed by a group of individuals, the court stated gracefully that "one of the aims of the common law has always been to protect every person against the wrongful acts of every other person, whether committed alone or in culmination with others; and it has provided an action for injuries done by disturbing a person in the enjoyment of any right or privilege which he has." The court reasoned as follows with regard to the existence of a legal cause of action for the injury which Carew had suffered:

> Every man has a right to determine what branch of business he will pursue, and to make his own contracts with whom he pleases and on the best terms he can. He may change from one occupation to

another, and pursue as many different occupations as he pleases, and competition in business is lawful. He may refuse to deal with any man or class of men. And it is no crime for any number of persons, without an unlawful object in view, to associate themselves together and agree that they will not work for or deal with certain men or classes of men, or work under a certain price, or without certain conditions.

The *Carew* court tried to invoke cases involving the general exploitation of the other party, as where payment had been induced "by menaces, duress or taking undue advantage of the other's situation" or cases where money had been received "tortiously without any color of contract or cases dealing with duress of goods". See *Carew v. Rutherford*, at 11 and 12.

> Without undertaking to lay down a precise rule applicable to all cases, we think it clear that the principle which is established by all the authorities cited above, whether they are actions of tort for disturbing a man in the exercise of his rights and privileges, or to recover back money tortiously obtained, extends to a case like the present. We have no doubt that a conspiracy against a mechanic, who is under the necessity of employing workmen in order to carry on his business, to obtain a sum of money from him, which he is under no legal liability to pay, by inducing his workmen to leave him, and by deterring others from entering into his employment, or by threatening to do this, so that he is induced to pay the money demanded, under a reasonable apprehension that he cannot carry on his business without yielding to the illegal demand, is an illegal, if not a criminal, conspiracy; that the acts done under it are illegal; and that the money thus obtained may be recovered back, and, if the parties succeed in injuring his business, they are liable to pay all the damage thus done to him. It is a species of annoyance and extortion which the common law has never tolerated.

The interesting thing about this case is that it implicitly recognizes the circumstance of need and its importance in the duress of goods cases. The reason that Carew was induced to comply with the workmen's demand was that he was "under a reasonable apprehension that he cannot carry on his business without yielding to the illegal demand...". That is, Carew was not in fear of his life, he was not in fear of having his goods destroyed or an imminent fear of imprisonment. The fear was that he would lose money. The courts broke through the old forms of action simply to say that such an attaining of money is wrongful, that the law will not permit money to be obtained freely in that manner.

The difficulty which the court faced, though, in addition to the lack of precedent on which to rely and the lack of relationship between this action and the traditional forums of lawsuits, was the apparent contradiction of the workmen's freedom. At this time, the formation of the Association of Stonemasons was not, according to the Superior Court of Massachusetts, illegal. Nor was it illegal for them to agree not to work except upon certain conditions. As the court strongly put it:

> This freedom of labor and business has not always existed. When our ancestors came here, many branches of labor and business were hampered by legal restrictions created by English statutes; and it was a long time before the community fully understood the importance of freedom in this respect ... . One of the colonial acts ... punished by fine and imprisonment such indisposed persons as may take the liberty to oppress and wrong their neighbors by taking excessive wages for their work, or unreasonable prices for merchandises or other necessary commodities as may pass from man to man ... . Another act regulated the price of bread...the towns fixed the prices of labor, provisions and several articles of merchandise, as late as the time of the Revolutionary War.

Having thus strongly supported the policy of freedom of contract, the court noted that "all persons who have been born and educated here, and are obliged to begin life without property, know that freedom to choose their own occupation and make their own contracts not only elevates their condition, but secures to skill and industry and economy their appropriate advantages". *Carew v. Rutherford*, at 15. In its statement, of course, the court expressly adopted the economic policy of *laissez faire* as well as the concept of a civil right to economic freedom. That is, the court was holding that freedom of contract would promote the greatest good and greatest justice as well as generally promoting freedom. If, however, freedom to choose their own occupation would secure to skill and industry its own appropriate advantages, then why was it wrongful for the workmen to unite against the stonemason? The court decided that "freedom does not imply a right in one person, either alone or in culmination with others, to disturb or annoy another, either directly or indirectly in his lawful business or occupation, or to threaten him with annoyance or injury for the purpose of compelling him to buy his peace ...". *Carew v. Rutherford*, at 15.

Therefore, on one court's view, the workmen could unite and could strike lawfully to obtain higher wages or additional conditions of their work; they could not, however, lawfully strike to obtain a payment to their association to enforce the rules of that association where the master mechanic was not a member of it and therefore had no contractual obligation to the association. Such an exercise of their economic power was, in the view of this mid-nineteenth-century court, extortion and entitled the stonemason to the return of his money.

HOUGH V. HUNT

The Supreme Court of Ohio in 1826 decided a case of economic duress, *The Administrators of Hough v. Hunt*, 2 Ohio (2 Ham.) 495, 15 Am. Dec. 569 (1826). Hough was deeply in debt in September 1818 and was being pressed for payment of a loan due to the Branch Bank of the United States at Lexington. Being under such economic pressure, he went to defendant Hunt for a loan of money in the amount of $2600. Hunt agreed to lend Hough $10,000 upon the condition that Hough would buy 593 acres of land at $20 per acre. The land, however, was worth only about $10 per acre. Hough, of course, was never able to make the payments, and the full $10,000 was never advanced. Instead, by September 1819, Hough was dead. His heirs sued in Chancery (equity) to have the contract for land cancelled and the loan from Hunt to Hough declared paid. Hough's heirs' lawyers argued:

> The purchaser [Hough] was in distressed circumstances; and here the principle to be extracted from the cases does not appear to be that the distress of one party affords proof of *imposition* by the other, but rather that the distress has rendered the first *incompetent to act freely*, and that therefore there need be no fraud on the other side.

Hunt's lawyers, on the other hand, argued that the mere inequality of the price demanded and the knowledge of Hough's financial circumstances were not enough to set aside the transaction, claiming that the law was that the inequality which was challenged "must be so strong and manifest as to shake the conscience and confound the judgment of any man of common sense...". *Hough v. Hunt*, at 501.

The court relied upon the simple fact that no one in Hough's position would voluntarily have entered upon the transaction at issue. The court noted that "the imprudence of the proceeding, on the part of Hough, was so gross that it could be justly attributed to no other cause". *Hough v. Hunt*, at 502.

The court then stated the law with regard to those who deal with a person in distress:

> When a person is encumbered with debts, and that fact is known to a person with whom he contracts, who avails himself of it to exact an unconscionable bargain, equity will relieve upon account of the advantage and hardship. Where the inadequacy of price is so great that the mind revolts at it, the court will lay hold on the slightest circumstances of oppression or advantage to rescind the contract. *Hough v. Hunt*, at 502-503.

It is significant that in this case there is no suggestion that Hunt was responsible for Hough's being in distress. Hunt's only fault was that he had preyed upon that distress to exact a grossly unfair bargain, which the court would not enforce.

WILKERSON V. BISHOP

The case of *Wilkerson v. Bishop* 47 Tenn. (7 Coldw.) 24 (1869) presents an interesting case in its description of the effect of the Civil War upon ordinary commercial contracts. In 1857 the plaintiff, Wilkerson, agreed to sell the defendant, Bishop, a tract of land in eastern Tennessee. Bishop was unable to pay for the land, and in 1863 it was sold to a man named McIntyre. McIntyre paid $1530 in Confederate money to Wilkerson. In 1863, the court noted: "The Rebel authorities at this time held possession of east Tennessee, and the country was under military occupation and control." *Wilkerson v. Bishop*, at 26. Wilkerson sued Bishop in November 1864, seeking essentially to undo the transaction with McIntyre and to enforce his vendor's lien upon the property. In other words, Wilkerson was seeking to enforce the original agreement with Bishop, although McIntyre had not paid for the property. The ground given by Wilkerson for setting aside the payment by McIntyre was that he, Wilkerson, had accepted the payment in Confederate money under duress, arguing that

> it was generally understood in the community that E. Kirby Smith, the general in command of the Rebel forces in this region, had issued an order requiring all persons to accept Confederate money in payment of debts; and that disobedience to the order might subject persons, and especially Union men, at the pleasure of the military authorities to forced transportation to the south, and imprisonment. Men of known Union sentiments were objects of suspicion, and the situation was one usually of some peril, as was generally understood.

The trial court agreed that the deed to McIntyre and the receipt of money by Wilkerson from McIntyre were both under duress, and essentially ordered the transaction undone.

There are two points of interest in the appellate opinion in this case. The first is the court's statement that mere danger will not invalidate a contract.

> When threats, or other attempts at intimidation, are proven, then the fact of the danger to which the party disregarding the threat is exposed, is a fact, which, proven in connection with the threat, may complete the duress. But mere proof of the existence of the danger, without proof that it in fact, operated upon the mind of the party, or that such threats or other means were employed as must tend to cause it to operate upon the mind, will not be sufficient to

establish the fact of duress. If it were otherwise, every contract, the consideration of which was Confederate money, entered into during the reign of terror spoken of by the witnesses in this case, might be set aside. To constitute duress, the danger must not only exist, but must be shown to have actually operated upon the mind, and to have constituted the controlling motive for the performance of the act sought to be avoided.

Second, the court recognized the factual difficulty of determining whether a person had acted under duress, saying:

It is very difficult to declare what circumstances of fear and terror, operating upon the mind of a party, shall constitute such duress as shall avoid a contract; for, from the nature of the case, no testimony can show with certainty what the actual mental condition of the party was.

Having noted the difficulty of proving it, the court cited the following evidence as tending to show that Wilkerson did not act under duress: (l) No threats were made by anyone to induce him to act; (2) he did not object at the time that the Confederate money was paid; (3) he had been anxious to have the transaction consummated; (4) part of the money paid in the transaction had been paid in bank notes at his request; (5) he received payment of Confederate money for another debt which was owed to him at the same time without objection; and (6) he invested the money into tobacco at a later date. Therefore, the appellate court found *as a matter of fact* that Wilkerson had not acted under duress even though he may have acted in circumstances of great danger.

APPENDIX C

Encyclopedia of Law Analysis

The American and English Encyclopedia of Law (1899) contains an interesting and instructive discussion of the state of the law of duress, particularly as it involved consideration of the subjective effect of the threat on the particular victim. It is from the end of the nineteenth century, and is worth quoting at length:

The Rule of the Roman Law differed from that of the old common law, and its doctrine accorded more with reason and with that which, according to what is believed to be the weight of modern authority, is now prevalent in the *United States*. Wharton, in his work on contracts, vol. § 147, says: "In the Roman law we have several rulings to the effect that in determining whether consent was extorted by fear we are to take into consideration the physical condition, the sex, the mental and nervous condition, the education, and the peculiar social and domestic relations of the party threatened."

It is to be remarked, that seeing all persons have not the same courage to resist violence and threatening, and that many are so weak and fearful that they cannot stand out against the least impressions, we ought not to limit the protection of the laws against threatenings and violence so as to restrain only such acts as are capable to overcome persons of the greatest courage and intrepedity. But it is just likewise to protect the weakest and most fearful, and it is chiefly on their account that the laws punish all acts of violence and oppression. Domat's Civil Law, pt. I, bk, I, tit. 18, § 2, art. 1244.

The civil law still recognizes this as the proper test to ascertain whether or not duress exists in the particular case. "We judge of the degree of fear by the quality of the person on whom it is exercised and by the circumstances which cause it." (Fieffe'-Lacroix, tom. I, p. 99). Mr. Bishop thus lends the weight of his authority to the proposition as stated in the text: "In duress, there are some propositions of law, or, at least, propositions accepted in the common-law courts, which seem a little technical. In reason, any lawful exercise of physical force, the effect whereof is to induce a person to become a party to an apparent contract, should be deemed duress. And the test of it should be simply and only, whether or not, in the particular instance, it produced this effect.

Not quite so, we have seen, is the language of the books; yet the authorities are not so conclusive against this view as to render hopeless the urging of it upon an intelligent court, in a proper case." *Bishop on Contracts*, § 730.

Statements of Existing Doctrine in the United States--Reason Therefor--In the case of *Jordan v. Elliott*, 12 W.N.C. (Pa.) 56, 22 Am. L. Reg. N.S. 180, where a note had been obtained from a woman seventy-seven years old, in payment of a debt due by her son, by means of implied threats, which, considering the state of her health, were regarded as sufficient to have coerced her will, the court said: "As we have already said, the fantastic heroics of Jordan would not have been sufficient to induce a courageous man to do that which he was not disposed; hence, if this rule is to be applied to the case in hand, the defense is insufficient. But fortunately for the weak and timid, courts are no longer governed by this harsh and inequitable doctrine, which seems to have considered only a very vigorous and athletic manhood, overlooking entirely women and men of weak nerves." Pothier regards this rule as too rigid, and approves the better doctrine, that regard must be had to the age, sex, and condition of the parties, since that fear which would be insufficient to influence a man in the prime of life and of military character might be deemed sufficient to avoid the contract of a woman, or man in the decline of life. Evans's Poth. on Oblig., i. 18. And we think the opinion of Mr. Evans expresses the doctrine which is now approved by the judicial mind, both of this country and of England; that is, that any contract produced by actual intimidation ought to be held void, whether as arising from a result of merely personal infirmity or from circumstances which might produce a like effect upon persons of ordinary firmness.

In the case of *Earle v. Norfolk, etc., Hosier Co.*, 36 N.J. Eq. 192, it was held that wherever a contract is made under and because of a pressure which destroys free agency, whether such pressure be exercised by physical force, threats, importunity, or any other species of physical or mental coercion, it may be avoided for duress. In this case the vice-chancellor said: All that can be safely said in the way of formulating a definition of what the law calls undue influence is to say that whatever destroys free agency and constrains the person whose act is brought in judgment to do what is against his will, and what he would not have done if left to himself, is undue influence, whether the control be exercised by physical force, threats, importunity, or any other species of mental or physical coercion. The extent or degree of the influence is quite immaterial, for the test is, Was the influence, whether slight or powerful, sufficient to destroy free agency and render the act brought in judgment rather the result of the determination of the mind of another than the expression of the mind of the actor?"

In *Parmentier v. Pater*, 13 Oregon 121, where a debtor obtained the relinquishment of a debt from his creditor, a man of weak mind, by threats which, though not of such a character as are calculated to operate on a person of ordinary intelligence, health, and character, were shown to have actually operated to coerce the creditor's will, it was held that the relinquishment might be avoided for duress. In this case Mr. Justice Thayer, speaking for the court, said: "It was claimed upon the argument that, in order to constitute duress by threats, they must be of such a character as are calculated to operate on a person of ordinary firmness, and inspire a just fear of injury. This is frequently said by courts and text writers. Bouvier, in his *Law Dictionary*, says it; but he immediately adds the following: "The age, sex, state of health, temper, and disposition of the party, and other circumstances calculated to give greater or less effect to the violence or threats, must be taken into consideration." It would be very remarkable if these circumstances could not be taken into consideration in such a case; and yet I do not see how the test that "the violence or threats must be such as are calculated to operate on a person of ordinary firmness" is consistent therewith. The doctrine of duress, as understood at common law, was also alluded to, but the duress claimed in this case to have been resorted to by the appellant was of a different character. * * * It was a restraint or fear incited by threats that an impending calamity would befall the unfortunate Parmentier unless he complied with the demands of the appellant. The threats may have been vague, and the danger remote; but they were just as effectual in the accomplishment of their purpose as a double-barrel shotgun would have been, if loaded and leveled at the party's head. * * * Persons of a "weak or cowardly nature" are the very ones that need protection. The courageous can usually protect themselves. Capricious and timid persons are generally the ones that are influenced by threats, and it would be great injustice to permit them to be robbed by the unscrupulous because they are so unfortunately constituted. The important question in the case was whether the appellant was indebted to Louis Parmentier, as testified to by the respondent. If it be true that he was so indebted, then he should have paid it, notwithstanding he had succeeded by artifice in securing a surrender of the evidence of the debt. That a person should, in such a case, be allowed to profit by his own wrong, would be a monstrous proposition."

This rule was recognized by the Court of Appeals of Illinois in a case where a defendant was being sued on a note given by him on

account of the implied threats of the payee to prosecute him for larceny, of which crime he was in fact innocent. The court said: "The fact, if it was one, that appellee did not act as a reasonable man in yielding to threats in signing the note might be a circumstance from which the jury might find he did not yield and sign the note on that account, but it is not an estoppel to the plea of duress."
Overstreet v. Dunlap, 56 Ill. App. 487 (1894).

In 1915, Roscoe Pound noted that the actual cases tended toward a subjective criterion, although courts were divided in their statement of the rule.[1] He briefly discussed four aspects of the progression from an objective to a subjective standard, in arguing that the subjective standard was the proper one: preventing fraud; "maintaining the social interest in security of transactions"; individualism; and "reluctance to set aside acts done in due legal form."[2] Fraud and impairment of the parties' ability to rely on contractual agreements were two fears expressed in connection with the proposed subjective standard; if a party to a contract could impeach that contract by simply alleging that the circumstances and conduct of the other party had coerced him, even though such circumstances were not such as would have intimidated an ordinary person, then persons would not be able to rely upon the bargains which they had entered. Pound felt that these interests were legitimate, but they could be accomodated by "requiring a proper quantum of proof" and "by treating considerations of what a reasonable man would do as of evidentiary value."[3] On the other hand, Pound argued that objective standard represented "extreme individualism" and an undue regard for the formalities of contracts.[4] By "extreme individualism" Pound probably meant the notion that each individual was expected to look out for his own interests with a reasonable degree of resolution.

NOTES

CHAPTER ONE

1.   See Eugene Kamenka, *Ethical Foundations of Marxism*, London, Routledge & Kegan Paul, 1972; hereinafter "Kamenka"; Shlomo Avineri, *The Social and Political Thought of Karl Marx*, London, Cambridge University Press, 1968, hereinafter "Avineri".

2.   Karl Marx, 'On the Jewish Question' in Karl Marx, Frederick Engels, *Collected Works*, Vol. 3, New York, International Publishers, 1976, hereinafter "3 *Collected Works*", p. 164; also in Lloyd D. Easton and Kurt H. Guddat, *Writings of the Young Marx on Philosophy and Society*, New York, Doubleday & Co., 1967, p. 237, hereinafter "*E and G*." Where parallel references are given, the translation is from the "*Collected Works*" series unless otherwise noted, and references will be to the appropriate volume thereof, e.g. "5 *Collected Works*." Frequently cited works by Marx or Engels will be referred to by title only after the first complete reference.

3.   Karl Marx and Frederick Engels, *The German Ideology*, in Karl Marx, Frederick Engels, *Collected Works*, Vol. 5, London, Lawrence & Wishert, 1976, p. 91 hereinafter 5 *Collected Works*; *E and G*, p. 409; *The German Ideology* in Robert C. Tucker, *The Marx-Engels Reader*, New York, W.W. Norton & Co., 1972, p. 113, hereinafter "Tucker". See also Karl Marx, *Capital*, in Tucker, p. 192.

4.   Karl Marx, *Capital* in Tucker p. 196; *The German Ideology*, 5 *Collected Works*, pp. 90-91; *E and G*, p. 414.

5.   See Alexander Balinsky, *Marx's Economics, Origin and Development*, Lexington, Mass., D. C. Heath and Co., 1970, p. 41. But see James F. Becker, *Marxian Political Economy*, London, Cambridge University Press, p. 3.

6.   See, e.g., Karl Marx, 'Preface' to *A Contribution to a Critique of Political Economy,* 1859, trans. by T.B. Bottomore, in Lord Lloyd of Hampstead, *Introduction to Jurisprudence*, New York, Praeger Publishers, 1972, p. 655. See also Karl Marx, *Grundrisse*, trans. by David McLellan, New York, Harper & Row, 1972, pp. 16-17, hereinafter "McLellan".

7.   'On the Jewish Question', 3 *Collected Works*, p. 167; *E and G*, pp. 234-237.

8.   See, e.g., 'On the Jewish Question', 3 *Collected Works*, p. 167; *E and G*, pp. 240-241.

9.   *Grundrisse*, McLellan, p. 111; See also Karl Marx, *Grundrisse*: *Foundations of the Critique of Political Economy*, trans. by

Martin Nicolaus, New York, Random House, 1973, hereinafter "Nicolaus".

10.   See Alexander Balinsky, *Marx's Economics: Origin and Development*, Lexington, Massachusetts, D. C. Heath & Company, 1970.

11.   Karl Marx, '*Enquête Ouvrière*', *Revue Socialiste*, April 20, 1880, reprinted in T. B. Bottomore and M. Rubel, *Karl Marx, Selected Writings in Sociology and Social Philosophy*, London, Watts & Co., 1956, pp. 204 and 302, hereinafter "Bottomore and Rubel".

12.   Karl Marx ,'Preface' to the '*Enquête Ouvrière*',' *Revue Socialiste*, April 20, 1880, quoted in Bottomore and Rubel, p. 203.

13.   Karl Marx, *Eighteenth Brumaire of Louis Napoleon*, in Tucker, pp. 436 f.

14.   Roberto Mangabiera Unger, Lecture, 'Law and Social Theory', Spring, 1976, Harvard University; see also Kamenka, p. 6.

15.   Karl Marx, *The Civil War in France*, in Tucker, pp. 526 f.

16.   For a similar comment, see Alexander Balinsky, *Marx's Economics*, *supra*, p. 49.

17.   See Karl Marx, *Grundrisse*, Nicolaus p. 472.

18.   Ernest Mandel, *The Formation of the Economic Thought of Karl Marx;1843 to Capital*, trans. by Brian Pearce, London, Monthly Review Press, 1971, especially pp. 120 f.

19.   See, e.g., Erich Fromm, 'Foreword', to *Karl Marx: Early Writings, E and G*, p. viii; Shlomo Avineri, *The Social and Political Thought of Karl Marx*, London, Cambridge University Press, 1975, p. 123.

20.   Eugene Kamenka, *The Ethical Foundations of Marxism*, London, Routledge & Kegan Paul, 1972.

21.   See *The German Ideology*, 5 *Collected Works*, pp. 35-36; Tucker, p. 118; *E and G*, p. 424.

22.   Karl Marx, *Grundrisse*, trans. by David McLellan, New York, Harper and Row, 1971, p. 131.

23.   *The German Ideology* in 5 *Collected Works,* p.91; E and G, p.471.

24.   The phrases "juridical illusion" and "illusion of lawyers" in the Easton and Guddat translation or "illusion of the jurists" in the *Collected Works* version are assumed here to be synonymous.

25.   Roscoe Pound, *Jurisprudence*, St. Paul, Minn., West Publishing Co., 1959, p.172. See also pp. 170-174. The will theory, assuming for the moment that there is one such theory, emphasizes the subjective nature of legally significant acts, particularly in the sphere of promises, and that philosophical exposition of the role of the will in creating legal relationships affected the development of contract law.

26.   To utilize for a moment the terminology of philosophy of

science, if Marx were perfectly consistent in his endeavour to be a social scientist, which I will contend he was not, his sentences about the content of other theories of society would be "observation sentences" about the subject matter of his inquiries into the nature of ideology, while he would also formulate theoretical remarks about the nature of those rival theories. On the other hand, as a critic, Marx would deal with those same theories on a theoretical level. This is complicated by Marx' view of himself as transcending contemporary theory.

27.   *The German Ideology*, 5 *Collected Works*, pp. 51-52; Karl Marx, 'Comments on James Mill, *Elémens d'économie politique*', 3 *Collected Works*, pp. 227-228; See also *Grundrisse*, McLellan, pp. 74-75.

28.   *The German Ideology*, 5 *Collected Works*, p. 91; *E and G*, p. 471. Emphasis supplied. *E and G* translation.

29.   Robert Payne, *Marx*, New York, Simon & Schuster, 1968, p. 43.

30.   Payne, *Marx, supra*, p. 43.

31.   Franz Mehring, *Karl Marx: the Story of his Life*, trans. Edward Fitzgerald,   London, George Allen and Unwin Ltd., 1951, p. 10.

32.   K. Marx, 'Letter to His Father', November 10, 1837, Karl Marx, Frederick Engels,   *Collected Works*, Vol.1, New York, International Publishers, 1976, pp.10-21; *E and G*, pp. 40-50.

33.   Marx, 'Letter to His Father', 1 *Collected Works*, pp. 15 and 19; *E and G*, pp. 43 and 47.

34.   Payne, *Marx, supra*, p. 78; Mehring, *Karl Marx, supra*, p.10.

35.   Saul K. Padover, *Karl Marx: An Intimate Biography*, New York, McGraw-Hill Book Company, 1978, pp.73-74; Payne, *Marx, supra*, p. 78.

36.   Karl Marx, 'The Philosophy Manifesto of the Historical School of Law', 1 *Collected Works*, p. 203.

37.   'Letter to his Father', 1 *Collected Works*, pp. 12-17.

38.   See, e.g., Karl Marx, 'Contribution to Critique of Hegel's Philosophy of Law', 3 *Collected Works*, pp. 161, 165; *E and G*, pp. 252-215; Bottomore, pp. 59-198.

39.   'Letter to his Father', *supra*.

40.   'On the Jewish Question', 3 *Collected Works*, pp. 161, 165; *E and G*, pp. 222, 235.

41.   Karl Marx, *Capital*, in Robert C. Tucker, *The Marx-Engels Reader*, New York, W. W. Norton & Co., Inc., 1972, p. 264.

42.   Mehring, *Karl Marx, supra*, p. 10.

43.   *E and G*, p. 129

44.   *E and G*, p. 96.
45.   *E and G*, p. 97.
46.   *Loc. cit.*
47.   'Contribution to the Critique of Hegel's *Philosophy of Law*. Introduction" 3 *Collected Works*, p. 180. *E and G*, p. 255.
48.   This translation is from *E and G*, pp. 251-252; see also 3 *Collected Works*, p. 177.
49.   Sidney Hook, *From Hegel to Marx: Studies in the Intellectual Development of Karl Marx,* Ann Arbor, University of Michigan Press, 1968, pp. 164 f.
50.   See also *Grundrisse*, McLellan, p. 36.
51.   *E and G*, p. 403.
52.   *Grundrisse*, McLellan.
53.   As an example of the vagueness of Marx' references, it can be observed that Marx could be referring to the works of John Austin. This attribution is sustainable both as a matter of logic and of historical connection. Although Austin's famous lectures were unpopular when first given in England, his work was well received by German scholars, including Savigny, during the 1840s, when Austin himself was living in Dresden and Berlin. By that time, in fact, *The Province of Jurisprudence Determined* had become a classic. Marx was then living in exile in Paris, and he could easily have encountered Austin's work either while he was a student in Germany or while living in France. The attribution is sustainable as a matter of logical and theoretical congruity because Austin espoused the theory that law was the command of the sovereign, which is in turn clearly a matter of will.
54.   *The German Ideology*, 5 *Collected Works*, p. 90; *E and G*, p. 470.
55.   As discussed below, the general structure of Theses I, V, VI, and VII leads from the general to the specific, from the "juridical illusion" to specific points of law or fact, as can be seen from an examination of Thesis I in particular. That progression suggests that the juridical illusion is either a meta-legal principle or an axiom of law, since such general postulates might be considered to lead to specific statements.
56.   The theory may be modified to allow for dissent, as in typical majority rule situations, or it may be expanded to a more general model of what may be called the "hypothetical consent" embodied in John Rawls' theories. These modifications are not of significance here, however.
57.   Interestingly, it does not appear that the basis will theory must be true in order for the normative theory to be meaningful. In other words, it is not necessary that laws be *caused* by acts of will in order for people meaningfully to consent to them. Suppose, for

example, that the act of voting were not what brought a law into being but that political and economic forces caused that particular law to exist. Would the consent expressed by the vote be, by virtue of that fact, less morally effective?

58.   *Berry v. Donovan*, 188 Mass. 353, 74 N.E. 603, *appeal dismissed* 109 U.S. 612 (1905).

59.   *Dunn v. Chambers*, 4 Barb 376, N.Y. App. Div. (1848).

60.   The first and perhaps simplistic step, which is applicable to all seven theses, is to assure ourselves that they actually are statements about an ideology and not about some other phenomenon. On their face, they are about law, and Marx held that law is part of the state and that the state is part of the "idealistic superstructure". Therefore, these statements by Marx are about the idealistic superstructure - in other words, about ideology. It should be noted here that the terms "law" and "lawyers" are not defined by Marx. He treated these social phenomena as apparent to the observer or reader, and for that reason no further attempt will be made to define these terms here.

61.   Normative versions of those theories can be created, but as noted above, do not necessarily follow from the descriptive premises above, as follows,

> 1a.   A law is morally binding if and only if it is con-
> sented to by all members of a society. (Normative basis
> theory)
>
> 2a.   Just or fair laws of property and contract recognize
> the relationship between an individual's will and an object
> or another's will. (Normative recognition theory)

62.   *Grundrisse*, Nicolaus, pp. 83-84; McLellan, pp. 16-17.

63.   See also Karl Marx, 'Manifesto of the Communist Party', in Tucker, p. 349; *The German Ideology*, 5 *Collected Works*, p. 37; *Grundrisse*, McLellan, pp. 35-36.

64.   *The German Ideology*, 5 *Collected Works*, p. 91; *E and G*, p. 471.

65.   Consider Rousseau's famous "Man is born free but everywhere he is in chains."

66.   In fact, that tautology seems to make a descriptive reading rather meaningless. The situation can be remedied, perhaps, by contrasting contractual exchange relationships with forced exchange.

67.   Put in other terms, this ambiguity in reference indicates that this category could perhaps be subdivided into two kinds of descriptive statements, those which are about a particular society and those which are descriptions of the concepts or entities called "property" and

"contract". These two interpretations are respectively historical or anthropological claims and "pure" meta-legal statements, the latter being statements about legal entities.

68.   In an attempt to express the accidental/necessary distinction in legal terms, as opposed to metaphysical terms, I have interpreted the term "accidental" here to mean that the persons who are members of capitalist society do not stand in a contractual relationship with each other prior to the time when they enter the contract, i.e., that they do not have contractual obligations to one another.

Second, there are, of course, legal relationships and obligations in society which are not obviously or expressly contractual, such as the reciprocal obligations of parent and child, the duty to pay taxes, and one's liability to military service. Interestingly, the question of whether marriage was essentially a contractual relationship was disputed by Hegel and Kant. Clearly, the citizen has legal obligations to others that do not arise from a contract with the other individual, although it may be argued that these obligations do arise from a general or social contract. Among these social contract obligations are those not to inflict injury carelessly on others, as by a negligent act; the duty to drive carefully does not arise from a contract entered with other motorists, although it may be derived from a Rawlsian social contract in which each party "agrees" that all will drive carefully in order that conducting an automobile will be proportionately safer.

Third, if statement 2b is read as "No person has a contractual obligation to another until and unless those two persons enter into a contract with each other", then it appears tautological. Contractual relationships are by definition consensual; a relationship is not a contractual one unless it arises from a contract between the related persons. That statement, however, is not inconsistent with the idea that two people may have obligations to each other irrespective of whether they have entered into a contract, as for example, if there were a law requiring that a baker give away five loaves of bread per week to the deserving poor. The baker and the poor would not then stand in a contractual relationship, but the baker would nonetheless have a legal obligation to the poor.

69.   This subjective interpretation may be restated more carefully as follows:

Thesis I - Subjective Interpretation
    The belief that law is a matter of will causes the belief that title is separable from actual use.

Thesis V - Subjective Interpretation
    The belief that law is a matter of will causes the belief that "it is altogether accidental that individuals enter into relationships with each other, such as contracts".

Thesis VI - Subjective Interpretation
  The belief that law is a matter of will causes the belief that
  contractual relationships "can be entered into or not at
  will".
Thesis VII - Subjective Interpretation
  The belief that law is a matter of will causes the view that
  the content of contracts rests entirely on the individual free
  will of the contracting parties.

70.   *The German Ideology*, 5 *Collected Works*, p. 92.

71.   A less loaded interpretation would be to replace the term
"causes" with the term "is connected with", but this simply leaves open
the nature of this vague "connection".

72.   *The German Ideology*, 5 *Collected Works*, p. 36.

73.   See *The German Ideology*, 5 *Collected Works*, pp. 36-37,
90; *E and G*, p. 470.

74.   G.W.F. Hegel, *The Philosophy of Right*, in Frederick A.
Olafson, *Society, Law, and Morality*, New Jersey, Prentice-Hall, Inc.,
1961, p. 227.

75.   The above discussion of Hegel's reaction to Savigny is
from Huntington Cairns, *Legal Philosophy From Plato to Hegel*,
Baltimore, Md., Johns Hopkins Press, 1949.

76.   Karl Friedrich von Savigny, 'On the Vocation of Our Age
for Legislation and Jurisprudence', translated by Abraham Hayward,
London, 1831, in Jerome Hall, *Readings in Jurisprudence*, New York,
The Bobbs-Merrill Company, 1938, p. 87.

77.   Savigny, 'On the Vocation of Our Age', *supra*, at 91; see
also Rudolf Stammler, *Fundamental Tendencies in Modern
Jurisprudence*, 21 Michigan Law Review 623, 1923, in Jerome Hall,
Readings in Jurisprudence, supra, pp. 97-98.

78.   Ernest Barker, *Introduction to Gierke, Natural Law and the
Theory of Society*, Cambridge University Press, 1934, and Roscoe
Pound, 'Interpretations of Legal History', Cambridge University Press
and The MacMillan Co., 1930, both in *Readings in Jurisprudence,
supra*, at pp. 91 and 100, respectively.

79.   *Hegel's Philosophy of Right*, trans. by T.M. Knox, Oxford, 1942, pp. 42-44 and 50.

80.   *Ibid.* p. 50.

81.   *Ibid.* p. 52.

82.   'Comments on James Mill, *Elémens d'économie
politique*', 3 *Collected Works*, pp. 218, 224; 'Excerpt Notes of 1844',
E and G, pp. 267 and 273.

83.   See 'Economic and Philosophical Manuscripts of 1844', *E
and G*, pp. 278 and 280.

84.   *Hegel's Philosophy of Right, supra*, pp. 57-60.

85.   Karl Friedrich von Savigny, 'On the Vocation of Our Age for Legislation and Jurisprudence', *op.cit.* p. 87.

86.   *The German Ideology*, 5 *Collected Works*, p. 91; *E and G*, p. 471. (*E and G* translation).

87.   *The German Ideology*, 5 *Collected Works*, pp. 36-37; *E and G*, p. 415.

88.   'On the Vocation of Our Age', in Jerome Hall, *Readings in Jurisprudence, supra* at p. 88.

89.   'On the Jewish Question', 3 *Collected Works*, p. 167. See also 'On the Jewish Question', 3 *Collected Works*, p. 162.

90.   *The German Ideology*, 5 *Collected Works*, p. 60; *E and G*, p. 439.

91.   "Pour que des créatures libres, ainsi mises en présence, puissent s'aider mutuellement et ne se gêner jamais dans le déploiement de leur activité, il faut qu'une ligne de démarcation invisible circumscrive les limites au sein desquelles le développement parallèle des individus trouve indépendence et sécurité. La règle qui fixe ces limites et garanti cette liberté s'appelle droit." Karl Friedrich von Savigny, *Traité de Droit Romain,* trans., into French, by Charles Genous, Paris, Firman Didot Frères, 1840, Vol. I, p. 326.

92.   'On the Jewish Question', 3 *Collected Works*, p. 162; *E and G*, p. 235. (*E and G* translation)

93.   "Sous le point de vue où nous nous sommes placés, chaque rapport de droit nous apparaît comme une relation de personne à personne déterminée par une règle de droit, et cette règle déterminante assigne à chaque individu un domaine où sa volonté règne indépendante de toute volonté étrangère. ... Mais dans le monde extérieur se rencontre la nature non libre, puis des volontés libres comme la nôtre, c'est-à-dire, des personnes étrangères à notre personnalité." *Traité de Droit Romain, supra*, pp. 327 and 329.

94.   'Comments on James Mill', 3 *Collected Works*, p. 225; *E and G*, p. 278.

95.   'On the Vocation of our Age', in *Readings in Jurisprudence, supra*, p. 298.

96.   'Philosophical Manifesto', *E and G*, pp. 99 and 104.

97.   "Nous ne pouvons dominer la nature non libre dans sa totalité, mais dans une portion déterminée, détachée de son ensemble. La portion ainsi détachée se nomme chose, et ici commence la première éspèce possible de droits, le droit à une chose, qui, sous sa forme la plus pure et la plus complète, s'appelle propriété." *Traité de Droit Romain, supra*, p. 332.

98.   "Il faut au contraire signaler une analogie bien autrement essentielle entre les obligations et les rapports du droit des choses, dont

la propriété forme la base. Il est vrai que dans la propriété nous ne rencontrons pas les deux personnes isolées, qui sont de l'essence de l'obligation. Mais en revanche ces deux institutions ont ce charactère commun, que l'obligation, comme la propriété, consiste dans la domination d'une personne determinée sur une fraction du monde extérieur. Aussi constituent-elles, par leur union le droit des biens, dont elles sont les deux parties correlatives, en effet le droit des choses comprehends le principe du droit des biens abstraction faite de toute relation, de l'homme à l' homme, tant que cette relation est précisément l'objet des obligations.....″ Karl Friedrich von Savigny, *Le Droit des Obligations*, trans., into French, C. Gerardin and Paul Jozon, Paris, Ernest Thorin, 1873, Vol. I, p. 19.

99.   Roscoe Pound, 'Interpretation of Legal History', in *Readings in Jurisprudence, supra*, p. 103.

100.   "Mais si nous voulons nous représenter un rapport de droit qui establisse notre domination sur une personne étrangère sans détruire sa liberté, un droit qui resemble à la propriété et néanmoins s'en distingue, il faut que notre domination n'atteigne pas la totalité de la personne étrangère, seulement un de ces actes, et alors cet acte, soustrait au libre arbitre de cette personne, passe sous l'empire de notre volonté. Les rapports de droit en vertu desquels nous dominons un acte déterminé d'une personne étrangère s'appellent obligation."

"On appelle déclarations de volonté cette espèce de faits juridique qui non seulement sont des actes libres, mais qui, d'après la volonté de l'agent, ont pour but immediat d'engendrer ou détruire un rapport de droit." *Traité de Droit Roman,* Vol. I, p. 333 and *Traité de Droit Roman*, trans. Charles Genous, 1845; Vol. III, p. 103.

101.   John Locke, *Two Treatises on Civil Government*, in *The Great Legal Philosophers, supra*, p. 137.

102.   *Loc. cit.*

103.   *Loc. cit.*

104.   *Loc. cit.*

105.   Jean-Jacques Rousseau, *On the Social Contract*, trans. Roger O. Masters and Judith R. Masters, New York, St. Martin's Press, 1978, p. 57.

CHAPTER TWO

1.   *Hegel's Philosophy of Right, supra*, p. 52. References to fragmentary quotations have been omitted.

2.   It remains the fact, however, that nineteenth-century property law in general would permit the situation described by Marx where a person owned property which he could not for financial reasons fully utilize. The existence of the doctrine of adverse possession establishes, on the other hand, that it was not completely possible to have title completely separate from use, at least where another person proceeded to use the property without hindrance by the titleholder.

3.   The presence of Theses VI and VII, however, which deal with individual will as relevant to contracts, would make Thesis V superfluous, since it would then be interpreted as only restating more generally the conclusions of those later theses.

4.   See, e.g., 'On the Jewish Question', 3 *Collected Works*, pp. 153-154 and 168; *E and G*, p. 247. See also Karl Marx, 'Comments on James Mill', 3 *Collected Works*, p. 217.

5.   Hegel, *Philosophy of Right*, quoted in Karl Marx, 'Contribution to the Critique of Hegel's Philosophy of Law', 3 *Collected Works*, p. 5; *E and G*, p. 158. Emphasis omitted. Easton and Guddat translate this more clearly:

> Individuals *en masse* contain in themselves spiritual natures and thus two aspects: at one extreme, related individuality as knowing and willing, and at the other extreme, universality as knowing and willing what is substantial... . In those spheres... individuals acquire their right in the first of these two aspects directly. In the other aspect they find their essential self-consciousness in social institutions, the universal implicit in their particular interests ... .

6.   'Contribution', 3 *Collected Works*, p. 10; *E and G*, p. 158. Emphasis omitted.

7.   'Contribution', 3 *Collected Works*, p. 41; *E and G*, p. 179. Emphasis omitted.

8.   'Contribution', 3 *Collected Works*, pp. 5 f.; *E and G*, p. 152 f.

9.   *The German Ideology*, 5 *Collected Works*, p. 71; *E and G*, p. 471.

10.   'Comments on James Mill, *Elémens d'économie politique*', 3 *Collected Works*, pp. 226-228; 'Excerpt Notes of 1844', *E and G*, pp. 278-281.

11.   'Comments on James Mill, *Elémens d'économie poli-tique'*, 3 *Collected Works*, pp. 217-219. See also 'Excerpt Notes of 1844', *E and G*, p. 280. Emphasis omitted.

12.   'Comments on James Mill, *Elémens d'economie poli-tique'*, 3 *Collected Works*, p. 227-228; 'Excerpt Notes of 1844', *E and G*, p. 281.

13.   It may be asked whether these legal philosophers them-selves believed that the result premises expressed rules of law. It appears that Savigny and Hegel did, although I have not found much evidence as to Locke. The question is of less interest here, since the real issue is whether those premises were rules of law, rather than whether these philosophers thought that they were.

14.   The more classic free will issue, perhaps, is that of causation; it is argued that the will is not truly free unless it acts independently of the chain of causation which governs the actions of inanimate objects, such as bricks. The reason for avoiding this issue here is not only that it is not, apparently, the concept which Marx was discussing in this section of *The German Ideology*, but that it presents large difficulties of construction for all four philosophers, especially Marx. Marx must resolve not only the question of political action in the context of an almost mechanistic theory of history but must also resolve issues of individual human action in that context.

15.   5 *Collected Works*, p. 91; *E and G*, p. 471.

16.   John Locke, *Two Treatises of Government*, in *The Great Legal Philosophers*, *supra*, p. 152.

17.   Karl Friederich von Savigny, *Traité de Droit Romain*, trans., into French, Ch. Guenoux, Paris, Firmin Didot Frères, 1845, see esp. Vol. III, Chapter III, pp. 102 f.

18.   *Ibid.* pp. 120-121.

19.   *Ibid.* p. 120.

20.   *Ibid.* pp. 104-105.

21.   *Ibid.* p. 121. Emphasis supplied.

22.   G.W.F. Hegel, *Philosophy of Right*, in *The Great Legal Philosophers*, *supra*, §§ 45 and 71, pp. 307-308.

CHAPTER THREE

1.   T. Parsons, *The Law of Contracts*, (ed.2), Boston, Little, Brown and Company, 1855).
2.   *The American and English Encyclopedia of Law*, (ed.2), New York, Edward Thompson Company, 1898.
3.   Matthew Bacon, *A New Abridgment of the Law*, ed. Sir Henry Gwyllim, Charles Edward Dodd, Bird Wilson and John Bouvier, Philadelphia, T. & J.W. Johnson, 1854. Vol. 1.
4.   F. A. Hayek, *The Road to Serfdom*, Chicago, University of Chicago Press, 1944.
5.   Robert Nozick, *Anarchy, State and Utopia*, Oxford, Blackwell Publishers, 1975.
6.   C. Fried, *Contract as Promise*
7.   M. Horowitz, *The Transformation of American Law*, Cambridge, Mass., Harvard University Press, 1977.
8.   P.S. Atiyah, *The Rise and Fall of Freedom of Contract*, Clarendon Press, Oxford, 1979; hereinafter *Freedom of Contract*. This wonderfully detailed study provides and illuminating review of the history of nineteenth-century contract law. I disagree with the central conclusion which emphasizes the role of fairness in the courts' decisions. Regrettably, the book was not known to me when this chapter was written.
9.   See *Carew v. Rutherford*, 106 Mass. 1, 1871.
10.   Atiyah, *op. cit.* pp. 528-544.
11.   J. Dickinson, *New Conceptions of Contract in Labor Relations*, 43 Col. L. Rev. 688, 692, 1943.
12.   Brandeis, J. dissenting in *Hitchman Coal & Coke Co. v. Mitchell*, 245 U.S. 229, 271, 1917, quoted in Dickinson, *New Conceptions, supra* at 693. Atiyah argues - wrongly, I believe, that the doctrine of duress was "whittled away in the nineteenth century ... until virtually nothing was left of it." *Freedom of Contract, supra,* at 435.
13.   Dickinson, *op. cit.* p. 693.
14.   *Maisel v. Sigman,* 205 N.Y.S. 807, Sup. Ct. 1924); *Wasserstein v. Beim*, 294 N.Y.S. 439, N.Y. Sup. Ct. 1937, discussed in Dickinson, 'New Conceptions', at 693; *Cappy's Inc. v. Dorgan*, 46 N.E.2d 538, 1943, discussed in R. Hale, *Bargaining, Duress, and Economic Liberty*, 43 Columbia L. Rev. 603, 1943, at 615, n. 24.
15.   See, e.g., M. Radin, *Contract, Obligation, and the Human Will*, 43 Col. L. Rev. 575, 582, 1943.
16.   *The German Ideology*, 5 *Collected Works*, p. 90; *E and G*, p. 470; *Capital*, Tucker, p. 192.
17.   Sir William Searle Holdsworth, *A History of English Law*, London, Methuen, 1915-1966, hereinafter "Holdsworth". Footnotes

omitted.

18. W. Story, *Treatise on the Law of Contracts*, 1844, cited in Horowitz, *Transformation, supra*, p. 185.

19. *Printing and Numerical Registering Co. v. Sampson*, 1875, L.R. 19 Eq. at p. 465, also quoted in Atiyah, *infra*, p. 3.

20. Halsbury's *Laws of England, supra*, 'Contract', § 202, p. 80.

21. See discussion in Friedrich Kessler and Grant Gilmore, *Contracts; Cases and Materials*, 2d. Ed., Boston, Little, Brown & Company, 1970, pp. 39 and 40, hereinafter "Kessler and Gilmore".

22. The nature of contract as private planning and the role of state enforcement of executory contracts, as opposed to the state's merely remaining uninvolved in individual bargains, is an important element in Hayak's thought and is ably - but wrongly, I believe - discussed by Atiyah.

23. Kessler and Gilmore, *supra*, p. 3, n. 7.

24. See, e.g., 'On the Jewish Question', 3 *Collected Works*, pp. 166-167; *E and G*, p. 240.

25. *Hurley v. Eddingfield*, 156 Ind. 416, 59 N.E. 1058, 1901.

26. Kessler and Gilmore, *supra*, p. 38, and cases cited therein; but see *Freedom of Contract*, pp. 742 ff., regarding the erosion of this doctrine.

27. Atiyah, *Freedom of Contract*, at 167 ff.

28. M.J. Horowitz, *Transformation of American Law*, p. 184.

29. See Kessler and Gilmore, *supra*, at 186-187; see Holdsworth, *supra*, at 17, n. 3; *Freedom of Contract*, pp. 169 ff., 448 ff.

30. *Parmelee v. Cameron*, 2 Hand. 392, N.Y., 1869, at 395, citing *Dunn v. Chambers*. 4 Barb. 376, 436 New York, 1848; see also the discussion of Nathan Dane's *Treatise on Contracts* in Horowitz, *Transformation, supra*, p. 183.

31. 8 Holdsworth, *supra*, at 17.

32. Parmelee v. Cameron, *supra*.

33. 8 Holdsworth, *supra*, at 56. Footnotes omitted.

34. *Parmelee v. Cameron, supra; Freedom of Contract*, pp. 172-173, and 450 (regarding the nineteenth-century rule).

35. *Dunn v. Chambers* 4 Barb. 376, New York, 1848.

36. Dawson, *Economic Duress - An Essay in Perspective*, 45 Mich. Law. Rev. 253, 260, 1947.

37. *Bishop v. Kitchen*, 38 L.J.Q.B. 20, 1868, cited in Williston, *Freedom of Contract, supra*, p. 374, where this same point is made.

38. Locke, *Second Treatise of Government*, in John Locke, *Two Treatises of Government*, P. Laslett (ed.), Cambridge, New

American Library, 1968, p. 325.

    39.   H. Maine, *Ancient Law*, 1884, quoted in Kessler and Gilmore, p. 4, and discussed in *Freedom of Contract*, pp.259-260.

    40.   Kessler and Gilmore, p. 18, n. 1; M. Radin, *Contractual Obligation and the Human Will*, *supra*, 582.

    41.   S. Williston, *Freedom of Contract*, 4 Cornell L.Q. 365, 379 (1921) (hereinafter "Williston").

    42.   *Children's Hospital v. Adkins*, 284 F. 613 (Ct. of Appeals, D.C. 1922), aff'd 261 U.S. 525 (1923), discussed in *Williston*, *supra*, pp. 377 and 379.

    43.   M. Radin, *op. cit.* p. 582.

    44.   'Ordinance and Statute of Laborers', 23 Edw. III St. 1 (1349) and 25 Edw. III St. 12 (1350); discussed in L.E. Blades, *Employment at Will vs. Individual Freedom: On Limiting the Abusive Exercise of Employer Power*, 67 Columbia L. Rev. 1404 (   ), at 1424, n. 102.

    45.   See, e.g., *Carew v. Rutherford*, *supra*, at 14; *Freedom of Contract*, pp. 128, 167 ff.

    46.   *Loc. cit.*

    47.   Williston, *supra, p. 373.*

    48.   *Loc.cit.*

    49.   *Loc.cit.*

    50.   P.S. Atiyah, *An Introduction to the Law of Contract*, Oxford, Clarendon, 1961, p. 1.

    51.   *Ibid.* p. 2.

    52.   W.G. Miller, *Lectures in the Philosophy of Law* (1884), quoted in *Kessler and Gilmore*, p. 4.

    53.   Sidgewick, *Elements of Politics*, quoted in Kessler and Gilmore, *supra.*

    54.   *Freedom of Contract,* pp. 515 ff. See I. Parsons, *The Law of Contracts* 3, 1855, cited in Kessler and Gilmore. For a Marxist critique of this aspect of "bourgeois" law, its commodity exchange conception, see Pashukanis, 'The General Theory of Law and Marxism', reprinted in 5 *Twentieth Century Legal Philosophy Series, Soviet Legal Philosophy*, 111-225, (1951); Kessler and Gilmore, *supra*, p. 4, n. 10.

    55.   For the most impressive operation of *laissez-faire*, see Marshall, *Principles of Economics* 246-247, 8th ed. 1938: "This doctrine of natural organization contains more truth of the highest importance to humanity than almost any other... . But its exaggeration worked much harm, especially to those who delighted most in it, for it prevented them from seeing and removing the evil that was intertwined with the good in the changes that were going on around them... ." See further Moos, 'Laissez-faire, Planning and Ethics', *The Economic*

Journal 17, 1947. Kessler and Gilmore, *supra*, p. 4, n. 11.

56.   Adam Smith, *Wealth of Nations,* 423, Cannan (ed. 1937). For a more guarded expression of this idea, see Knight, *Freedom and Reform* 45, 54, 1947. Kessler and Gilmore, *supra*, p. 51, n. 12. Quotation taken from Kessler and Gilmore, *supra*, pp. 3-5.

57.   Williston, *supra*, p. 367.

58.   *Carew v. Rutherford* 106 Mass. 1, 15, 1871.

59.   P. S. Atiyah, *Law of Contract, supra*, at 3.

60.   M. Radin, *op. cit.* p. 583.

61.   *Great Atlantic & Pacific Tea Co. v. Cream of Wheat Co.,* 227 F. 46, 48-49, 2d Cir. 1915. (emphasis supplied)

62.   *Lochner v. New York,* 198 U.S. 45, 1905.

63.   *Lochner v. New York, supra* at 53.

64.   *Loc. cit.*

65.   *Capital,* Tucker, pp. 256-258.

66.   Williston, *supra*, p. 376.

67.   *Muller v. Oregon,* 208 U.S. 412, 1908. See discussion in Williston, *supra*, p. 377.

68.   Kessler and Gilmore, *supra*. See Llewellyn, 'What Price Contract? - An Essay in Perspective', 40 Yale L.J. 704, 717, 1931).

69.   Kessler and Gilmore, *supra*, pp. 2-3 (some citations deleted). See also 9 Halsbury's *Laws of England*, "Contract", § 202, p. 80.

70.   It should be noted that there are many early statutes making extortion a criminal offense.

By the Gen. Sts. c. 160, § 28, which is cited by the plaintiff's counsel, "whoever, either verbally or by a written or printed communication, maliciously threatens an injury to the person or property of another, with intent thereby to extort money or any pecuniary advantage whatever, or with intent to compel the person so threatened to do any act against his will, shall be punished" as the section prescribes. As this is a penal statute, perhaps it does not extend to a threat to injure one's business by preventing people from assisting him to prosecute it, whereby he loses his profits and is compelled to pay a large sum of money to those who make the threat, though the threat is quite analogous to those specified in the statute, and may be not less injurious. *Carew v. Rutherford.*

71.   *Carew v. Rutherford, supra.*

72.   See e.g., *Jordan v. Stevens,* 51 Me. 78, 81 Am. Dec. 556, Me. 1863); *Howe v. Howe* 9, 9 Mass. 88, Mass. 1868.

73.   *Dunn v. Chambers, supra*, at 379.

74.   *Parmelee v. Cameron,* 2 Hand. 392, 1869.

75.   *Wilkerson v. Bishop, supra.* See also *Earle v. Norfolk and New Brunswick Hosiery Co.,* 30 N.J. Eq. 188, 9 Stew. 188,

1882, which states this requirement with regard to undue influence.

76.   *Sturtevant v. Sturtevant*, 116 sec. 340, 6 N.C. 428, sec. 1886, held, mere influence, if fairly and honestly acquired, is not grounds for setting aside a deed if the grantor acted freely, See also *Howe v. Howe, supra.*

77.   *Freeman v. Wilson*, 51 Miss. 329, Miss. 1875, held, the fact that husband was violent, turbulent, intemperate, prone to violence when drunk, and domineering to his wife was not sufficient to invalidate her consent unless the particular transaction at issue was the result of clearly proven duress. But see *Tapley v. Tapley* 10 Minn. 448, Gil. 360, 88 Am. Dec. 76, Minn. 1865 (held, threat of physical injury by husband not required to constitute duress of the wife).

78.   See *Jenkins v. Page* 37, U.S., 12 Pet., 241, 9 L. Ed. 1070, U.S. 1838; *Taylor v. Taylor*, 49 U.S., 8 How., 183, 12 L. Ed. 1040, U.S. 1850.

79.   See Holdsworth, 'Assumpsit', 1 *Bouvier's Law Dictionary,* 8th ed., 1913, pp. 270 f.

80.   10 *The American and English Encyclopedia of Law*, pp. 326-327.

81.   'Debt', 1 *Bouvier's Law Dictionary* (8th ed. 1913), pp. 787 f.

82.   *Loc. cit.*

83.   'Assumpsit', 1 *Bouvier's Law Dictionary*, 8th ed. 1913, pp. 270 f.

84.   Ames, *The History of Assumpsit*, 2 *Harv. L. Rev.* 1 and 2 *Harv. L. Rev.* 52, at 15, 1888; 1 *Williston on Contracts*, (3d ed. 1957), § 99, p. 368. Even Atiyah bows out of the effort to explain the law's progress from debt to assumpsit. *Freedom of Contract*, pp. 119-120.

85.   See *Bacon's Abridgement of the Law,* Vol. I, pp. 398-399, 1854.

86.   *Green v. Wood*, 2 Vern. 632, as described in 1 *Bacon's Abridgement of the Law,* 1854, p. 398; see also the discussion in *Bosanquet v. Dashwood*, 8 Geo. II, 1734, Chancery, Dec. Term, 5. Michaelis, 25 English Rep. 648, at 649.

87.   1 *Bacon's Abridgement of the Law*, 1854, p. 399., citations omitted.

88.   Matthew Bacon, *Abridgement of the Law*, ed. Sir Henry Guyllim, Charles Edward Dodd, Bird Wilson, and John Bouvier, Philadelphia, McCarty and Davis, 1844, Vol. 4, p. 160.

89.   *Bosanquett v. Dashwood*, 25 Eng.Rpts. 648 at 649, 1734.

90.   *Heathcote v. Paignon*, 1 Bro. C.C. 173, 24 Eng. Rpts 96, Court of Chancery 1787; *Freedom of Contract*, pp. 448 ff.

91.   Y.B. of Edw. IV, 17, p. 32, cited in Dawson, 'Economic

Duress', p. 254, n. 3, and discussed in the text thereat. Duress by false imprisonment was the focal point of these discussions, with cases of threatened physical harm being less discussed.

92.   *Coleman v. Mercantile National Bank,* 6 Ohio Dec. 1063, Ohio, 1881.

93.   See *Kistler v. State,* 54 Ind. 500, Ind. 1876 (held, threat to print accusations of immoral sexual conduct is extortion).

94.   Bracton, *De Legibus,* nn. 16b-17, *Bracton's Notebook,* cases 182, 200, 229, 750, 1126, 1643, 1913, discussed in Dawson, 'Economic Duress', p. 254, n. 2.

95.   Coke, *Second Institute* 483, 1642, *Coke on Littleton* 253b, 1633, discussed in Dawson, 'Economic Duress', p. 255.

96.   Blackstone, *Commentaries,* Chitty ed., 131, 1859, cited in Dawson, *Economic Duress, supra.*

97.   See *Baker v. Morton,* 79 U.S. 159, 1870; *Brown v. Pierce,* 74 U.S., 7 Wall, 205, 1868; *Adams v. Stringer,* 78 Ind. 175, Ind. 1881.

98.   *Harmon v. Harmon,* 61 Maine, 1 Smith, 227, 34 Am. Rpts. 556, Maine 1873; *Simmons v. Trumbo,* 9 W. Va. 358, 1876; *Foshy v. Ferguson,* 5 Hill, (n.v.), 154.

99.   10 *The American and English Encyclopedia of Law* 325, 2d. ed. 1899.

100.   See *U.S. v. Huckabee,* 83 U.S., 16 Wall, 414, 1872.

101.   See *Cadaval, Duke v. Collins,* 1836, 4 Ad. & El. 858 ; 2 Har. &. W. 54; 111 E.R. 1006; *Bromley v. Norton,* 1872, 27 L.T. 478; sub. nom. *Re Bromley, Bromley v. Norton,* 2 W.R. 155; *Cumming v. Ince,* 1847, 11 Q.B. 112, 17 L.J.Q.B. 105, 116 E.R. 418, discussed herein, and other cases collected in The English and Empire Digest, vol. 12, pp. 120-121, 1973); see also 9 Halsburg's *Laws of England,* 1924, § 297, p. 172, although there may be some doubt as to the accuracy of the statements therein.

102.   See *Cumming v. Ince,* 1847, 11 Q.B. 112, 17 L.J.Q.B. 105; 116 E.R. 418, discussed below.

103.   10 *The American and English Encyclopedia of Law* (2d ed. 1899), pp. 434.

104.   *Williams v. Bayley,* 6 Ruling Cases 455 (1895).

105.   *Davies v. London & Provincial Marine Ins. Co.,*1878, 8 Ch. D. 469; 38 L.T. 478 and *Seear v. Cohen,* 1881, 45 L.T. 589 D.C. and other cases referred to in *The English and Empire Digest* Vol. 12, p. 119, 1973 ed.,

106.   *Osbaldiston v. Simpson,* 1843, 13 Sim. 513; 1 L.T.O. 335; 7 Jur. 734; 60 E.R. 199.

107.   *Shattuck v. Watson,* 53 Ark.147.

108.   See, for example, the cases discussed in *Bosanquett v.*

Dashwood, supra.

109. See *Biffin v. Bignell,* 1862, 7 H. & N. 877 31 L.J. Ex. 189; 6 L.T. 248; 8 Jur. N.S. 647; 10 W.R. 322, 158 E.R. 725.

110. *Vernon v. Pethell,* 2 Eden 110, 113, 1762, as discussed in J. Dickinson, *New Conceptions,* at 692.

111.   *Morgan v. Palmer,* 2 Barn. & C. 735, 1824, cited in J. Dickinson, *New Conceptions,* at 693.

112. Dawson, *Economic Duress, supra,* p. 255, text and n. 4.

113. *Loc. cit.*

114. *Loc. cit.*

115. *Astley v. Reynolds,* 93 E.R. 939, 40, 1732.

116. 10 *The American and English Encyclopedia of Law,* at 345-346.

117. *C. & A. RR Co. v. Chicago, etc., Coal Co.,* 79 Ill. 121-130 as cited in *News Publishing Co. v. Associated Press, supra,* with several other citations to the same effect, at 255; *Freedom of Contract,* p. 556.

118.   *Astley v. REynolds, supra; Freedom of Contract, supra,* pp. 434 ff.

119.   *Summer v. Ferryman,* ll Mod. Rep. 201, 88 E.R. 989, 1709.

120.   *Atlee v. Blackhouse,* 3 M.&.W. 633; 7 L.J.L. Ex. 234; 150 E.R. 1298.

121.   *Parker v. Bristol & Exeter Ry. Co.,* 6 Exch. 702, 155 E.R. 726.

122.   *Skeate v. Beall,* 11 Ad & El 983; 9 L.J.Q.B. 233; 113 E.R. 688.

123.   See *Kohler v. Wells Fargo & Co.,* 26 Cal. 606, 1864.

124.   *Chase v. Dwinal,* 7 Me., 7 Greenl., 134, 20 Am. Dec. 352, Me. 1830, See also *Casenov v. Cutler* 45 Mass., 4 Metc., 246, Mass. 1842 (held, excessive payment demanded by mortgagee for redemption may be recovered), and *Forbes v. Appleton,* 59 Mass., 5 Cush., 115, Mass. 1849; *Weber v. Aldridge,* 2 N.H. 461, 1822. But see *contra Quinnett v. Washington,* 10 Mo. 53, 1846, and *Austin v. Durant,* 2 Strob. 257, 49 Am. Dec. 596, S.C. 1848.

125.   *Evans v. Gale,* 18 N.H. 397, N.H. 1846; but see *Sartwell v. Horton,* 28 Vt., (2 Williams) 370 (Vt. 1856).

126.   *Powell v. Hoyland,* 6 Exch. 67, 155 E.R. 456 (1851).

127.   *Hackley v. Headley,* discussed herein; *Miller v. Miller,* 68 Pa. St. 486, 1871; but see *Dana v. Kamble,* 34 Mass. 545, Mass. 1836 (held, actor's threat of refusal to perform is duress).

128. See *Carew v. Rutherford, supra.*

129.   *Ohio C. & Co. v. Whitcomb,* 123 Fed. Rep. 359, at 362; *Freedom of Contract, supra, at 556.*

130. See *New Publishing Co. v. Associated Press*, 114 Ill. App. 241 (1904), and cases collected therein.

131. *C. & A. RR. Co. v. Chicago, etc., Coal Co.*, 79 Ill. 111.

132. *Copper v. Crane*, 61 L.J.P. 35 sub. nom. *Crane (orse Cooper) v. Crane*, 40 W.R. 127.

133. See *Simmons v. Trumbo,* 9 W. Va. 358, W. Va. 1876.

134. That encyclopedia's discussion is reported further in Appendix C.

135. See *Crowell v. Gleason,* 10 Me. (1 Fairf.), 325 (Me. 1833); *Freeman v.Wilson, supra*; *Bosley v. Shannon,* 36 Ark. 280, (Ark. 1870).

136. *Barrett v. French,* 1 Conn. 354, 6 Amer. Dec. 41 (Conn. 1815).

137. *Fisk v. Stubbs*, 30 Ala. 335 (Ala. 1857), *Van Deventer v. Van Deventer*, 46 N.J. Law (17 Vroom), 460 (N.J. 1884).

138. *Willetts v. Willetts*, 104 Ill. 122 (1882). See also *Pulliam v. Pulliam*, 1 Freem. Ch. 348 (Miss. 1843).

139. *Kellog v. Kellog,* 21 Colo. 181, 40 P.358 (Colo. 1895); *Kocourek v. Merak*, 54 Tex. 201, 38 Am. Rpts. 623 (Tex. 1881); *Capley v. Capley*, 10 Minn. 448, Gil. 360, 88 Amer. Dec. 76 (Minn. 1865).

140. *Freeman v. Wilson*, 51 Miss. 329 (Miss. 1875).

141. *Rexford v. Rexford,* 7 Lans. 6 (N.Y. 1872).

142. *Feller v. Green, supra*.

143. *Fairbanks v. Snow*, 145 Mass. 153, 154 (1887). See also *The Eliza Lines*, 109 U.S. 119, 130-131 (1905).

144. *Barry v. Equitable Life Assurance Society*, 59 N.Y. 587, at 591 (1875).

145. Hale, *Economic Liberty*, p. 616.

146. *Fairbanks v. Snow*, cited in Hale, *op. cit.*, p. 618, emphasis supplied.

147. 10 *The American and English Encyclopedia of Law*, p. 338. See also 9 Halsbury's *Laws of England*, §§ 296 and 297, p. 172.

148. 10 *The American and English Encyclopedia of Law*, p. 334.

149. 10 *The American and English Encyclopedia of Law*, p. 327 and cases cited therein.

150. *Town of Ligonier v. Ackerman*, 46 Ind. 552, 15 Am. Rpts. 323 (Ind. 1874).

151. *Atwell v. Zeluff*, 26 Mich. 118 (1872); *McKee v. Campbell*, 27 Mich. 497 (1873).

152. *Meek v. McClure*, 49 Cal. 6 (1875). See *Klein v. Bayer*, 81 Mich. 233, 45 N.W. 991, (Mich. 1890).

153. *United States v. Union National Bank* (U.S. 1879), 10

Ben. 408, Fed. Cases No. 16,597. But see *Spense v. Thompson,* 11 Ala. 746, 1847; *Weatherford v. McIvor,* 21 Ala. 750 (1852).

154. *Talley v. Robinson's Assignee,* 22 Grat. 888, Va. 1872; *Accord City of Baltimore v. Lefferman,* 4 Gill. 425, 45 Am. Dec. 145, (Md. 1846); *Elson v. City of Chicago,* 40 Ill. 514, 89 Am. Dec. 361, (Ill. 1866).

155. *Hough v. Hunt, supra.* But see *Wilkinson v. Stafford,* 1789, 1 Ves. 32, 30 E.R. 216 holding that a compromise could be set aside where one party was in jail at the time, even though the other had not caused his imprisonment.

156. See *Allore v. Jewell,* 94 U.S. 506, 24 L. Ed. 260 (1876); *Harding v.Wheaton,* Fed.Cas. No. 6,051 [2 Mason 378] modifying *Same v. Handy,* 1826, 24 U.S. (11 Wheat.), 103, 6 L. Ed. 429 (1826).

157. See *Taylor v. Taylor,* 49 U.S. (8 Howe), 183 (1850), (conveyance from daughter to parents); *Pye v. Jenkins,* Fed. Cases No. 11, 487, 4 Cranch, C.C. 541 (1835) (transfer from daughter, who was impoverished thereby, to wealthy father; *Sears v. Shaeffer,* 6 N.W., 2 Seld 268, affirming 1 Barb 408 (N.W. 1852).

158. *Baldwin v. Dunton,* 40 Ill. 188 (1860); *Harkness v. Fraser,* 12 Fla. 336 (1869), on the issue of legitimacy of pressure; *Cruger v. Cruger,* 5 Barb. 225 (N.Y. 1849).

159. *Millican v. Millican,* 24 Tex. 426 (1859).

160. *Corbett v. Smith,* 7 Iowa 7, Clarke, 60, 71 Am. Dec. 431 (Iowa 1858).

161. *Loc. cit.*

162. *Sturtevant v. Sturtevant,* 116 Ill. 340, 6 N.W. 428 (Ill. 1886).

163. *Howe v. Howe,* 99 Mass. 88 (1868).

164. *Jordan v. Stephens,* 51 Maine 78, 81 Amer. Dec. 556 (Maine 1863).

165. *Powers v. Powers,* 48 How. Prac. 389 (N.Y. 1872).

166. *Harding v. Weaton,* Fed. Cases No. 6,051, 2 Mason 378, modifying *Same v. Handy,* 24 U.S. (11 Wheat), 103 (1821).

167. *Guest v. Beson,* 2 Houst. 246 (Del. 1860).

168. *Wray v. Wray,* 32 Ind. 126 (1869); *Buffalow v. Buffalow,* 22 N.C., 2 Dev. & Beq., 241 (N.C. 1837); *Amis v. Satterfield,* 40 N.C., 5 Ired. Eq., 173 (N.C. 1848); *Oldham v. Oldham,* 58 N.C., 5 Jones Eq., 89 (N.C. 1859); *Gibson v. Fifer,* 21 Tex. 260, 1858; *Brice v. Brice,* 5 Barb. 533 (N.Y. 1849); *Freeland v. Eldridge,* 19 Mo. 325 (1854).

169. 'Culpa in Contrahendo', Kessler & Fine; Williston, *supra,* p. 368; *Freedom of Contract,* especially at pp. 213, 216, 406-408, and 455-464.

170. Williston, *supra*, p. 368.

171. An interesting aspect of this argument lies in those cases where one party guessed correctly about the increased or actual value of the subject of the contract. A case debated to this day in contracts classes is the famous case about a cow; the seller believed that the otherwise valuable animal was barren and sold her at a slaughter price, while the buyer gambled correctly that the animal was fertile. When the cow proved to be with calf, the court rescinded the transaction on the ground of mistake.

172. 'Culpa in Contrahendo', *supra*; *Freedom of Contract, supra*, at 407.

173. Dawson, *Economic Duress - An Essay in Perspective*, 45 Mich.Law.Rev. 253, 1947; *Note, Economic Duress after the Demise of Free Will Theory, A Proposed Tort Analysis*, 53 Iowa Law Rev. 892, (1968).

174. *Loc. cit.; Freedom of Contract, supra,* at 435.

175. *Union Pacific Railroad Co. v. Public Service Comm. of Mo.*, 248 U.S. 67 (1918), at 70.

176. 8 Holdsworth, *supra*, p. 51.

177. See Appendix A for a detailed discussion of Dawson's analysis of this view.

CHAPTER FOUR

1.   It is to be remembered that some political philosophers, such as Sedgwick, whose *Elements of Politics* was quoted earlier, said that, without contractual relations, "the members of the human community are atoms that cannot effectively combine ...."

2.   *Cooley on Torts, supra,* at p. 278.

3.   'On the Jewish Question', 3 *Collected Works,* p. 165; *E and G,* p. 238.

4.   'On the Jewish Question', 3 *Collected Works,* p. 166; *E and G,* p. 237-238.

5.   See, *Corbett v. Smith, supra.*

6.   This argument may appear to ignore the distinction between the continental rule and the English and American rule as to assent. As discussed above, the continental legal theory held that assent was a purely subjective act, while Anglo-American legal theory tended to rely upon the objective expression of assent. That distinction, while important in other areas of contract law, is of lesser importance in the area of duress, for the simple reason that the duress and undue influence cases govern the situation where there is an apparent, objective act of assent, such as by signing a contract or a will, but where the necessary subjective state is lacking.

7.   *Earle v. Norfolk, etc., Hosiery Co.,* 36 N.J. Eq. 192, 9 Stew. 188 (1882).

8.   See 10 *The American and English Encyclopedia of Law,* 325 (2nd Ed. 1899).

9.   Some commentators, such as Mr. Duncan Kennedy, have argued that such a reading of the cases involves a "logical" error since there is no such thing as a contract, and hence, there can be no criteria for its existence, and hence, the courts must really have been concerned with social justice or some other reason for their decision. That argument not only is itself flawed but is irrelevant - the *courts* wrote about the will and about the criteria for the existence of a contract. No adequate reason has been advanced for interpreting those decisions as "actually" being about some other issue.

10.   In this regard, Mr. Justice Holmes' writings on the subject are of interest. Holmes said that this notion of apparent vs. real consent was a fiction since a person under threat or pain might very well heartily wish to enter the disputed contract. A moment's thought reveals Holmes' error. If the person desired the contract, why would it later be repudiated? Moreover, simple introspection reveals that we sometimes superficially say things which we do not mean.

11.   10 *The American and English Encyclopedia of Law, supra.*

12.   This discussion has not dealt with the "other minds"

problem which may be inherent in the duress and undue influence cases. If I may venture an analysis of these cases in the context of that problem, it would be something like this; these cases are begun because one person says that their psychological state at the moment of entering into a contract was not such as constituted assent. In the absence of such an assertion, the case, of course, would never arise - the absence of the other party's assent is seldom asserted, only the party who is under duress makes such an assertion. The factual discussion of these cases, therefore, may be taken as an evaluation of those circumstances under which such an assertion of the lack of subjective assent may be considered as believable.

13.   *French v. Shoemaker, supra*, emphasis supplied.

14.   'On the Jewish Question', 3 *Collected Works*, p. 163; *E and G*, p. 236.

15.   'On the Jewish Question', 3 *Collected Works*, p. 162; *E and G,* p. 235. , *E and G,* translation.

16.   *Grundrisse* pp. 127-31.

17.   *Cooley on Torts, supra.*

CHAPTER FIVE

1.   Avineri, p. 92.

2.   See e.g., *Grundrisse*, McLellan, pp. 16-18, Nicolaus, p. 83; Avineri, p. 82; *The German Ideology*, 5 *Collected Works*, pp. 36, 46-47, and 91; *E and G*, pp. 414, 441, and 472.

3.   Some scholars, such as Erich Fromm and Eugene Kamenka, hold that Marx was advancing a universal theory of ethics, which was somehow to be immune from his own criticisms of ideology. The tension between the supposedly scientific bent of Marx and the interpretation of him as a proto-existentialist humanist is evident in the foreword by Erich Fromm and the introduction by T.B. Bottomore to *Karl Marx; Early Writings*, trans. T.B. Bottomore, New York, McGraw-Hill, 1964.

4.   See, e.g., 'On the Jewish Question', 3 *Collected Works*, *E and G*, pp. 236-238; 'Economic and Philosophical Manuscripts of 1844', 3 *Collected Works*, pp. 274-278, pp. 299-300, 337-338; Bottomore, pp. 156-157; "Economic alienation is that of real life..."; Karl Marx, 'Toward the Critique of Hegel's Philosophy of Law, Introduction', *E and G*, pp. 272-273 and 306-307, ("private property is only the sensuous expression of the fact that man becomes objective for himself and at the same time becomes an alien and inhuman object for himself, that his expression of life is his externalization of life...").

5.   *The German Ideology*, 5 *Collected Works*, p. 39; *E and G*, p. 417.

6.   John Rawls, *A Theory of Justice*, Cambridge, Mass., Harvard University Press, 1971; Robert Nozick, *Anarchy, State and Utopia*.

7.   *The German Ideology*, 5 *Collected Works*, pp. 35-36, *E and G*, pp. 413-414. Emphasis supplied.

8.   See 'Economic and Philosophical Manuscripts of 1844', 3 *Collected Works*, p. 299; *E and G*, p. 306. : ("Above all we must avoid postulating 'society' again as an abstraction vis-à-vis the individual. The individual is the social being."); See also Avineri, p. 92.

9.   'Contribution to the Critique of Hegel's Philosophy of Law." 3 *Collected Works*, pp. 7-11; see also *E and G*, p. 179; *Capital*, Tucker, p. 197.

10.   Certainly Marx and Engels were aware of the question of how much, if any, efficacy to attribute to the superstructure, which includes ideology, and to the actions of individuals or classes under certain historical conditions.

11.   von Savigny, 'On the Vocation of Our Age for Legislation and Jurisprudence', trans. Abraham Hayward, in erome Hall, *Readings in Jurisprudence*, p. 87.

12.   See, e.g., 'Theses on Feuerbach', Tucker, p. 108.

13.   Avineri, p. 82; See *Grundrisse*, Nicolaus, p. 83.

14.   This conclusion about Marx is subject to some quali-
fication. It seems clear that Marx did not believe that the individual's
perception of an ideal society could precede the actual existence of at
least some elements of that society. Equally it seems clear that Marx
believed that ideas succeeded and were caused by social institutions,
rather than the other way around. Last, but not least, it is not apparent,
however, precisely what Marx thought about the will's ability to
influence the progress of history.

15.   *The German Ideology*, 5 *Collected Works*, p. 35; *E and G*,
p. 414. In the discussion of Savigny and Locke, a distinction was
made between those theories which held that laws arose from a general
will of the people and those theories which held that law arose from the
consent of each individual member of the society. That distinction,
while philosophically interesting, is not crucial here. Marx, to the best
of my knowledge, did not make the distinction, nor do his remarks, if
persuasive, depend upon that distinction.

16.   *The German Ideology*, *Collected Works*, p. 91; *E and G*,
pp. 470-471.

17.   See Karl Marx, *Critique of the Gotha Program*, Tucker,
pp. 382-398.

18.   See, e.g., *Economic and Philosophic Manuscripts*, *E and
G*, p. 305; ("[communism] is the true resolution of the conflict between
existence and essence, ... freedom and necessity, individual and
species. It is the riddle of history solved and knows itself as this
solution.")

19.   *Grundrisse*, McLellan, pp. 16-17, see also pp. 35-36.

20.   *Economic and Philosophic Manuscripts of 1844*, *E and G*,
p. 305.

21.   *The German Ideology*, 5 *Collected Works*, p. 92; *E and G*,
p. 472.

22.   *Grundrisse*, McLellan, pp. 16-17; see also *Grundrisse*,
Nicolaus, pp. 83-84. Emphasis supplied.

23.   *The German Ideology*, 5 *Collected Works*, p. 62; *E and G*,
p. 441. "The historical method which reigned in Germany and
especially the reason why, must be explained from its connection with
the illusion of ideologists in general, for example, the illusions of the
jurists...this is explained perfectly easily from their practical position in
life, their job, and the division of labour."

24.   *The German Ideology*, *E and G*, p. 490.

25.   It is my opinion that, just as Marx was probably as a matter
of historical fact guilty of the genetic fallacy, so too he did at least
sometimes arrogate to himself the ability to make universal, trans-

cultural moral judgments. This is particularly true of his theory of the true nature of freedom as discussed in the *Grundrisse*. See *Grundrisse*, McLellan, pp. 128-131.

26.   Roberto Mangabeira Unger has tried to formulate a quasi-Marxist moral theory which adopts both positions, i.e., that ethical judgments are simply the consensus of a given society and that those judgments can be true or false as representing a more or less accurate conception of human nature. That position has the continuing problem that there can be no way to judge the true human nature without knowledge independent of social norms. Roberto Mangabeira Unger, 'Lectures in Law and Social Order' and 'Jurisprudence', courses taught in Harvard College and Harvard Law School, respectively, in the Spring of 1976.

27.   *The German Ideology*, 5 *Collected Works*, p. 80; *E and G*, p. 460.

APPENDIX A

1. Dawson, *Economic Duress, supra*, p. 287 f.
2. *Ibid.* p. 255
3. *Ibid.* p. 256.
4. *Ibid.* n. 9.

APPENDIX C

1. Pound, 'Interests of Personality', 28 Harv. L. Rev. 343, 1915, p. 359.
2. *Ibid. p. 359*
3. *Loc. cit.*
4. *Loc. cit.*

BIBLIOGRAPHY

The American and English Encyclopedia of Law, 2d Ed., New York, Edward Thompson Company, 1898.

Ames, *The History of Assumpsit*, 2 Harv. L. Rev. 1 and 2 Harv. L. Rev. 52, at 15, 1888.

P. S. Atiyah, *An Introduction to the Law of Contract,* Oxford, Clarendon Press, 1961.

Shlomo Avineri, *The Social and Political Thought of Karl Marx*, London, Cambridge University Press, 1968.

Alexander Balinsky, *Marx's Economics: Origin and Development*, Lexington, Mass., D. C. Heath and Co., 1970.

Ernest Barker, *Introduction to Gierke, Natural Law and the Theory of Society*, London, Cambridge University Press, 1934.

James F. Becker, *Marxian Political Economy*, London, Cambridge University Press.

L.E. Blades, *Employment at Will vs. Individual Freedom, On Limiting the Abusive Exercise of Employer Power*, 67 Columbia L. Rev. 1404, at 1424.

Huntington Cairns, *Legal Philosophy from Plato to Hegel*, Baltimore, Md., Johns Hopkins Press, 1949.

Cooley on Torts.

John P. Dawson, *Economic Duress - An Essay in Perspective*, 45 Mich. Law. Rev. 253, (1947).

J. Dickinson, *New Conceptions of Contract in Labor Relations*, 43 Columbia L. Rev. 688, 1943.

Lloyd D. Easton and Kurt H. Guddat, *Writings of the Young Marx on Philosophy and Society*, New York, Doubleday, 1967.

A New Abridgement of the Law, Sir Henry Guyllim, Charles Edward Dodd, Bird Wilson and John Bouvier (eds.), Philadelphia, T. & J.W. Johnson, 1854.

F. A. Hayek, *The Road to Serfdom*, Chicago, University of Chicago Press, 1944.

G.W.F. Hegel, *The Philosophy of Right*, in Frederick A. Olafson, *Society, Law, and Morality*, New Jersey, Prentice-Hall, 1961.

Hegel's Philosophy of Right, trans. by T.M. Knox, Oxford, 1942.

Sir William Searle Holdsworth, *A History of English Law*, London, Methuen, 1915-1966.

Sidney Hook, *From Hegel to Marx: Studies in the Intellectual Development of Karl Marx,* Ann Arbor, University of Michigan Press, 1968.

M.J. Horowitz, *The Transformation of American Law, 1780-1860,*

Cambridge, Mass., Harvard University Press, 1977.
Eugene Kamenka, *Ethical Foundations of Marxism*, London, Routledge & Kegan Paul, 1972.
Friedrich Kessler and Grant Gilmore, *Contracts; Cases and Materials*, Boston, Little, Brown & Company, 1970.
John Locke, *Two Treatises of Government*, P. Laslett (ed), Camb., New American Library, 1968.
Ernest Mandel, *The Formation of the Economic Thought of Karl Marx; 1843 to Capital*, trans. by Brian Pearce, London, Monthly Review Press, 1971.
Karl Marx, *Grundrisse: Foundations of the Critique of Political Economy*, trans. by M. Nicolaus, New York, Random House, 1973.
_____, Frederick Engels, *Collected Works*, Vols. 1, 3, and 5, London, Lawrence & Wishart, 1976.
_____, 'Preface' to *Contribution to the Critique of Political Economy*, (1859) trans. by T.B. Bottomore, in Lord Lloyd of Hampstead, *Introduction to Jurisprudence*, New York, Praeger Publishers, 1972.
_____, *Grundrisse,* trans. by David McLellan, New York, Harper & Row, 1972.

The following works by Marx and Engels, as translated by various persons, are discussed herein:

Karl Marx, 'Contribution to the Critique of Hegel's *Philosophy of Law*'.
_____, 'Manifesto of the Communist Party'.
_____, 'Letter to His Father', November 10, 1837.
_____, *Capital.*
_____, Frederick Engels, *The German Ideology.*
_____, 'On the Jewish Question'.
_____, '*Enquête Ouvrière*', *Revue Socialiste*, April 20, 1880.
_____, *Eighteenth Brumaire of Louis Napoleon.*
_____, *The Civil War in France.*
_____, 'Comments on James Mill, *Élémens d'économie politique*'.
_____, *Critique of the Gotha Program.*
_____, *Economic and Philosophic Manuscripts of 1844.*
_____, *Grundrisse.*
_____, 'Theses on Feuerbach'.
Franz Mehring, *Karl Marx: The Story of his Life*, trans. Edward Fitzgerald, London, George Allen and Unwin Ltd., 1951.
Note, Economic Duress after the Demise of Free Will Theory, A Proposed Tort Analysis, 53 Iowa Law Rev. 892, 1968.

Robert Nozick, *Anarchy, State and Utopia*, Oxford, Blackwell Publishers, 1975.

T. Parsons, *The Law of Contracts* (2d. ed.), Boston, Little, Brown and Company, 1855.

Robert Payne, *Marx*, New York, Simon & Schuster, 1968.

Roscoe Pound, *Interpretations of Legal History*, Cambridge University Press and The MacMillan Co., 1930.

_____, *Jurisprudence*, St. Paul, Minn., West Publishing Co., 1959.

M. Radin, *Contract, Obligation, and the Human Will*, 43 Col.L.Rev. 575, 582, 1943.

Jean-Jacques Rousseau, *On the Social Contract*, trans. Roger O. Masters and Judith R. Masters, New York, St. Martin's Press, 1978.

Rudolf Stammler, *Fundamental Tendencies in Modern Jurisprudence*, 21 Michigan Law Review 623, 1923.

W. Story, *Treatise on the Law of Contracts*, 1844.

Robert C. Tucker, *The Marx-Engels Reader*, New York, W.W. Norton & Co., 1972.

Roberto Mangabeira Unger, Lecture, 'Law and Social Theory', Spring, 1976, Harvard University.

Karl Friedrich von Savigny, 'On the Vocation of Our Age for Legislation and Jurisprudence', translated by Abraham Hayward, in Jerome Hall, *Readings in Jurisprudence*, New York, The Bobbs-Merrill Company, 1938.

_____, *Ibid.*, trans.by Abram Hayward in *The Great Legal Philosophers*, London, Littlewood & Co.,1931.

_____, *Traité de Droit Romain* (trans. into French), Ch. Guenoux, Paris, Firman Didot Frères, 1840.

_____, *Le Droit des Obligations*, (trans. into French), C. Gerardin and Paul Jozon, Paris, Ernest Thorin, 1873.

Samuel Williston, *Freedom of Contract*, 4 Cornell L. Q. 365, 379, 1921.

1 *Williston on Contracts*, (3d ed. 1957) 6 Cornell L. Q. 365.

INDEX

Abbott, Chief Justice
    quoted: 119
"abuti" 73
adverse possession 62, 64–65, 85
alienation of property
    restrictions on: 96, 97
America(n) 73, 108, 118, 162
    cases: 121
American and English Encyclopedia of Law, The 84, 120, 123, 145
    quoted: 115, 126, 127, 203–206
Ancient Law (Maine)
    quoted: 97–98
Anglo–American Law 82
    courts: 93
    society: 115
antitrust laws 115
arson 120
Ashmole v. Wainwright 122
assumpsit 112
assent 143
Astley v. Reynolds 120, 122, 124, 177, 193, 194–195
    quoted: 177–178
Atiyah, P.S. 101, 104
    quoted: 101, 104
Atlee v. Blackhouse 121
Austin 10, 17
Avineri, Shlomo 152–153, 158
    quoted: 5, 158

Bacon's Abridgment
    See *A New Abridgment of the Law*
bargaining power 119
Barry V. Equitable Life Assurance Society 126, 127
basis will theory 5,31, 79, 80, 155–158, 158–161, 162, 164,
    169–171
battery 116
Bauer, Bruno 16, 17
Bentham, *A General View of a Complete Code of Laws* 91
Berry v. Donovan 26–27
Bethlehem Steel 126
Black, Justice 126
Black Death (plague) 99
blackmail 115